D1518150

Proclaiming a Classic

Proclaiming a Classic

THE CANONIZATION OF *ORLANDO FURIOSO*

Daniel Javitch

PRINCETON UNIVERSITY PRESS
PRINCETON, NEW JERSEY

Copyright © 1991 by Princeton University Press
Published by Princeton University Press, 41 William Street,
Princeton, New Jersey 08540
In the United Kingdom: Princeton University Press, Oxford

Library of Congress Cataloging-in-Publication Data

Javitch, Daniel
Proclaiming a classic : the canonization of Orlando Furioso / Daniel Javitch.
p.   cm.
Includes bibliographical references and index.
ISBN 0-691-06549-7
1. Ariosto, Lodovico, 1474–1533. Orlando furioso. 2. Roland (Legendary
character)—Romances—History and criticism.   I. Title.
PQ4569.J38   1991
851'.3—dc20   90-19609

This book has been composed in Adobe Galliard

Princeton University Press books are printed on acid-free paper,
and meet the guidelines for permanence and durability of the
Committee on Production Guidelines for Book Longevity of the
Council on Library Resources

Printed in the United States of America by Princeton University Press,
Princeton, New Jersey

1   3   5   7   9   10   8   6   4   2

In Memory of Lucie Javitch (1908–1988)

———————————

CONTENTS

ACKNOWLEDGMENTS

First, I wish to thank the American Council of Learned Societies for the grant-in-aid that helped me start this project in 1983. It has taken long enough to complete it that some of the individuals who read portions of this book when it was first taking shape may well have forgotten by now that they gave me useful advice and encouragement. Robert Hanning, James Mirollo, Joseph Solodow, and Edward Tayler were among these early readers, and I wish to thank them for their help. I also benefited from the information that Riccardo Bruscagli and Rosanna Pettinelli gave me in the early stages of my research. I am particularly grateful to Professor Pettinelli for having provided me with several indispensable sixteenth-century texts which the Vatican Library generously allowed to be photocopied. I also wish to thank Amedeo Quondam, who not only gave me encouragement, but also made Italian readers aware of my work-in-progress by publishing a translated shorter version of my second chapter in *Schifanoia*.

Relatives, colleagues, and friends read or heard portions of this book at various stages of its development and offered valuable criticism. I would like to thank in particular Albert Ascoli, Pellegrino D'Acierno, Oscar Kenshur, Dennis Looney, Lawrence Rhu, and Richard Sieburth. My colleague Timothy Reiss gave me most useful editorial advice after reading an early version of the entire manuscript. I wish to thank him, too, for his unflagging support. By listening to me with good humor and curiosity on numerous summer afternoons, Brendan Gill and Crosby Kemper made me clarify my thoughts, and also helped me choose the title. I am also very grateful to my father-in-law, James Laughlin, for his encouragement and for his editorial scrutiny. It is very sad for me that I will not be able to show the published book to the late Ann Laughlin, who went out of her way to facilitate my writing it during my many stays at Meadow House.

My wife, Leila, has borne this project with great patience and goodwill, and I am enormously grateful to her for so often freeing me of daily responsibilities to enable me to work undisturbed.

Michael Hays was the friend who helped me most. I am not only indebted to him for making me realize more fully than I did when I began this book that cultural processes and needs bring about the canonization of poetic works. Michael was always ready to listen to my descriptions of problems I faced while I was shaping my argument, and to offer constructive suggestions when I was blocked. In retrospect, I feel that it was in large part thanks to his intellectual sympathy and his midwifery that I was able to complete this book.

In the course of preparing the final version I incurred more debts. Judy Sauli and Dain Trafton looked over my translations, and I thank them for helping me make some of them less inaccurate. My daughter Arielle helped print the first hard copy, and Joseph M. Caporale, aside from assisting me in various other ways, helped me print the last. I owe special thanks to David Quint, my first reader for Princeton University Press. After reading the manuscript with intelligence and care, he made numerous suggestions that I heeded in my final revision, and that have improved the book as a result. I owe thanks as well to Annette Theuring for her skillful and sympathetic copyediting.

Chapter 3 appeared originally in the *Harvard Library Bulletin* (1986); a portion of Chapter 4 appeared in the *Journal of Medieval and Renaissance Studies* (Spring 1981); and an earlier version of Chapter 5 appeared in *Modern Language Notes* (January 1988). I wish to thank the editors of these respective journals for allowing me to incorporate this material in the present book.

Proclaiming a Classic

INTRODUCTION

IN THE contemporary debate about the literary canon there are those who believe that canonicity is created by a culture for specific reasons. The canon, maintain some in this camp, is the institutionalization of those literary texts that appear best to convey and sustain the interests of the dominant social order. The "essentialists" in the opposing camp deny this by pointing to the internal qualities of canonical works, arguing that such qualities constitute the superiority of these works and earn them their canonical status. Those who maintain that canonicity is a cultural production challenge these claims of innate superiority by invoking the changing fortunes of literary works—for example, texts deemed canonical cease being so—or by pointing to the ways in which interests and ideology shape canon formation. While I concur with those who hold that canonicity is created by a culture, I have found that their arguments tend to lack sufficient historical specificity and corroboration. After all, if one maintains that canonicity is conferred upon literary texts and is not automatically earned by them, one should be able to indicate the specific cultural processes that bring about the canonization of these works. Moreover, by establishing with more precision than has heretofore been attained what characteristics or signs mark the presentation of a text that has become canonical one can demonstrate quite persuasively that canonicity is a cultural production rather than something that literary works innately possess.

The present study seeks to make up for this shortage of specific historical documentation by investigating how a particular poem first entered the European poetic canon. The poem is Ludovico Ariosto's *Orlando Furioso*, originally published in its final form in 1532. What makes it possible to examine, in some detail, the processes that brought about the canonization of this poem is the extraordinary (at least for the early modern period) body of extant sixteenth-century commentary about it. In fact, no vernacular work of poetry provoked as much discussion and commentary in the sixteenth century as did the *Furioso*. Much of this commentary accompanied the numerous midcentury editions of the poem constantly reissued by Venetian publishers. The work also generated an extraordinary series of critical responses. It came up repeatedly in the large body of theory that emerged in the second half of the cinquecento, and it was a central object of contention in several of the literary quarrels of this period.[1] But it is not simply the sheer amount of commentary that enables my study. I can describe the processes by which the poem was canonized because the aim of much of that commentary—and this has until now not been fully appreciated—was to establish that the *Furioso* either descended from or was the modern equivalent of the canonical epics of antiquity.

My commitment to demonstrating the extratextual process of canonization is reflected in this study by my virtual disregard of the internal features of the *Furioso*. I do not doubt that the *Furioso* possessed particular features that enabled it to be deemed a classic. We know that the universal appeal of the poem in the sixteenth century (about which I shall say more in the first chapter) stemmed from Ariosto's ability to adapt the old "lowbrow" romances of the popular *cantastorie* into a "higher" form of literature that incorporated classical poetic models and that conformed, as well, to the new linguistic norms being established for a courtly and learned vernacular. The extraordinarily broad appeal that the poem achieved by such means was repeatedly invoked by its champions to confirm the poem's legitimacy as a new classic. One could show that other internal aspects of the poem—for instance, its recurring imitations of the *Aeneid*, or the moral wisdom that the narrator readily proffers in the proems of each canto— facilitated, even invited some of the processes of canonization that I will describe. However, I am not as interested in the intrinsic attributes of the poem as in the ways its early readers determined its value. I leave, therefore, to other scholars the task of ascertaining which features of Ariosto's poem played a role in guaranteeing its good fortune. My primary concern will be with how sixteenth-century readers interpreted and manipulated the text in their efforts to establish its poetic aristocracy. Occasionally, however, I do consider certain aspects of Ariosto's poetry. In my fifth chapter I briefly discuss Ariosto's narrative technique, but only in order to elucidate the first critical reactions to the discontinuities of his poem. Also, in my last chapter, devoted to Harington's Elizabethan translation, I compare the English version with the Italian text, and I make some comments about Ariosto's playful intentions, but, again, only to illustrate how Harington suppressed these intentions so that the English rendering would conform to his idea of a modern heroic poem. Except for these brief discussions of the *Furioso* "as such," my study is concerned almost exclusively with the reception and the perception of the poem in the sixteenth century.

My task has been facilitated by prior studies of the poem's early reception. A pioneering work, which was very useful as a preliminary guide, was Giuseppina Fumagalli's study of the poem's sixteenth-century *fortuna*, published at the beginning of the century.[2] The most recent work—in fact, it appeared too late for me to benefit from it fully—is Klaus Hempfer's *Diskrepante Lektüren* (see note 1). Hempfer's important book is the most comprehensive survey to date of the poem's reception in the sixteenth century. It is limited, however, by the author's determination to show that every interpretation, on whatever aspect of the poem, was countered by an oppos-

ing view. His systematic and too neatly balanced account of the contradictory readings of the poem aims, ultimately, to affirm the ambivalent, ironic,
even paradoxical nature of *Orlando Furioso*, and there lies the fundamental
difference between Hempfer's approach and mine. Whereas he presumes
that the contradictory responses to the *Furioso* were the product of the
poem as an intrinsically "problematischer" text, I assume that the responses, contradictory or not, were more the product of the different agendas and needs of the poem's various readers.

In English the only extensive treatment of the early responses to the
Furioso are the two chapters Bernard Weinberg devotes to "The Quarrel
over Ariosto and Tasso," in his *History of Literary Criticism in the Italian
Renaissance*.[3] While I am indebted to Weinberg's work, my study provides
a much fuller account of the reception of the *Furioso* before the publication
of Tasso's epic. On the other hand, because Weinberg has provided an
adequate treatment of the prolonged dispute that took place between
Tasso's and Ariosto's champions at the end of the century, I focus on only
part of this quarrel. One of the limitations of Weinberg's account is that it
does little to dispel a commonly held but erroneous view: namely, that by
the last decades of the cinquecento, proponents of neoclassical and especially neo-Aristotelian standards of poetic art had gained such ascendance
among Italian literati that they succeeded in dislodging Ariosto's poem
from its eminent position. It is also assumed that Tasso's *Gerusalemme
Liberata* (originally published in 1581), which the new classicists deemed
the first genuine vernacular equivalent of ancient epic, contributed decisively to this eclipse of the *Furioso*. My study should serve to revise, or at
least refine, these views by showing that the neoclassical opposition to the
poem only affirms how important a part of the literary culture the poem
had become. In fact, by provoking articulate defenses of the *Furioso*, this
neoclassical opposition actually helped to secure the canonical status that
the poem had so rapidly won. But this is to anticipate the last part of my
history, which is, first of all, about how Ariosto's poem acquired that status.

I stated earlier that there is a need in the contemporary debate over
canons for more historical specificity about the cultural mechanisms that
bring about the canonization of poetic texts. My study answers that need
by describing the processes by which *Orlando Furioso* was elevated to the
rank of a classic.[4] It should be understood that I do not intend to develop a
theory of canon formation from this one case. Yet many of the processes by
which the *Furioso* was canonized consisted of typical strategies of legitimation which can be shown to recur in subsequent efforts to canonize new
literary works. For instance, the first and foremost of these processes was to
affiliate the *Furioso* to the "great" poems of antiquity. Throughout the
second half of the sixteenth century Ariosto's poem was shown to descend
from or resemble Homer's and Virgil's epics, as well as Ovid's *Metamor-*

phoses. Aside from anchoring it to a tradition, such affiliation of the new poem to the aristocratic poems of the past often constitutes the first stage of canonization in that it confers upon the new poem a genealogy of already established classics.

Allegorization, which had been the traditional way of preserving the normative character of the pagan epics in a Christian culture, and which was itself a sign that a poetic text deserved to be institutionalized, was another process that the *Furioso* underwent in the sixteenth century. In the various midcentury editions of Ariosto's poem one regularly finds supplemental *allegorie* which indicated how each canto of the poem exemplified virtues to be emulated and vices to be shunned. Since such moral allegorizations had already become a traditional appendage to Virgil's and especially Ovid's major poems, attaching them to the *Furioso* was another way of affiliating the Italian poem to those ancient ones. But this allegorization was also part of another process of canonization, namely, domestication. By domestication I mean the ways in which a poem's objectionable or problematic aspects are suppressed or ignored so that it can be shown to conform not only to conventional ethical and religious values, but to artistic ones as well. To be sure, moral allegorization was the most frequent technique used to domesticate the *Furioso*, but exegetes and translators made the form and content of the poem safe and normative in other ways. Both affiliation and domestication served to stabilize the poem by giving it clearly identified origins, and by reducing the complexity and ambivalence of its meanings. Such stabilization is itself a typical process that a text undergoes as it becomes a classic.

Another important process of canonization, and one that some would consider necessary before a text can be deemed truly canonical, is its adoption in educational curricula. The *Furioso* did, in fact, enter some classrooms in the sixteenth century, and it seems to have been the only vernacular classic to have attained this status.[5] But whether school adoption is a sine qua non of a text's canonization is highly questionable in the case of vernacular poetry in the premodern period given that the curricula in standard grammar schools before the eighteenth century were predominantly of Latin works. Texts of vernacular poetry, for example, Petrarch's, can be shown to have achieved canonical status long before they became school texts. These texts were seen to possess educational value, but for an adult reading public rather than for classroom students. And what can be discerned about a vernacular text that is proclaimed a classic in the sixteenth century is that it assumes an institutional physiognomy as a book. Publishers "package" it in a format that resembles the one adopted for the ancient classics, to advertise as well as to facilitate its educational uses. The textual "physiognomy" of the *Furioso* was so altered. From the midcentury on, editions of the poem acquired paratextual features—the *allegorie* mentioned above, notes about the poem's normative linguistic and rhetorical features, commentaries about Ariosto's imitative practice—that betoken its institutionalization as clearly as its eventual entry into Italian classrooms.

Besides processes of canonization, there are, as I have just suggested, various signs that a poetic text is acquiring or has acquired canonical status. The most prevalent sign is that the text becomes a model. It is made to seem exemplary not only in ethical terms, but in linguistic, rhetorical, and prosodic ones as well. Its form and themes become the object of repeated imitations. The *Furioso* rapidly became such a model. Although I do not examine in any detail the influence of the *Furioso* on sixteenth-century poetry, in the fourth chapter I will consider its influence on cinquecento translations of ancient narrative poetry, in particular, Ovid's *Metamorphoses*. (This phenomenon, I might add, whereby translations of the ancient classics are made to look like the new poem is as telling a sign of the new poem's eminent status as its being made to look like the ancient classics.) But, on the whole, my discussion of the poem's role as a model focuses more on the ways it functioned as such in poetic theory than in practice.

In poetic treatises and theories of the latter half of the sixteenth century Ariosto is cited increasingly alongside vernacular "masters" such as Petrarch, Boccaccio, and Dante, as well as ancient authors such as Homer, Virgil, and Ovid. This kind of exemplarity offers perhaps the clearest indication that the poem is becoming part of the canon. An equally important sign is that, in these treatises, Ariosto's poem is made to represent different poetic principles—often contradictory ones. For example, in some treatises the poem is made to embody the postulates of poetic neoclassicism, in others the contrary ones of modernism. To those who believe that a text proves itself canonical by withstanding changing assaults of interpretation, the *Furioso*'s capacity to bear such different and often conflicting interpretations would already confirm its potential as a classic. Since not all texts, moreover, are equally amenable to the conflicting readings the *Furioso* was subjected to, it might be argued (as Klaus Hempfer does) that the text's capacity to accommodate these interpretations stemmed from its innate ambiguity. I would not deny the poem's ambiguity, nor that this ambiguity facilitated its role as a locus of conflicting interpretations. But the ambiguity itself does not account for the poem's cultural function as a site onto which readers could project quite opposing values and ideologies, and it is this function that offers perhaps the most notable sign of the poem's canonicity.

On the one hand, Ariosto's poem was made to embody the formal, thematic, and functional characteristics of what some deemed the noblest poetry, namely, ancient heroic poetry. On the other hand, some critics used the poem to validate those forms and functions, different from ancient ones, that they thought poetry should have in modern times. It is in the latter role that the poem became increasingly important in the last half of the sixteenth century. At first, critics exploited the poem's manifest success to proclaim the legitimacy of chivalric romance as a new genre. Rather than assimilating the poem to already canonical works of the past, the "moderns" took advantage of the *Furioso*'s tremendous popularity to try to open up the generic system that the conservative "ancients" sought to confine. The latter, in turn, fiercely contested the modernists' effort to grant the *romanzo* a separate generic identity because to recognize the chivalric romance as a new genre was to deny one of the fundamental premises of the neoclassicists: that poetic art has universal and unchanging norms. There were some "ancients" who eventually conceded that the *Furioso* was a romanzo, but they did so only to disqualify it as poetry, given that the romance was not part of Aristotle's generic system. This exclusionary tactic provoked some defenders of Ariosto to persist in classifying his poem as a traditional epic in order to be sure that the *Furioso* lost none of its legitimacy, an eventuality that could threaten the status of all the modern vernacular achievements that Ariosto's poem stood for.

In this prolonged debate about whether the *Furioso* was an epic or a romance, and if it was a romance, whether it was a legitimate poem, one can gradually perceive that it was no longer the status of Ariosto's poem that was really at stake as much as what the poem was made to stand for. And what, as we shall see, the poem was most often made to stand for by the final decades of the century was one or another kind of poetic modernism. More generally, the work became a site of contestation, a text upon which various and often conflicting ideologies (not only poetic) were projected. As I have already suggested, such a development—when a poetic work becomes a locus where the culture debates artistic or other issues that may be central to the culture but that bear less and less on the poem as such—is one of the surest indications that the poem in question has achieved canonical status.

These preliminary observations should suggest why it is important to understand the canonization of *Orlando Furioso* and the debates it provoked: this body of discourse plays a central and inaugural role in the formation of the European poetic canon. To be more precise, Ariosto's poem was being proclaimed a new classic at the same time that critics were defining the neoclassical canon and establishing the standards by which modern works of poetry were or were not to be included in it. While some deemed that the *Furioso* fully merited inclusion in this canon, the more conservative Aristotelians chiefly responsible for erecting it did not. As a result, Ariosto's poem was the first modern work of European poetry whose canonical eligibility became an issue of extensive debate. The contestation bears quite directly on the later history of canon formation because both the arguments for and against inclusion were to recur in future debates about the canonicity of new literary works. But the contestation also serves to illustrate more general truths about canon formation, the primary one being that the aristocratic attributes of texts that become canonical—and what is the canon if not an aristocracy of texts?—are not inborn but are conferred upon them.[6] A work like the *Furioso* did not automatically enter the canon because of its inherent superiority. It did so because some individuals persuaded the readers of their time that it deserved to be there by proclaiming the poem's aristocratic status and lineage. Other individuals sought to challenge such claims by persuading these same readers that Ariosto's work did not belong in the company of the best poems to which it had been compared. The very fact that critics wanted to divest the poem of its aristocratic status confirms that this status was conferred and not innate. Nor did opponents of the poem fail to "decanonize" it because of its innate superiority. This failure was due, rather, to the fact that readers continued to value the poem for many of the same reasons for which Ariosto's champions valued it. But, again, the value that the *Furioso* possessed for these readers was mediated by cultural and historical factors outside of the poem, the primary one being the need, by the midcentury, for a modern heroic poem comparable to the epics of antiquity.

The capacity of the *Furioso* to satisfy this need had, I will soon propose, much to do with the large volume of commentary that the poem provoked. But another, and perhaps prior, reason for the extraordinary volume of discussion it received was that it quickly became the most widely read work of modern Italian poetry in the sixteenth century, and, thanks to its promoters, became known to be such. I should begin this history, therefore, with some remarks about the tremendous publishing success that the poem enjoyed in the cinquecento.

Chapter One

THE SUCCESS OF *ORLANDO FURIOSO* IN THE SIXTEENTH CENTURY

IT HAS BEEN assumed that *Orlando Furioso* became a best-seller only after it appeared in its final form in 1532. But the second version of the poem, first published in 1521, had already been reissued at least fifteen times and had, in the decade after it appeared, a significant impact on the development of Italian chivalric romance. The third and final version of the poem, originally published in 1532 (Ariosto died the following year) enjoyed an even greater success: it was republished sixteen times by 1540, and after that it began to be reprinted every year by several different publishers, primarily in Venice. Scholars have estimated that, in this period, an average edition of nondevotional literature ran to about a thousand copies. The original 1516 edition of the *Furioso* comprised about fifteen hundred copies; the third and definitive edition of 1532 seems to have had an unusually large print run of about three thousand copies.[1] The Venetian publisher Gabriel Giolito alone published no fewer than twenty-seven editions of the poem between 1542 and 1560. G. A. Valvassori published nine more between 1553 and 1567, and another Venetian rival, Vincenzo Valgrisi, found enough continuing demand to publish yet another seventeen editions between 1556 and 1579.[2]

In Chapter 2 I will say more about the format and content of these midcentury editions. To begin with, however, I simply want to indicate how frequently the work was reprinted. In the decade between 1550 and 1560 publishers issued thirty-four editions of the poem (if one includes dialect and incomplete versions), and thirty editions appeared in the following decade. In comparison, Petrarch's *Canzoniere*, until that point the most frequently published work of Italian poetry, appeared in thirty-three editions between 1550 and 1560, but in only thirteen editions in the following decade. In other words, by the 1560s, *Orlando Furioso* was being republished more often than the already canonical lyrics of Petrarch. Altogether, from 1540 to 1580 there appeared at least 113 editions of Ariosto's poem.[3]

A decade after Italian readers had enjoyed his editions of the *Furioso*, the Venetian publisher Gabriel Giolito announced in a letter prefacing the Spanish translation of the poem he published in 1553 that Ariosto's work

was so perfect and so "stimata comunemente da tutti" that it deserved to
be translated not only in Spanish but in all languages so that it could be
understood by all nations. By 1560 Lodovico Dolce maintained that the
work was acclaimed by every kind of reader "con lode e grido universale."[4]
This claim is corroborated by the learned Bartolomeo Ricci. In a letter to
Ariosto's sons dated 1560 Ricci writes that "patris vestri scripta omnia ab
omnibus summa cum voluptate legantur [all your father's writings are read
with the greatest pleasure by all]." *Orlando Furioso*, he goes on to say, has
won special acclaim. It is such a rich source of learning, of artifice, and of
delight "ut cum ab Auctore suo primum ederetur, summo cum omnium
plausu acciperetur, neque vel legendo, vel audiendo non attente saepius
iteraretur [that ever since it was first published by its author, it has met with
the greatest applause of all, and it is often eagerly repeated in reading or in
listening]."[5]

Aside from such testimonies, the great success of *Orlando Furioso* in this
period is also made evident by the various kinds of imitations it prompted.
There were, to begin with, sequels to the poem which already began to
appear after the 1521 edition. These multiply in the wake of the 1532
edition: for example, Dolce's *Primo libro di Sacripante* (1536), Pesca-
tore's *La morte di Ruggero* (1546), Brusantino's *Angelica Innamorata*
(1550), and, later, Cataneo's *Amor di Marfisa* (1562).[6] New translations
of ancient narrative poems also assume the formal and prosodic aspects of
Ariosto's poem. For instance, Lodovico Dolce's 1553 translation of Ovid's
Metamorphoses is presented as a romanzo in "ottava rima" and is published
by Giolito in a format virtually indistinguishable from the editions of the
Furioso constantly reissued by his press (the influence of the *Furioso* on the
"volgarizzamenti" of Ovid's *Metamorphoses* will be discussed at length in
Chapter 4).

New narrative poetry also imitated "la maniera ariostesca" even though
poets wishing to compose heroic poetry in the 1550s were already being
constrained by the demands of neoclassical literati to conform to the norms
of epic composition exemplified by Homer and Virgil. Still, the obvious
success of Ariosto's modern romanzo spurred some of these poets to resist
such strictures. Thus, in a letter to Benedetto Varchi dated 6 March 1559,
Bernardo Tasso (the father of Torquato) invokes the broad appeal of Ariosto's unclassical poem to explain why he, too, opted to compose his
Amadigi as a romanzo rather than making it conform to the formal norms
of ancient epic. In the course of attesting to the popularity of the *Furioso*
he maintains that "non è dotto, ne artegiano, non è fanciullo, fanciulla, nè
vecchio che d'averlo letto più d'una volta si contenti [there is not a learned
person, nor a craftsman, not a boy, a girl, nor an old man who is contented
even after reading it more than once]." And if comparative sales are a

measure, the work, he goes on to suggest, is clearly more appealing to the reading public than the classical epics of antiquity: "Io non credo che in tanto spazio di tempo, quant'è corso dopo che quel dottissimo Gentiluomo mandò in man degli uomini il suo Poema, si sian stampati, nè venduti tanti Omeri, nè Virgili, quanti Furiosi [I do not believe that in the length of time that has passed since this most learned gentleman made his poem available as many Homers or Virgils have been published and sold as Furiosos]."[7]

Bernardo's claim that the *Furioso* enjoyed a universal readership was meant to challenge militant neoclassicists—for example, G. G. Trissino—who had maintained that all *romanzi*, Ariosto's included, were lowly popular forms of literature that could not possibly appeal to the discriminating *dotti* for whom the only valid narrative poetry was one that imitated ancient epic models.[8] Benedetto Varchi himself, the addressee of Tasso's letter, had already acknowledged on an earlier occasion that Ariosto was to be distinguished from "poeti plebeij" like Pulci who "scrivono solo per piacere alla Plebe, e far ridere il Volgo [write solely to please the people and make the vulgar sort laugh]." Although Varchi still had reservations about the *Furioso*, he recognized that Ariosto deserved "infinita comendazione, havendo usato nel suo poema & arte, & ingegno, e giudizio, e dottrina, & ancora eloquenza [infinite praise for having used in his poem both art and wit, judgment, learning, and also eloquence]."[9] Bernardo, in turn, was suggesting to Varchi that Ariosto's elevation of the romanzo had been so effective that it had undermined the notion that all modern romances were merely trivial entertainment catering to the populace. Actually, as Bernardo's testimony already suggests, Ariosto's romanzo was unusual not only because it captivated the *dotti* in an unprecedented way: it captivated everybody.[10]

The poem's universal appeal is affirmed repeatedly as the century progresses. For example, in the dedicatory letter of his 1567 edition Comin da Trino speaks of publishing "la non mai a bastanza lodata opera dell' Ariosto, la quale ben che al volgo diletti, nondimeno con la sua altezza da che pensare a' savi huomini [the never sufficiently praised work of Ariosto, which, pleasing though it is to common people, nonetheless manages with its loftiness to make wise men ponder]." The preface of the 1568 *Furioso* published by Domenico Guerra declares that "vediamo tutto il giorno haversi in mano il suo leggiadro Poema da ogni sorte di persone: e vediamo ciascheduno cavarne gusto equale a la sua capacità [all day long one sees every sort of person reading his lovely poem: and one sees each one enjoying it according to their individual capacity]." And here is how an anonymous commentator presents the work "to the readers" in the 1580 edition of the poem published by Horatio de' Gobbi. The *Furioso*, he writes, is a work

che fin qui tante volte da tanti in tante forme è stato dato alla stampa; è opera
così ben da voi conosciuta, Begnini Lettori, che non v'ha alcun grado di persona, grande, mezano, o picciolo, non v'ha alcun dotto, nè mezanamente
versato negli studi, nè alcuno ignorante, il quale pur che sappia leggere, che
non prenda gusto e dilettatione in questo Poema.[11]

[that up to now has so often been published by so many in so many forms; a
work so well known by you, gentle readers, that there is not a person of whatsoever rank, great, middle, or small, not a learned person, nor someone of
average learning, nor anyone ignorant but who can read, who does not derive
pleasure and delight from this poem.]

Such claims that the *Furioso* was enjoyed by everyone who could read
in the latter half of the cinquecento are corroborated by the various
types of editions of the poem ("da tanti in tante forme è stato dato
alla stampa") published in this period, ranging from the lavish, illustrated
"signorile" editions in quarto, designed for the more cultivated and afflu-
ent segment of readers, to less costly, more "popular" octavo editions
which at first appeared in cruder type (*gotico* or *semi-gotico*), to even smaller
formats also printed in semi-gothic type and in double columns. In her
study of the *fortuna* of Ariosto's poem, Giuseppina Fumagalli had observed that the numerous editions in octavo (more than a third of the
editions published in the course of the century were in this more eco-
nomical format) revealed that an important segment of the poem's readership consisted of the "piccola borghesia" rather than the "popolino
minuto" or the "plebe" as some of the highbrow literati of the period
complained. Despite the "carattere popolare" of these octavo editions
before the 1540s, a growing number of them in the second half of the
century were printed in roman and even italic type, and contained relatively
erudite annotations suggesting that they were not aimed at "la plebe af-
fatto mancante di cultura ma per il ceto medio che voleva spendere poco
[a wholly uncultured populace but at the middle class who wanted to
spend little]."[12] We still lack a comprehensive study of the different ways
Venetian publishers of this period "packaged" books for different groups
of readers. But it is immediately apparent to anyone looking at the various
books they produced that the typographical features and paratexts (for
example, title pages, prefaces, illustrations, glossaries) of an edition of
an esteemed Latin author, aimed at learned readers, differed from those
of an anthology of modern sonnets devised for more worldly or even
courtly readers, and that these, in turn, differed from the configurations of
inexpensive, "lowbrow" works of popular piety or chivalric adventures.
What was extraordinary about Ariosto's poem—and this confirms its
universal appeal—is that between 1521 and 1584 it seems to have embodied virtually every one of the particular typographical physiognomies that

Venetian publishers had devised for the different kinds of readers who made up their market.

Proof of this broader readership can also be found in surviving book inventories. For example, inventories of books owned by Florentine merchants, a group that had no predilection for "opere cavallaresche," reveal that in the period from 1531 to 1569 the vernacular author they most frequently read after Petrarch and Dante was Ariosto. Aside from these sober merchants we know that the poem had courtly and academic readers from the upper strata of society, and from the lower ones craftsmen, apprentices, and even rural readers. A recent study points out that by the final decades of the sixteenth century, vernacular schools training boys for the world of work adopted the *Furioso* as part of their curricula.[13] Given this evidence, one can well believe Francesco Caburacci when, in the course of defending the poem in 1580, he proclaims that he has seen "l'opera sua [that is, Ariosto's] essere manegiatta dai vecchi, letta dai gioveni, havuta cara da gli huomini, pregiata dalle Donne, tenuta cara da i dotti, cantata da gl'indotti, star con tutti nelle Città, andar con tutti in villa [his work handled by the old, read by the young, cherished by men, valued by women, prized by the learned, sung by the ignorant, possessed by all in the cities, and taken with them to the country]."[14] One of the champions of Ariosto's poem in Malatesta's dialogue, *Della nuova poesia* (1589), provides a similar but more elaborate testimony to the poem's broad readership and ubiquitous presence:

> Se voi pratticate per le Corti, se andate per le strade, se passeggiate per le piazze, se vi ritrovate ne' ridotti, se penetrate ne' Musei, mai non sentite altro, che, o leggere, o recitar l'Ariosto. Anzi, che dico Corti, che dico Musei? Se nelle case private, nelle ville, ne' Tugurij stessi, & nelle capanne ancora si trova, & si canta continuamente il Furioso. Lascio stare, che non sia scuola, nè studio, nè Academia, dove non si faccia conserva di questo mirabil poema, ma diciam pure delle inculte villanelle, & delle rozze pastorelle.[15]

> [If you frequent the courts, if you walk along the streets, or through the squares, if you find yourself in salons, if you enter academies, you never hear anything but Ariosto being read and recited. Indeed, why do I say courts and academies when in private homes, in country houses, even in hovels and huts one also finds the *Furioso* continually recited. Leaving aside that there is not a school, a study, or an academy where this wonderful poem is not held dear, I am speaking as well of uneducated country lasses and crude shepherdesses.]

Aside from the fact that it was the most popular work of modern poetry in the sixteenth century, there was another major reason why the *Furioso* provoked so much commentary: it was perceived to best fill the need for a modern equivalent of the canonical epics of antiquity at a time when such a need was felt with particular intensity. One must bear in mind that the idea of a vernacular classic was still very new when Ariosto's poem was published in its final form in 1532. It was not until the first decades of the sixteenth century that the writings of the great trecento writers, Petrarch, Boccaccio, and Dante, began to gain the status accorded the best-known ancient Greek and Roman authors, and even then this status was granted unreservedly only to Petrarch and Boccaccio. The work usually credited for having played a vital role in canonizing these two writers is Bembo's *Prose della volgar lingua* (1525). While Bembo (whose legislations about proper poetic style influenced Ariosto's revisions of his 1521 version of the poem) firmly established Petrarch and Boccaccio as master authors, he did not bestow such prestige on Dante. Actually, Bembo's assessment of Dante's poetic style was rather unfavorable, and he questioned the appropriateness of writing poetry on Christian theology. At one point in the *Prose*, one of the speakers in the dialogue, commenting on the author of the *Commedia*, points out

> quanto sarebbe stato più lodevole che egli di meno alta e di meno ampia materia posto si fosse a scrivere, e quella sempre nel suo mediocre stato avesse scrivendo contenuta, che non è stato, così larga e così magnifica pigliandola, lasciarsi cadere molto spesso a scrivere le bassissime e le vilissime cose; e quanto ancora sarebbe egli miglior poeta che non è, se altro che poeta parere agli uomini voluto non avesse nelle sue rime.[16]

> [how much more praiseworthy it would have been if he had set himself to write of a less high and less ample subject and if he had, in writing, constantly maintained this subject in its middle level, than it was to take so broad and so magnificent a subject and to allow himself to fall very frequently into writing of most base and vile things. And, moreover, how much better a poet he would be than he is, if he had not wished to appear to men, in his rhymes, as something else than a poet.]

Objections of this sort diminished Dante's standing in relation to Petrarch and Boccaccio. It was not that the *Commedia* lacked admirers in the first half of the sixteenth century; but it was valued for its scholastic and theological wisdom, and was not thought of as an "ordinary" epic. Whether it could even be considered an epic at all did not become an issue of debate until the final decades of the cinquecento.[17] The fact, moreover, that no other trecento or quattrocento poem (for example, Boccaccio's *Teseide*) could be favorably compared to the ancient epics meant that there was both room and need for a narrative poem in Italian to serve as such an exemplar. With Petrarch and Boccaccio as models, Bembo could establish stylistic norms for "high" Italian lyric and prose, but the absence of a similar model in narrative poetry left a gap in that generic field.

The need to fill that gap became all the more pressing the more Italians felt they could boast about the poetic accomplishments that their vernacular but no other had yet achieved. Obviously their pride could be all the more justified if, besides the writings of their trecento laureates, they could boast of a heroic poem that measured up to the ones of Greece and Rome. Ariosto's poem fulfilled their need. By the 1540s, the *Furioso* began to be hailed as the first long Italian poem to equal the great epics of antiquity. It had been Ariosto's intent, his promoters began to maintain in retrospect, to match the ancient epic bards and to raise the Italian language to its loftiest and most illustrious level. A great deal of the commentary that the poem received in the middle of the century aimed, as will become clear in the next two chapters, to confirm its identity as the heretofore missing Italian *epos*. And once the *Furioso* began to be identified as such, it also became an object of critical discussion that, as Marina Beer points out, could fill "lo spazio lasciato aperto dalle *Prose della volgar lingua* alla regolamentazione narrativa prima che venga interamente occupato dalla teorizzazione aristotelica [the space that the *Prose della volgar lingua* left open to the regulation of narrative poetry before it became totally occupied by Aristotelian theorizing]."[18]

This last comment points to a third major reason why the *Furioso* was the object of so much discussion between the 1540s and the 1580s. It was exactly during this period—when the poem enjoyed its greatest success and was being hailed as the modern equal of ancient epic—that Aristotle's *Poetics* was being assimilated and conflated with Horace's *Ars poetica* to shape rules of poetic art that, at least in Italy, quickly became normative. Although the *Poetics* was known by late quattrocento humanists, and a Latin translation (by Giorgio Valla) was available as early as 1498, it was not until the 1540s that Aristotle's treatise really began to be valued and assimilated by Italian literati. Its spreading influence was due to the efforts of scholars connected to the school of Aristotelian philosophy at Padua who began, in the 1540s, to lecture on, retranslate, and comment on the text. Some scholars maintain that the full impact of the treatise did not occur until the 1548 publication of Robortello's *Explicationes*, the first major commentary on the *Poetics*. Robortello's commentary was followed by Segni's Italian translation in 1549 and then a series of rival commentaries which mark as well as contribute to the full assimilation of Aristotle's theory in the latter half of the cinquecento: the *Explanationes* of Lombardi and Maggi in 1550; Vettori's *Commentari* in 1560; and Castelvetro's Italian commentary in 1570. One should also bear in mind that by 1547–1548 Giangiorgio Trissino had published his *Italia liberata dai Goti*, the first major effort to re-create epic according to the models of Homer and Virgil and Horatian-Aristotelian rules ("avendo io," Trissino boasted in his preface, "co i precetti di Aristotile . . . e con la idea di Omero, composto questo mio Eroico Poema, cosa che non si è fatta più ne la nostra lingua Italiana"). And, shortly before his death in 1550, Trissino composed *La quinta e la sesta divisione della Poetica*, which contained the first Italian codification of epic poetry based on Aristotelian norms, and which already criticized chivalric romances for violating the Aristotelian requisite of a plot with a single action of a single hero.[19] It is hardly accidental that the *Poetics* gained importance as a regulatory text in Italy at the same time that the reform of the Catholic church, beginning with the Council of Trent, ushered in a new climate of conformity. In fact, the homology between Counter-Reformation demands for greater unity and orthodoxy and the demands of the new Aristotelians for narrative unity, as well as for a single neoclassical standard, suggests that the rapid ascendance of Aristotelian poetics in the mid–sixteenth century was spurred by the new religious and moral climate.

My intent is not to discuss, in any more detail, the good fortune of the *Poetics* in the late Renaissance, or its causes, but rather to point out that the impact of Aristotle's treatise on Italian literary culture occurred at the very same time that *Orlando Furioso* became the best-selling work of modern poetry in Italy. This conjunction could not but provoke critical controversy given that Ariosto's poem was quickly perceived to flout what were understood to be Aristotle's prescriptions for narrative poetry. In fact, no sooner had Robortello's *Explicationes* appeared in 1548 than Aristotelian enthusiasts began to criticize the *Furioso* for failing to observe the requisites set down by the Greek philosopher.

We know about this early neo-Aristotelian attack because it was reported and refuted by Simone Fornari in his *Spositione sopra l'Orlando Furioso* (1549), the first extensive commentary on the Italian poem. To be precise, it was in the "Apologia brieve sopra tutto l'Orlando Furioso," preceding his commentary, that Fornari listed the complaints of the new Aristotelians. What were their objections? The foremost complaint was that the *Furioso* consisted of multiple actions, and told not of one but of many knights, rather than the single complete action and one hero called for by Aristotle.[20] The next main objection was leveled at the obtrusive presence of Ariosto as narrator, a phenomenon quite contrary to the narratorial self-effacement that Aristotle had praised in Homer (see *Poetics* 24).[21] Criticism was also leveled at the disposition or unfolding of Ariosto's narrative, particularly Ruggiero's story, which lacked the art shown by Virgil and Homer in the disposition of their plots. The critics, says Fornari, maintain that if Ariosto wished to sing about Ruggiero he had to "incominciar dal mezzo dai suoi gesti e poi far, che egli raccontasse di se dal principio innanzi a qualche huomo di conto, o donna . . . come Virgiliano Enea dinanzi a Dido, e Ulisse Homerico al cospetto d'Alcinoo [begin in the middle of his exploits and then arrange it so that Ruggiero himself narrates his earlier deeds to some man or woman of note, like Virgil's Aeneas does to Dido, and Homer's Odysseus in the presence of Alcinoos]."[22] This demand that the epic observe an *ordo artificialis*, which Ariosto failed to meet, was not an Aristotelian as much as a Horatian requisite (see *Ars poetica* 146–48, where Horace states that the epic poet ought not to begin "ab ovo" but in "medias res"). It reflects how these so-called Aristotelian critics tended to conflate Horace's principles of poetic construction with Aristotle's. More Aristotelian, perhaps, was the next objection Fornari reports, namely, that Ariosto's poem was fantastic and lacked credibility. "Molti biasimano il Poeta," he writes, "del raccontar cose troppo maravigliose, & tali, che par che eccedino il termine della verità [Many blame the poet for narrating matters too marvelous and such that they seem to exceed the limits of truth]."[23] There were, finally, complaints about the title, given that the poem was not primarily concerned with Orlando's madness.

How Fornari refuted, or tried to refute, these objections will be discussed in the next chapter. For the moment, I merely wish to point out that the objections Fornari singles out would be made repeatedly as the century progressed, and more vociferously as neo-Aristotelian (combined with neo-Horatian) poetics gained ascendance. The predominant and recurring complaint of the neoclassicists was that Ariosto's plot was multiple, involving many protagonists, rather than unified around a single hero. But the other objections—about the poem's faulty structure, its obtrusive narrator, its lack of verisimilitude—were also frequently voiced. Despite these complaints, the *Furioso*'s popularity did not wane. While the proponents of the new classicism were establishing rules for all future narrative poets, a poem that often flouted those rules not only had become the most widely read work of narrative poetry in the period, but was also being acclaimed as the first such work in Italian to match the ancient epics. This paradoxical conjunction could hardly escape the notice of practicing poets.

In the 1559 letter, cited earlier, in which Bernardo Tasso reminds Benedetto Varchi of the tremendous success of the *Furioso*, he acknowledges beforehand that for the "maggior parte de' dotti, i quali s'hanno preposto per una vera forma d'un perfetto Poema la maravigliosa Iliade d'Omero, e l'Eneide di Virgilio, non piace Poema di molte azioni [majority of the learned, who take as the real form of a perfect poem Homer's marvelous *Iliad*, and Virgil's *Aeneid*, a poem of many actions is not pleasing]." Yet despite the bias of learned readers, modern audiences preferred, as the success of the *Furioso* manifests, poems of multiple actions. Bernardo maintains that it would be hard for a modern poet to find readers without providing a narrative plot possessing the *varietà* of Ariosto's. In this, as in his other letters to fellow *literati* discussing his *Amadigi*, Bernardo was trying to justify the multiple plot structure of his own romanzo, because, by 1559, despite the acclaim won by the *Furioso*, one could not write a romanzo *all'Ariosto* without being anxious about having disregarded Aristotle. All Bernardo could propose, to rationalize his choice of the "maniera ariostesca" and not seem impervious to classical doctrine, was that if Aristotle had now been alive, and could have witnessed the pleasure produced by *Orlando Furioso*, he would have modified his rules to accommodate Ariosto's practice.[24]

In the face of a similar dilemma, Torquato Tasso, Bernardo's more famous son, opted to follow Aristotle's demand for a unified plot, all too aware that the most successful Italian poem of the century flouted this requisite. In fact, when, in his early epic theory, Torquato Tasso is about to recommend unity of action in the heroic poem, he acknowledges what his father had ascertained earlier: that modern taste and experience challenge the call for such unity. The opponents of unity, he writes,

> veggendosi che l'Ariosto, partendo da le vestigie degli antichi scrittori e delle regole d'Aristotele, ha molte e diverse azioni nel suo poema abbraciate, è letto e riletto da tutte l'età, da tutti i sessi, noto a tutte le lingue, piace a tutti, tutti il lodano, vive e ringiovinisce sempre nella sua fama e vola glorioso per le lingue de' mortali.[25]

> [see that Ariosto, who abandoned the path of ancient writers and the rules of Aristotle, and who embraced many and diverse actions in his poem, is read and reread by all ages and both sexes, is known in all languages, liked and praised by all, lives forever in his fame and is ever young, and soars in glory on the tongues of mortals.]

One might well argue that the issue Tasso raises in this passage—the resounding success of the *Furioso* in the face of the ascending authority accorded Aristotle's poetic rules—was a central preoccupation of anyone concerned with narrative poetry in the latter half of the cinquecento. The contradiction became an important enough issue in the learned academies that it was in itself a topic of debate. One of the surviving Latin disquisitions on the subject, "Disceptatur cur Ariostus probetur omnibus qui tamen Aristotelis praeceptis non satisfecit," sums up in its title a question that literati of the later sixteenth century could not help but ask themselves.[26]

Obviously, had the *Furioso* not been a best-seller from the 1540s to the 1580s, and had it not been hailed as a modern version of ancient epic, it would not have been so intensively discussed, its failure to conform to neo-Aristotelian standards notwithstanding. The *Furioso*, we may recall, was a sequel to Boiardo's *Orlando Innamorato* (originally published in 1482–1483). One need only consider the relative absence of discussion concerning the *Innamorato*—a romanzo equally at odds with the ascending classical standards but one that, by midcentury, had lost most of its original appeal—to realize how much the ongoing popularity and reputation of the *Furioso* had to do with the critical attention it was given.[27] But it was not simply the success of the *Furioso* that provoked discussion. Much of that discussion was defensive. Those who acclaimed Ariosto's poem for having fulfilled the need for a vernacular equivalent of ancient heroic poetry had to contend with those who attacked the poem for flouting the so-called classical rules of poetic art which were so rapidly gaining authority. Ariosto's champions had already been promoting the idea that his poem was a modern classic before neo-Aristotelian (and neo-Horatian) critics contested it, but, as I will show in the next chapter, it took this challenge to intensify as well as to shape the counterclaims made on behalf of the *Furioso*.[28]

Chapter Two

THE LEGITIMATION OF *ORLANDO FURIOSO*

HAD THE NEW Aristotelians not so persistently denied that the *Furioso* equaled the greatest ancient heroic poems, the volume of discourse generated by the poem would have been significantly diminished. Such adversarial criticism clearly provoked the first extensive appraisals of the *Furioso* produced in the cinquecento.[1] We already saw that Simone Fornari's 1549 "Apologia," one of the earliest defenses of the poem, was written explicitly as an answer to the neo-Aristotelian attack he records. The same sort of opposition is described in a letter from G. B. Pigna to Giovambattista Giraldi supposedly written in 1548, the year before Fornari attested to this hostility.[2]

Before Pigna lists the various objections leveled at Ariosto, he maintains that all of them "a questo s'indirizzano, che egli non abbi seguitato le vestigia degli antichi [address the fact that he did not follow in the footsteps of the ancients]." Specifically, the critics complain

> che il titolo propone una cosa della quale manco si parla in tutto il libro che d'altro, e seguitano argomentando che gli altri scrittori fanno rispondere insieme il principio e il fine, ma che il suo cominciamento è diversissimo da quello che nell'ultimo si conchiude. Dicono altresí che va per tutta l'opera saltando d'una cosa in un' altra intricando tutto il poema, e che piglia quelle sorti d'arme fatte con incantagione, e quelle donne ed uomini negromanti che sono fuori dell'usanza, e quello che molto più monta, vi aggiungono che si dee stare una sola azione, ma che egli molte ne piglia.

> [that the title proposes one subject about which less is said in the whole book than of any other; and they go on to argue that other writers make their beginnings relate to their ends, whereas his beginning is totally different from what he concludes with at the end. They also say that he jumps from one thing to another throughout the work, tangling up the whole poem, and that he brings in magical weapons and male and female wizards that violate contemporary usage; and what stirs them up above all is that, instead of having a single action, he chooses to have many.]

The objections go on: the poem regularly violates decorum; and, unlike Virgil and Homer, who set forth the noble deeds of "due generosissimi capitani," Ariosto presents the wicked example of a wise man who goes mad. These critics seek to show, as Pigna sums up, that Ariosto departed altogether from the rules of Aristotle's *Poetics*, "che egli si è del tutto scostato dalla Poetica di Aristotile."[3] How, Pigna concludes his letter, can one effectively defend Ariosto against these charges? He asks Giraldi to provide him with such a defense so that he can use it as a shield against the many "uomini dei nostri tempi che fanno professione di letteratissimi."

Giraldi obliged, first by defending Ariosto in the letter he sent back to Pigna, and later, in his *Discorso intorno al comporre dei romanzi* (1554), by justifying the rights of modern writers of romance to disregard ancient epic norms. In 1554 *I romanzi*, Pigna's own contribution to the counteroffensive, was also published. Pigna's and Giraldi's treatises have been taken to be similar because they both constitute the first extensive justifications of the modern romanzo. Moreover, Pigna's charges that Giraldi (his former mentor) plagiarized his ideas reinforced the notion that their views were similar. Actually, while both treatises played an important role in the early legitimation of the *Furioso*, their arguments differed. First of all, Pigna was more intent on defending Ariosto's singular achievement than the genre of chivalric romance, whereas Giraldi took advantage of the extraordinary success and reputation that the *Furioso* had already achieved to make a case for the romanzo in general, arguing that it was a more appealing and relevant kind of poetry for modern audiences than classical epic. As we will see shortly, there was another significant difference between their arguments. Pigna countered objections that Ariosto had not followed in the footsteps of the ancients by affiliating his poem in as many ways as he could to the epics of antiquity. Giraldi, on the other hand, met these same objections by acknowledging the modernity and difference of a romanzo like Ariosto's, and by justifying this difference on grounds of historical change.

Many of the objections that Pigna reported in his 1548 letter to Giraldi were leveled at formal aspects of *Orlando Furioso*: its beginning and end were unconnected; its title announced one subject and the poem treated another; the poet "va per tutta l'opera saltando d'una cosa in un'altra" and entangled the narrative as a result; the poem should have a single action instead of many; it has too many inappropriate digressions. The general complaint was that Ariosto did not follow in the footsteps of Virgil and Homer. The letter Giraldi sent back to Pigna eloquently defended the *Furioso* against these charges, especially the last one, by affirming the rights of the modern romanzo to disregard ancient epic norms.

After all, Giraldi wrote, the Italian language does not derive from ancient Greek, as does Latin, but from romance languages. As Virgil understandably imitated (and even surpassed) Homer, given that Latin derived from Greek, so have Italian poets imitated poets in romance languages "onde la nostra ha presa la maniera del comporre," namely, authors of "romanzi francesi, provenzali e spagnuoli." If Virgil chose to write in the same epic form as Homer, he did so, Giraldi explains, because that was the manner of poetry that the custom of their times introduced and that they judged capable of pleasing the people in whose time they were writing. So Ariosto and other Italian writers of romance found it necessary to

> seguire quella forma e quella maniera di poema, ch'era già acettata dell'uso dei migliori scrittori di questa lingua, quantunque ella fosse lontana da quella di Virgilio e di Omero, i quali ad altri tempi e in altre lingue scrissero, le quali avevano altri costumi e altri modi di poeteggiare.[4]

> [follow that form and that manner of poem which was already accepted by the usage of the best writers of this language, however distant it might be from that of Virgil and of Homer, who wrote for other times and in other languages which had other customs and other ways of poetizing.]

Custom or "uso" changes as history evolves, and so, as a result, do modes of poetizing. Romance compositions agree more with current usage and are therefore more pleasing to a modern audience. Giraldi points to the parallel example of Petrarch, whose successful lyric practice followed not the models provided by Horace and Pindar, but the usage of his times. Thus, if Italian "romanzatori" have followed in the footsteps of the authors of "l'Amadigi, Palmerino, Primaleon . . . Lancilotto, Tristano, la Tavola Ritonda e altri tali," they are not to be blamed.

Giraldi goes on to praise Ariosto for having raised the romanzo to new heights, and comments on the wide acclaim the poem has so rapidly won, a universal consent which itself serves to sanction Ariosto's departures from ancient poetic standards. In the last section of his letter, Giraldi replies to some of the criticisms that Pigna had itemized. Far from denying that Ariosto deviates from Homer's and Virgil's poetic norms, here he reaffirms Ariosto's decision to compose a poem of multiple plots, "seguendo il costume dei romanzi, non quello di Greci o di Latini," and he dismisses various objections about the poem's formal shortcomings on the grounds that they do not apply to Ariosto's modern, nonclassical composition. The whole thrust of his letter is to assert that the romanzo is different from the old epic and that *Orlando Furioso* has to be judged according to the norms of this modern genre, not those established by Homer and Virgil.

Giraldi's letter to Pigna anticipates, of course, some of his claims in the *Discorso intorno al comporre dei romanzi*, which was also published in 1554 (the earlier letter accompanied the treatise in some editions). There, again, Giraldi proclaims that contemporary Italian poets must follow the example of the best modern practitioners, not ancient poetic norms that can no longer satisfy modern tastes. The Italian poet, he writes,

> deve camminare per quelle strade, le quali hanno proposte i migliori poeti di questa nostra favella, con quella istessa autorità che hanno avuto i Greci ed i Latini nelle lingue loro; e questo è stato cagione che io mi sono molte volte riso di alcuni che hanno voluto chiamare gli scrittori de' romanzi sotto le leggi

dell'arte dataci da Aristotile e da Orazio, non considerando che né questi né
quegli conobbe questa lingua, né questa maniera di comporre.[5]

[must follow the paths that have been set by the best poets of our language,
with the same authority that the Greeks and Latins had in their languages: and
this is why I have laughed many times at those who wanted to submit writers
of romances to the rules of art given us by Aristotle and Horace, disregarding
the fact that neither one nor the other knew our language, nor this manner of
composition.]

Yet unlike his earlier letter, Giraldi's *Discorso* was not as concerned with
defending the *Furioso* as with establishing the differences between the
modern romanzo and ancient epic, and with justifying these differences.
Part of its unstated agenda was also to justify the kind of romanzo—about
the many actions of a legendary hero—that Giraldi was in the process of
composing, namely, his *Ercole*. Nonetheless, by showing that several of the
formal features that were being criticized in the *Furioso* by the new classicists were characteristic and "traditional" aspects of romance compositions, the modern equivalents of ancient epic, Giraldi was in effect validat-
ing Ariosto's practice.

When Giraldi defines some of the generic features of the romanzo, he
often appears to have specifically Ariosto's practice in mind. Occasionally
the normative status of the *Furioso* is made explicit. For example, the following passage begins by discussing, in general terms, how "romanzatori"
proceed from one canto to another, and how they differ from ancient epic
writers in this respect:

> Si dee considerare che questa poesia di romanzo ha altro modo di legare che
> non ha avuto l'eroico de' Greci e de' Latini, che hanno composte poesie di
> una sola azione, come ha fatto Omero e Virgilio. . . . Perché questi con con-
> tinua narrazione hanno congiunto un libro con l'altro solo con una certa
> dipendenza che hanno avuto insieme per rispetto della materia. Ma gli scrit-
> tori de' romanzi di maggior stima non si sono solamente contentati della
> dependenza, ma hanno usata un' altra diligenza, la quale è stata di porre di
> canto in canto, prima che sian venuti alla continuazione della materia, qualche
> cosa che abbia apparecchiata la via a quello che si doveva dire, nella qual cosa è
> riuscito maraviglioso l'Ariosto.

[One should take into account that romance poems have a way of being
linked that differs from the heroic poetry of the Greeks and Latins who wrote
poems of one action, as did Homer and Virgil. . . . These poets have joined
one book with another with continuous narration only by means of a certain
interdependence that they had on account of the subject matter. But the most
esteemed writers of romances have not only been content with this dependence but have striven further. In moving from one canto to another, before

continuing their matter, they insert something to prepare the way for what is going to be said. In this technique Ariosto succeeded marvelously.]

Having brought up Ariosto's narratorial interventions at the beginning of cantos—these, it will be recalled, were criticized by the new Aristotelians— Giraldi proceeds to justify them by reinvoking the dignified ancestry of the canto, a pedigree that he traces back to the heroic songs recited by ancient rhapsodes:

E perché vi sono di quelli che biasimano in lui, quel che a me par degno di grandissima lode, cioè i principij de' canti suoi, non mi pare fuori di proposito render ragione di questo, e mostrare quanto sia più lodevole cosí fare, che scegliere in questa qualità di poesia l'ordine di Virgilio e di Omero. E per meglio far nota questa parte, non mi sarà grave ricorrere a quello che prima dissi, cioè che si dividono questi componimenti in canti. Perché i poeti nostri o cantano, o si fingono di cantare innanzi ai gran principi, secondo i costumi degli antichi Greci e Latini. Laonde perché promettono nel fine de' canti loro di dover tornare a cantare e fingono nei principij de' canti di esserci ritornati per dir quel che avevano lasciato, è stato loro bisogno prima che vengano alla materia, la quale vogliono continuare, disporre gli animi di chi ascolta all'attenzione.

[And because there are those who reproach him for what seems to me worthy of the greatest praise, that is, the beginnings of his cantos, I think it is not remote from my purpose to account for this, and to show how much more praiseworthy it is to proceed in such a manner than to choose in this form of poetry the arrangement of Virgil and Homer. And to better emphasize this section, it will not be amiss for me to go back to what I said previously, namely, that these romance compositions are divided into cantos, for our poets either sing or feign to sing in the presence of great princes, as was the custom of the ancient Greeks and Latins. The reason why they promise at the end of their cantos that they will return to sing, and why they feign at the beginning of cantos that they have returned to sing what they had suspended, was their need to gain the attention of their listeners before resuming the matter they wanted to continue.]

After justifying Ariosto's "proemi" by invoking the precedent of ancient rhapsodes, Giraldi then generally warrants these narratorial addresses to the audience at the beginning of cantos, and, in effect, makes Ariosto's practice normative:

Così anco i poeti nostri, cercando di canto in canto nuova attenzione, con qualche bello cominciamento, destano gli animi di chi ascolta e poi se ne vengono alla continuazione della materia, legando un canto coll'altro con maravigliosa maestria.[6]

[So also our poets seeking renewed attention in the transition from one canto
to the next arouse the minds of the hearers with some pleasing beginning and
then proceed with the continuation of the matter, linking one canto to another with marvelous mastery.]

It is, in fact, by making the *Furioso* the exemplary poem of modern times
that Giraldi most enhanced its status. At one point Giraldi announces that
both Boiardo and Ariosto are the "migliori poeti" whose practice must
guide new "romanzatori."[7] But, as the passage cited above can serve to
illustrate, Giraldi's norms for the romanzo are more often determined by
Ariosto's practice. Later in the *Discorso* he openly affirms that Ariosto is the
master author for "romanzatori" in the same way that Petrarch has been
for lyric poets:

> Lasciò il Petrarca tutti gli antichi Toscani, che prima di lui avevano scritto,
> di gran lunga dopo sé, e il nostro Ariosto tale rimase appresso gli altri che a
> così fatte composizioni s'erano dati ch' egli solo tra tutti (parlando univer-
> salmente) si è scoperto degno di essere imitato.[8]

[Petrarch left far behind him all the Tuscan poets who had written before him,
and our Ariosto so stands in relation to those who took to writing romances
that he is the sole one, among all of them (speaking universally), who has
proved worthy to be imitated.]

Giraldi had said that, as ancient arts of poetry drew their principles from the
practice of their best poets, so a modern art of poetic composition should
be based on its preeminent practitioners. His *Discorso* on the composition
of romances ascribed to Ariosto the exemplary "autorità" for modern poets
that Homer and Virgil held for ancient epic. It did so, one should bear in
mind, not much more than twenty years after *Orlando Furioso* was first
published in its final form.

Giraldi's elevation of the *Furioso* to canonical status was extraordinary
not only because he did it so soon after it was written, but because he did it
by differentiating it from rather than assimilating it to the epics of antiquity. That is to say, he sought to add Ariosto's poem to the canon not by
maintaining that it replicated classical epic but on the grounds that it was a
new counterpart of it. This modernist stance, as I will demonstrate, was
untypical of the larger effort that began in the 1540s to make the *Furioso*
into a classic. Instead of asserting and justifying its differences from ancient
epics, most midcentury promoters of the *Furioso* sought to affiliate it in
every way possible to those prestigious classical poems. Even Pigna, Giraldi's correspondent, adopts this promotional stance when he defends Ariosto's poem in his treatise *I romanzi* (1554).

In this treatise (published the same year as Giraldi's), Pigna asserts that
the romances constitute an independent poetic form that originated in

Spain and France, and as such observe different rules of composition than those of Greek and Latin epic.[9] He distinguishes the feigned subject matter and multiple plot structure of the romanzo from the historical matter and single plot of classical epic. Nonetheless, insofar as the romance is an imitation of heroic actions (in which one protagonist is often prominent) and deals with matter that is exemplary, marvelous yet verisimilar, it is like classical epic. One finds Pigna censuring the earlier foreign, especially Spanish, *romanzi* for their disregard of verisimilitude (see *I romanzi*, pp. 40–41) because he seeks to show that, as the genre evolved into its superior Italian phase (culminating in the *Furioso*), it eventually embodied most of Aristotle's criteria for epic poetry. Giraldi had sought to show that, being a modern genre, the romance necessarily observed different norms from those Aristotle had prescribed for ancient epic. Pigna, on the other hand, generalizes Aristotelian poetics in such a way ("in speaking of romances," he claims at one point [p. 65], "Aristotle has been our guide although he never spoke of them") as to be able to maintain that the romance can, and in Ariosto's hand did, conform to Aristotle's prescriptions.[10] However, in his defense of the *Furioso*, which takes up the second book of his treatise, he is not as concerned with Ariosto's observance of Aristotelian principles as with showing his poem's numerous affiliations to the heroic poems of antiquity.

Pigna organizes his defense of Ariosto in book 2 around a biography of the poet, a life that aims to reveal the genesis of Ariosto's masterpiece but also to show "what true poets should be like." The biography bestows seriousness on the *Furioso* indirectly by showing the various kinds of knowledge (for example, of ancient mythology, of warfare) Ariosto had to acquire, the poetic apprenticeship he had to complete, before he could undertake his major composition. It becomes evident, too, that Pigna wants his readers to see parallels between Ariosto's and Virgil's careers, between the genesis of the *Furioso* and of the *Aeneid*. In fact, the parallels are made explicit when Pigna maintains that Ariosto's decision to write a sequel to Boiardo's *Orlando Innamorato* was analogous to Virgil's decision to continue Homer's story after the Fall of Troy. This analogy prompts the critic to interrupt his biography in order to point out various other parallels between the *Furioso* and Virgil's and Homer's epics. It becomes progressively clear that he draws these parallels in order to refute the basic objections against Ariosto that he had originally cited in his 1548 letter to Giraldi, the primary one being that Ariosto had not followed in the tracks of the ancient poets.

For instance, one of the specific objections was that the beginning and the end of the poem were disconnected, whereas good poets have always made them relate to each other. Rather than justifying such disconnectedness in terms of the multiple plots of the romanzo (this was Giraldi's response), Pigna shows that there is a relation between the beginning and the end of the *Furioso* in that canto 1 imitates the opening quarrel of the *Iliad* whereas the end of the poem imitates the final duel and closure of the *Aeneid*! Although Ruggiero's killing of Rodomonte at the end of the *Furioso* is ostensibly an imitation of Aeneas's killing of Turnus, the claim that the opening of Ariosto's poem is modeled on the quarrel between Agamemnon and Achilles is much more tendentious. Pigna points out, quite correctly, that Ariosto had to start with the rivalry between Angelica's various suitors, prompted by her presence in the Christian camp, because that was where Boiardo's poem had ended prematurely. But then he feels he has to bring in Homer to further justify the opening: "Et benché altrimenti introdur si potesse l'amor di Angelica; pure fu così in tal modo posto per esservi l'essempio dell'Iliade. la quale ha la prima attione fatta appunto in simil guisa: essendo ella una contesa tra Achille & Agamemnone per conto di Chriseide [And although he could have introduced the love of Angelica differently, it was placed in this way because of the example in the *Iliad* whose initial action is just the same: a quarrel between Achilles and Agamemnon on account of Chriseid]." Homer is not just invoked as a model this once; Pigna subsequently tries to ascribe as many Homeric origins as Virgilian ones so that he can finally propose that the beginning and end of the poem are emblematic of Ariosto's equal borrowing from Homer and Virgil: "Et per mostrare d'haver seguitato il Greco e il Latino poeta parimente, questo riguardo ha egli avuto di dar principio al suo poema alla via dell'Iliade: e di conchiuderlo secondo la forma dell'Eneide [And to show that he followed the Greek and the Latin poet equally, this consideration made him begin his poem in the same way as the *Iliad* and conclude it in the manner of the *Aeneid*]."[11] This drawing of parallels between Ariosto's poem and the epics of antiquity is characteristic of Pigna's defensive rhetoric. Thus, to the objection that Ariosto resorts too much to magical intervention and to the supernatural generally, Pigna again responds by pointing to analogues in the ancient epics. For example, he shows that Melissa's magical rescue of Ruggiero from Alcina in canto 7 is modeled on Mercury's similar effort to extricate Aeneas from Dido and Carthage. As for the miraculous transformation of rocks into horses and branches into ships that occurs in canto 39, Pigna recalls two similar precedents in ancient epic: the petrification of the Phaiakian ship that brought Odysseus back to Ithaca (*Odyssey* 13); and the transformation of Aeneas's ships into nymphs (*Aeneid* 9). Pigna also justifies a number of the fantastic occurrences in the poem by allegorizing them. Wishing to show that there is a coherent moral significance to the magical devices employed by several of Ariosto's protagonists, he tries to show that the horn, the shield, and the ring signify "Verità," "Inganno," and "Discorso," respectively. But his attempt to work out some overall schema of meaning for all the magical instruments in the poem breaks down. All he can construe as the meaning of the golden lance—given that it is gold, and that it unhorses all opponents—is that "i danari nel guerreggiare tanto importino, che chi in esso largamente può spendere abbatta ogni cosa [money matters so much in waging war that whoever can spend a great deal on fighting knocks down everything]."[12] Somewhat more successful is his allegorization of Ruggiero's experiences with Alcina and Logistilla, even though it fails to account for Ruggiero's recidivism. The point of his allegorization, however, is not to do justice to Ariosto's complex, ironic vision but to affirm "quanto moralità sotto le Romanzerie si ritruovi," in order to justify the fantastic aspects of the poem and to refute objections about its lack of didactic value. More broadly, against the charge that Ariosto failed to follow in the footsteps of the ancient poets, book 2 of *I romanzi* argues that, despite the formal differences between Ariosto's romance and classical epic, the Italian poem possesses or appropriates enough of the "serious" features of Virgilian epic to constitute a modern equivalent to it that is as grand and as edifying.

Pigna's effort to present the *Furioso* as a modern classic by advertising all the features it shared with the ancient ones was, as I proposed earlier, more characteristic of the midcentury promotion of Ariosto's poem than Giraldi's manifesto on behalf of the postclassical virtues of the Italian romanzo. But who, besides individual champions of the *Furioso* like Pigna and Giraldi, sought to elevate the poem to a more prestigious status? The main promotional effort—and one that had a wider impact than individual treatises like Pigna's—was undertaken by Venetian publishers and their editors. Indeed, the legitimation of *Orlando Furioso* can be said to have occurred primarily as a result of the vast number of Venetian editions, issued between the 1540s and the 1570s, that presented the poem as the new classic of the age. Before turning to this collective effort, however, we must mention another individual's contribution: Simone Fornari's *Spositione sopra l'Orlando Furioso* (1549–1550). This two-volume work contained a biography of Ariosto, an "Apologia" in his defense, an essay on the allusions in the *Furioso*, and an extensive commentary on each canto of the poem. The second volume opened with an essay justifying the allegorization of the poem and was followed by a detailed interpretation of what Fornari considered to be the principal allegorical segments of the poem: Ruggiero's adventures on Alcina's island followed by his moral reorientation at the hands of Logistilla (cantos 6–10); and Astolfo's various exploits, especially his extraterrestrial journey to the moon under the guidance of St. John (cantos 15 and 33–35). Fornari's detailed exegesis clearly enhanced the value of the poem by revealing what moral benefits and learning it contained.[13] But it is on his prefatory "Apologia" that I want to dwell, because this defense succinctly illustrates the kind of rhetoric that was adopted in the middle of the century to argue for the poem's legitimacy.

Like Pigna's defense, Fornari's "Apologia brieve sopra tutto l'Orlando

Furioso" also attempts to argue for the poem's classicism, but with a specific aim: to demonstrate that, whatever claims had been made to the contrary, *Orlando Furioso* complied with Aristotle's definition of epic poetry
set forth in the *Poetics*. As I pointed out initially, Fornari's "Apologia"
actually provides the earliest record of neo-Aristotelian criticism of the
poem, the primary objection being that it lacked unity of action. Other
such complaints, cited by Fornari, were that Ariosto speaks too much in
his own person, that the disposition of his work shows total lack of art,
and that the marvelous events in the poem exceed the limits of verisimilitude. Fornari's main task in the "Apologia" is to defend "l'ingegnoso
e dottissimo nostro poeta" against these objections, which he does by asserting that, the accusations against him notwithstanding, Ariosto does
satisfy Aristotle's requisites for epic. For instance, after reporting the objection against Ariosto's incredible marvels, he maintains that according to
Aristotle it is verisimilar to depict events that fall outside the verisimilar,
and, moreover, that epic requires marvelous events to achieve its wondrous
effects.[14]

Fornari is especially keen to deny the main accusation against the *Furioso*, namely, that Ariosto tells not of a single action "ma diverse et non un
cavalier solo, ma molti prese a dover cantare." He counters by claiming that
the poem does have a single plot, organized around Agramante's conflict
with Carlomagno. Just as the principal action of the *Iliad* is the anger of
Achilles, so, Fornari maintains, the ire and "giovanil furori d'Agramante"
constitute the main action of *Orlando Furioso*. To those who object to
Ariosto's title by arguing that it should have referred to the conflict between Agramante and Carlomagno, if that was its main action, Fornari
defends the existing title by again invoking Homer's authority. "Non sempre si vede," he claims, "che della prencipal attione viene il libro denomi-
nato. Il che si conosce al titolo della Iliade, nella quale quantunque Homero prendesse ad dire dell'ira d'Achille, pure Iliade, e non Achilleide gli
piacque, che si chiamasse [One does not always find a book named on the
basis of its main action, as can be seen in the title of the *Iliad*, which,
however much of it Homer devoted to the anger of Achilles, he chose
rather to call it the *Iliad* and not the *Achilleid*]."[15] As for the other plot
lines and the many other characters and events in Ariosto's poem, Fornari
explains that they are accidental elements that should be counted as episodes. Aristotle, he goes on to claim, allowed epic to have many episodes;
he then justifies their great number in the *Furioso* by maintaining that the
Odyssey has just as high a proportion of them in relation to its main plot.
His basic rhetorical strategy is to find, or rather impose, structural analogies between Ariosto's poem and Homer's epics, and then to adduce that
these aspects of the *Furioso* would have met with Aristotle's approval since
the Greek philosopher based his definition of epic on Homer's practice. In

a few instances he shows how the Italian poem fulfills Aristotle's requisites without bringing in Homeric parallels. For example, he points out that the "peripetie" Aristotle deemed so effective can be found in the changing fortunes of Agramante, or in the relations between Bradamante and Ruggiero. But, on the whole, he bases his defense of Ariosto's classicism on the claim that the poet "imitò diligentemente, in ogni parte e Homero, e Virgilio, & sempre a quelli hebbe gli occhi intesi [carefully imitated both Homer and Virgil everywhere, and he always had his eyes on them]."[16]

Pigna, as we saw, drew ingenious thematic parallels between the *Furioso* and the ancient epics. Fornari presents a similar kind of argument, except that he devotes his ingenuity to finding structural parallels. From our vantage point, both Pigna's and Fornari's efforts to show the resemblances of the *Furioso* to Homer's and Virgil's epics seem strained and less than convincing. However, at the time they were making these claims neoclassical criticism had not yet established the differences between the modern romanzo and the ancient epic clearly enough to deter them from assimilating Ariosto's practice to that of the ancients. How ready the Italian reading public was to accept this kind of assimilation is made evident by the fact that the basic promotional strategy of the Venetian publishers of the *Furioso* was also to advertise the poem's resemblances to Virgil's and Homer's epics.

The project of legitimizing the *Furioso*, as I mentioned already, was undertaken primarily by a group of Venetian publishers and their editors, beginning in the early 1540s. The publisher who initiated this promotional effort and who was largely responsible for its success was Gabriel Giolito. In fact, the presentation of the *Furioso* as a new classic begins with the publication in 1542 of the first of the numerous Giolito editions.[17] The full title of it was *Orlando Furioso di M. Ludovico Ariosto novissimamente alla sua integrita ridotto & ornato di varie figure. Con alcune stanze del S. Aluigi Gonzaga in lode del medesimo. Aggiuntovi per ciascun canto alcune allegorie et nel fine una breue espositione et tavola di tutto quello, che nell'opera si contiene.* For the next twenty years Giolito's was the most frequently reissued edition of the poem. By 1560 no less than twenty-seven editions both in quarto and in octavo had appeared. And even when other Venetian publishers such as Valvassori and Valgrisi began to produce rival editions in the 1550s, they continued to imitate the basic format that Giolito had introduced in 1542.

What made Giolito's presentation of the poem new was not simply the illustrations and "paratexts" announced in the title of the 1542 edition. It was also that these various texts (mostly composed by Lodovico Dolce) accompanying the poem aimed to convey its serious status and pedigree. Giolito's own dedicatory letter to the Dauphin of France affirmed from the start that the *Furioso* was not just another chivalric romance but one of the

rare poems of modern times that matched the perfection achieved by the
ancient poets. Ariosto, claims Giolito, "la bassezza de' Romanzi ha con l'ali
del suo raro e felice ingegno a tanta altezza recata, che per aventura a più
sublime segno il gran Virgilio non recò l'arme di Enea [has, with his rare
and happy genius, raised the lowliness of romances to such heights that
perchance even the great Virgil did not raise the feats of Aeneas to a more
sublime level]." The publisher's intention to present the poem as a work
comparable to Virgil's and Homer's epics becomes more apparent when he
advertises its moral utility. He does this by listing the various *exempla* of
good and evil conduct that the poem provides. Here is to be found, he
writes,

> la prudenza e la giustitia d'ottimo Principe; qui la temerità et la trascurazione
> di non savio Re accompagnata con la tirannide; qui l'ardire e la timidità: qui la
> fortezza e la viltà: qui la castità & la impudicità: qui l'ingegno, e la scioc-
> chezza: qui i buoni e i rei consigli sono in modo dipinti & espressi ch'io
> ardisco dire, che non è libro veruno, dal quale & con più frutto, et con mag-
> gior diletto imparar si possa quello, che per noi fuggire e seguitare si debbia.[18]

> [the prudence and justice of a perfect prince; the rashness and negligence of
> an unwise king, coupled with tyranny, daring and timidity, fortitude and cow-
> ardice, chastity and immodesty, intelligence and stupidity; here good and evil
> advice are so represented and expressed that I dare say not a single book exists
> from which one can learn with more profit and delight that which we must
> avoid or follow.]

This sort of claim had previously been made about the canonical poems of
antiquity. "Does Homer lack any sort of wisdom," Leonardo Bruni had
asked, "that we should refuse him the repute of being most wise? Some say
that his poetry provides a complete doctrine of life in peace and war. And
indeed in the affairs of war, what has he not told us of the prudence of the
general, of the cunning and bravery of the soldier, of the kinds of trickery
to be allowed or omitted, of advice, of counsel?"[19] Similarly, later humanists praise the *Aeneid* as a moral and political guide to the better life. In fact,
one of the best-known endorsements of this sort was Cristoforo Landino's
praefatio to Virgil's *Opera*, first published in 1487 and reprinted in numerous editions thereafter. "As to what pertains to living well and happily,"
claims Landino, "who does not see that all the precepts by which human
life is rightly governed are made visible by this poet"; he goes on to describe the various moral benefits the *Aeneid* provides.[20] In the preface to
the most frequently reprinted Latin edition of Ovid's *Metamorphoses* Raf-
faelo Regio proclaims that "there is nothing appertaining to the knowledge and glorie of warre, whereof we have not famous examples" in the
work. "Neither shall you finde any Author, from whom, a civill life may
gather better instructions."[21] Such claims were not usually advanced about

modern vernacular poems, at least not before Giolito started making them about *Orlando Furioso*. By ascribing the same didactic range and richness to the Italian poem he was obviously trying to equate its moral usefulness with that of the most edifying poems of antiquity.

The editor of the Giolito *Furioso* was Lodovico Dolce, who was to be, for the next twenty-five years, Giolito's (and one can even say Venice's) most important editor in the field of modern literature.[22] Dolce sought to reveal more specifically Ariosto's didactic intent proclaimed in the publisher's dedicatory letter by providing, for the first time, brief *allegorie* at the head of each canto. Here, for example, is the *allegoria* he devised for canto 8:

> In questo ottavo per Ruggiero; che vinti i ministri di Alcina se ne va a Logistilla; si comprende l'huomo superati gli assalti dell'appetito ritrarsi alla vita virtuosa. In Orlando, il quale per cercare Angelica abbandona la difesa di Parigi; altro non si contiene che la forza di Amore: il quale quando avviene, che troppo signoreggi l'huomo fa, che egli per conseguire suoi desideri le cose honeste & utili, alle biasimevoli & dannose pospone.

> [In this eighth [canto] Ruggiero overcomes the agents of Alcina and goes away to Logistilla. [His action] signifies a return to the virtuous life once he has overcome the assaults of the appetites. Orlando's abandoning the defenses of Paris in order to go in quest of Angelica signifies the force of Love, which when it rules a man too much, makes him, in pursuit of his desires, turn from things honest and useful to others both blameworthy and harmful.]

Despite his disregard of the various other events treated in the canto—most notably the Hermit's attempted rape of Angelica, her being kidnapped by pirates, and her exposure to the monster Orca—Dolce extrapolates from the opening and closing actions enough moral commonplaces to affirm the canto's didactic value.

Some *allegorie* consist of vague generalizations that are tagged on simply to give a canto some moral point. Hence, for example, the rather banal *allegoria* of canto 9: "In questo nono ne gli varij accidenti di Olimpia et di Bireno contengonsi i diversi mutamenti della Fortuna [In canto 9, the vicissitudes of Olimpia and Bireno demonstrate the changeableness of Fortune]." In general, one is struck by the selectiveness of Dolce's allegorizations. Whenever certain actions that violate moral conventions are treated sympathetically in a canto—for example, Ricciardetto's comic account of his seduction of Fiordispina in canto 25—Dolce ignores them and, instead, moralizes less prominent, even marginal events in that canto. Nonetheless, tangential and reductive though some of them are, when taken together (there are forty-six of them), Dolce's *allegorie* reinforce the publisher's initial claims about the poem's didactic usefulness. They also serve to make the text more ethically assimilable.

Another measure Dolce took to enhance the status of Ariosto's poem was to establish its ties to the epic poems of antiquity. Dolce had already equated Ariosto's and Virgil's epic achievements in the eulogistic sonnet he composed for the Giolito edition and which began "Spirito Divin, ne le cui dotte carte / Fra bei concetti al gran Virgilio equali." But he realized that to acclaim Ariosto as the Virgil of Ferrara was not enough. He had to establish more concretely the distinguished pedigree of the *Furioso*, which he did by providing the first separate commentary on Ariosto's imitations of the ancient poets. Entitled a "Brieve dimostratione di molte comparationi et sentenze dall'Ariosto in diversi autori imitate," it was appended to all the Giolito editions, and, as we shall see, it was also appropriated in rival editions.

Dolce's commentary aimed primarily to indicate the ancient models of the poem's extended similes. Ariosto, it will be recalled, resorted frequently to such comparisons and already among his first readers they were one of the poem's most admired features. Although the title of his "Dimostratione" announces that it will refer to the "diversi autori" from whose works Ariosto drew similes and other borrowings, it soon becomes apparent that Dolce is not interested in the diverse and complex sources of Ariosto's poem but primarily in its epic pedigree, and especially in its Virgilian ancestry. Almost all the similes Dolce selects—he cites nearly thirty of them—are shown to be derived solely from the *Aeneid*. To be sure, many of Ariosto's extended similes were modeled on ones in the *Aeneid*, even though a number of them had other ancestors than Virgil's or others besides his. It was precisely because Ariosto's similes could so often be shown to have demonstrable Virgilian origins that Dolce focused on them rather than on any other imitative feature in Ariosto's poem. It must be recalled, moreover, that, at least since Virgil's imitations of Homer's use of them, such similes had become a hallmark of literary epic. What better bias could Dolce take to assert the *Furioso*'s epic pedigree, and especially the Virgilian strain of that pedigree, than to focus primarily on Ariosto's borrowed similes?

Dolce's commentary will be examined in more detail in the next chapter. For the moment it should be observed that the "Brieve dimostratione" does not simply comment on the origins of Ariosto's similes, it also identifies the models of larger imitative episodes in the poem. But, as with the similes, Dolce chooses to cite primarily the passages that can be shown to be imitations of the *Aeneid*. For instance, he points out that Melissa's mission to extricate Ruggiero from the clutches of Alcina is modeled on Mercury's mission to urge Aeneas to leave Dido and Carthage, or that Rodomonte's single-handed battle against the Christians inside Paris is modeled on Turnus's similar exploits inside the Trojan camp in *Aeneid* 9, or again, that the night expedition of Cloridano and Medoro is modeled on that of

Nisus and Euryalus. It is true that these and other heroic exploits in the course of the war between Carlomagno and Agramante were modéled, at least in part, on Virgil's epic. Yet Ariosto also imitated various other authors, often more recent vernacular precursors. Frequently he imitated these vernacular precursors at the same time that he imitated Virgil. Dolce, however, in his effort to make the *Aeneid* appear to be the dominant model, virtually disregards the works of the *diversi autori* that make up the complex intertextual fabric of the *Furioso*. While he refers to a few classical authors other than Virgil whom Ariosto also chose to imitate, the only model besides the *Aeneid* that he cites several times is Ovid's *Metamorphoses*. However, far from citing all the imitations of Ovid's poem that he must have recognized (Dolce translated the *Metamorphoses* into ottava rima), he selects, rather, grand or heroic episodes that served as models—for example, Perseus's combat with the sea monster when he rescues Andromeda in book 4 of the *Metamorphoses*, or the "epic" storm described in book 11. Perhaps Dolce disregarded the other, mostly amatory, episodes Ariosto imitated in the *Metamorphoses* and the *Heroides* because he wanted to emphasize the Italian poem's ties to Roman epic and therefore focused on passages dealing with *arme* rather than *amori*. There was another reason why he chose not to identify all the imitations of Ovid in the *Furioso*: it would have diminished the dominant role he wanted the *Aeneid* to have as a model.

It made sense to have the "Brieve dimostratione" on Ariosto's borrowings follow, as it did, the dedicatory sonnet in which Dolce acclaimed Ariosto as Virgil's equal, since the commentary extended the claims of the sonnet by establishing more specifically the similarities between the *Furioso* and the *Aeneid*. Besides this commentary, Dolce provided two other aids for readers in the 1542 Giolito edition: an "Espositione di tutti i vocaboli et luochi difficili" that glossed difficult or archaic terms and names of remote places and regions, and that also elucidated mythological allusions in the poem; and an inventory of "Descrittioni, . . . proverbi, sentenze, & altre cose di memoria," intended to serve readers who quickly wanted to extract from the poem ornaments, beautiful descriptions, or pithy moral sayings with which to enrich their own rhetorical efforts. Dolce's final *florilegium* served in its own way to affirm the distinguished status of the *Furioso* by reminding readers that, like the canonical poems of antiquity whose rhetorical flowers and proverbial lore they were taught to collect, the Italian poem was equally a storehouse of *copia* that could be exploited to enrich their own eloquence.

These various paratexts were regularly reprinted in the numerous Giolito editions, but it was especially the "Brieve dimostratione" that enjoyed a wide dissemination, since, beginning with the Blado edition of the *Furioso* published in Rome in 1543, Dolce's commentary on the borrowed

similes was regularly appended to numerous editions other than Giolito's
for the rest of the century. That the entire format of *Orlando Furioso* con-
ceived by Giolito and Dolce satisfied midcentury readers is confirmed by
the fact that between 1542 and 1560 twenty-seven Giolito editions were
published. The success of their presentation of the poem is also affirmed by
the efforts of rival publishers to imitate and improve upon it. In the course
of providing similarly annotated and illustrated editions, Giolito's Venetian rivals helped to establish more firmly the status of the *Furioso* as a
modern classic.

    The first of these rival editions (the first, that is, to be reissued quite
regularly) was the one published by G. A. Valvassori in 1553. It was entitled *Orlando Furioso di M. Lodovico Ariosto. Ornato di nuove figure, &*
allegorie in ciascun canto. Aggiuntovi nel fine l'espositione de' luoghi diffi-
cili. . . . Although this edition had some peculiar characteristics—for example, an entirely new set of woodcut illustrations—its *allegorie* and other
paratextual features were imitative of the Giolito editions (in 1548 Valvassori had printed an earlier edition of the poem that was hardly distinguish-
able from the ones issued by Giolito).[23] One of these similarities was a
prefatory eulogy of Ariosto's work composed by Clemente Valvassori, a
prominent Venetian jurist and relative of the publisher. Clemente, however, goes beyond Giolito's prefatory claim that the *Furioso* was as edifying
a heroic poem as Homer's and Virgil's. He maintains that Ariosto's work
possesses superior didactic value because, as a Christian poem, it carries
none of the liabilities inherent in the pagan and polytheistic worldview of
the ancient epic poets. The "divino" Ariosto, he writes, has in Italian

> rilevata l'Eroica composizione a tanta altezza, a quanta giammai s'alzasse per
> Virgilio, ed Omero nella loro favella. Né però qui si legge la moltitudine de'
> Dei, né la lor discordia; non gli adulteri, né gli scelerati lor congiungimenti,
> che non senza gran rossore si potrebbono dir'eziandio degli animali ir-
> ragionevoli. Ma qui un solo Iddio, eterno, giusto, ed immutabile con per-
> petua providenza dispone, e governa le cose umane; qui si castigano i com-
> messi peccati; e si guiderdonano i beni; qui è innalzato il leggitimo Prencipe, e
> l'empio Tiranno è posto al fondo; qui si vede, quanto siano brevi l'umane
> allegrezze, e infinite le miserie. Ed in brieve, qui appariscono innanzi agli
> occhi le virtù tanto illustri, ed in tal maniera fulminati vizi, che niuno Filosofo,
> non che altro Poeta meglio insegna o esprime quel, che per noi seguitar, e
> fuggir si debba in questa vita mortale.

> [raised epic poetry to heights that Virgil and Homer never raised it in their
> languages. Here, therefore, one does not read about the multitude of gods, or
> their clashes, their adulteries and their wicked unions that could not even be
> spoken of in connection with irrational animals except with great shame. But
> here [is to be found] one sole, eternal, and unchanging God, who orders and
> governs human affairs with perpetual providence; here committed sins are

punished, and good behavior is rewarded; here the legitimate prince is elevated, and the wicked tyrant is cast down; here one sees how short-lived human happiness is, how endless are human miseries. In short, here the virtues are made to appear so noble and vices so castigated, that no philosopher nor any other poet teaches or expresses better what in this mortal life must be followed and what must be shunned.]

Valvassori substantiates his claims about Ariosto's Christian, more pessimistic vision of the world ("qui si vede, quanto siano brevi l'umane allegrezze, e infinite le miserie") by providing moralizations of each canto, as Dolce had done. Though more detailed than the ones in the Giolito editions, these *allegorie* also tend to single out only episodes and segments in individual cantos that can be made to exemplify conventional moral truths of a very general sort. Here, for example, is the *allegoria* that precedes canto 11:

Per Ruggiero, il quale scordatosi di Bradamante gitta l'asta e lo scudo per abbraciarsi con Angelica: si dimostra, che quando l'uomo obblia l'Amor divino, spogliatosi d'ogni fortezza d'animo si sottomette a cose terrene. Per Angelica, che se ne fugge da Ruggiero, e s'involge ne' panni rozzi; si loda la Vergine, che schifa gli amanti, e per onestà nasconde la sua bellezza. Per l'Ippogriffo, che trattosi il morso, libero saglie in aria; si dinota, che l'appetito senza il freno de la ragione, chiede sempre cose instabili, e vane. Per Ruggiero, che nel bosco si pone a seguire la falsa immagine di Bradamante; compredesi come in questa vita mortale ingannati dal senso apprendiamo per vere le cose apparenti, e false. Per gli abitatori di Ebuda, che vollero uccidere Orlando, il quale aveva morta l'orca, ch'essi per vana Religione pascevano di belle Donne; si vede il pericolo, che s'incorre cercando di liberar il volgo ignorante da qualche superstizione.

[Ruggiero, who, having forgotten Bradamante, casts off the lance and the shield to clasp Angelica, illustrates that when man forgets divine love he subjects himself to earthly things, stripped of all spiritual strength. In Angelica, who flees Ruggiero and puts on rough clothes, praise is given the virgin who shuns lovers and hides her beauty for the sake of honesty. The Hippogryph, who frees himself from the bit and rises up to the sky, denotes that the appetite, without reason to constrain it, always seeks unstable and vain things. Ruggiero, who, in the woods, decides to follow the false image of Bradamante, signifies how in this mortal life, deceived by the senses, we take false appearances for real things. In the inhabitants of Ebuda who wanted to kill Orlando after he slew the Orca, the monster to whom they fed beautiful damsels for the sake of false religion, one can see the danger risked in trying to free the ignorant rabble of some superstition.]

It hardly needs stating that this prefatory moralization does not dispose the reader to enjoy the comedy of Ruggiero's frustrated attempt to rape Angelica and of her ensuing escape, as well as that of the Hippogryph. These events, incidentally, take up only the first twenty stanzas of the canto, but it is this short initial segment that is made to generate the important moral lessons of the entire canto. Ruggiero's erotic misfortunes may receive disproportionate attention because his adventures, in general, since his arrival on Alcina's island in canto 6, are seen by all of the allegorizers to constitute the most important continuous allegory in the poem. Nonetheless, the fact remains that the major event in canto 11—Orlando's struggle with and killing of the Orca, and his rescue of Olimpia—is ignored in the *allegoria*, presumably because it cannot be made to yield enough moral instruction different from that derived from Ruggiero's preceding rescue of Angelica from the same Orca. Valvassori does dwell on the Ebudans' less than grateful reception of Olimpia's liberator. That he comments on this incident rather than on the happy outcome of Olimpia's liberation—her union with King Oberto—betrays his tendency to dwell on the negative or adverse events in Ariosto's narrative.

Defeats, delusions, frustrations, betrayals, and deaths of protagonists—when these occur in a canto, they are likely to be the events moralized. Whenever he can, Valvassori seeks to ascribe to the author a bleak and pessimistic view of "questa vita mortale," even when such pessimistic readings are clearly not warranted by Ariosto's fiction. Here, as a characteristic instance, is how he moralizes the fantastic and delightful scene in canto 4 when Bradamante, in the company of an innkeeper and his retainers, first catches sight of Atlante flying through the sky on the Hippogryph:

> Atlante, che rapisce, e seco ne porta prigionere le belle donne: significa il nostro affetto carnale, che 'n tutto spoglia della libertà l'anime nostre. L'ali dell'Ippogrifo grandi e di colore diverso: disegnano la violenza dell'appetito, e la varietà de' pensieri pronti ad ingombrarne il cuore.

> [Atlante, who kidnaps beautiful ladies and carries them off as prisoners, signifies our carnal desire that altogether deprives our souls of freedom. The large wings of the Hippogryph and their various colors designate the violence of the appetite and the many thoughts ready to encumber the heart.]

By repeated pessimistic interpretations of this sort Valvassori seeks to convince readers that a severe morality underlies the deceptively comic surface of the text. The world represented in the poem, according to his *allegorie*, is a vale of delusion and tears where desire, carnality, and blindness only lead to frustration and despair unless God's redeeming grace intervenes. To modern readers such a partial and totally humorless interpretation of the work may seem unresponsive to Ariosto's ironic but often sympathetic vision of the *comédie humaine*. But Valvassori was not seeking to do justice to Ariosto's humorous and ironic treatment of human folly. His severe readings, however strained, aimed to gain more respectability for the *Furioso* by making it appear to be a work full of edifying Christian morality. Ultimately they served to reinforce his prefatory claims that it was as a *Christian* epic, not simply as an epic worthy of the ancients, that Ariosto's poem deserved a place in the canon.

While Valvassori's editions were being republished with some frequency in the period 1554–1563, there appeared in 1556 another rival edition that became very popular in the course of the next fifteen years, the Valgrisi *Furioso*, edited by Girolamo Ruscelli. The "paratextual" features of the Valgrisi edition were announced on its title page: *Orlando Furioso. Di M. Lodovico Ariosto, tutto ricorretto, et di nuove figure adornato. Alquale di nuovo sono aggiunte le Annotationi, gli Avvertimenti, et le Dichiarationi di Girolamo Ruscelli, la Vita dell'autore, descritta dal Signor Giovambattista Pigna, gli scontri de' luoghi mutati dall'autore dopo la sua prima impressione, la Dichiaratione di tutte le favole, il Vocabolario di tutte le parole oscure, et altre cose utili et necessarie.* Girolamo Ruscelli, who had already produced an edition of Petrarch's *Canzoniere*, and an edition of Boccaccio's *Decameron* intended to rival Dolce's, and who had attacked Dolce as author, critic, and translator, now sought to rival him as the editorial custodian of Ariosto's poem.[24] Yet this competitive motive hardly deterred Ruscelli from imitating the format of the Giolito editions and, as I will point out shortly, from even appropriating some of Dolce's editorial matter. Like the Giolito edition, Valgrisi's contained *allegorie*, illustrations (the wood engravings in this edition are full-page and more lavish), and a *raccolto* of Ariosto's imitations from ancient poets, as well as glosses on difficult words, place names, and historical and mythological allusions. (These explanatory notes are now appended at the end of each canto.) But, as the full title above indicates, it also contained new paratexts that served to establish further the canonical status of the poem.

One of these new features was the addition of Pigna's "Life" of Ariosto, which, as I pointed out earlier, was originally part of book 2 of his 1554 treatise on *I romanzi*. To appreciate the illustrative (in the sense of making more illustrious) function of this biography one has to recall that part of the traditional commentary on Virgil was the poet's "Life" attributed to Donatus, and that this biography regularly prefaced quattrocento and early cinquecento editions of Virgil's *Opera*. Ovid's *Opera* were similarly prefaced with his biography. Given this convention of including a biography in the works of the major ancient poets, Valgrisi or Ruscelli must have deemed that the status of Ariosto as the age's poet laureate could be more strongly affirmed by including Pigna's "Life" at the beginning of his edition. Readers who may have failed to appreciate that the very inclusion of a "Life" conferred laureate status on Ariosto found that status affirmed in

the text of the biography itself, especially when Pigna recounts Ariosto's
efforts to elevate Italian poetry to the heights attained by the great ancient
poets. Here is his account of the ambition that spurred Ariosto to write the
Furioso:

> Ma veggendo egli quanto fosse il numero de'poeti Latini; e quello che più
> pesa, quanto alcuni di loro in alto saliti fossero, & dall'altro lato considerando
> che nella nostra lingua un luogo vi era non ancora occupato, & in che egli atto
> si sentiva a poter entrare; voltatosi alla Toscana poesia, prese per suo oggetto il
> comporre Romanzevolmente,   havendo   tal   componimento   per   simile
> all'Eroico, e all'Epico, nel quale egli conosceva di potere haver buona lena, &
> nel qual tuttavia non vedea alcuno che con dignità, & magnificamente poeteg-
> giato havesse.

> [But seeing how numerous were the Latin poets, and what is more important,
> to what heights some of them had risen, and considering, on the other hand,
> that in our tongue there was a place that had not yet been taken, and one that
> he felt he could suitably occupy, he turned to Tuscan poetry, and set out to
> write a romance. He deemed that such a composition was similar to heroic
> and epic poetry, and one in which he knew he had the necessary strength, and
> yet he saw no poet who had written such heroic poetry with magnificence and
> with dignity.]

As this passage already indicates, Pigna wanted to show the deliberateness
of Ariosto's epic undertaking. Whereas an editor like Giolito had simply
asserted that the *Furioso* was no mere chivalric romance but a poetic
achievement as grand as the ancient epics, Pigna devised a biography centered on Ariosto's deliberate conception and writing of a modern equivalent of those epics. I mentioned earlier, when discussing book 2 of *I romanzi*, that Pigna also sought to depict Ariosto as the Virgil of his age by
drawing parallels between their poetic procedures. In the excerpts of the
"Life" published by Valgrisi the most striking of these parallels occurs
when Pigna justifies Ariosto's decision to write a sequel to *Orlando Innamorato*. Critics of the *Furioso* were already citing this dependence on
Boiardo as evidence of Ariosto's lack of invention. But Pigna argues that
his decision to continue poetic matter made famous by Boiardo was the
modern equivalent of Virgil's choice to continue treating Homer's heroic
matter after the Fall of Troy. "Essendo," he writes,

> che i soggetti del Conte [Boiardo] erano già nella loro mente impressi, &
> istabiliti in tal guisa, che egli non continuandogli, ma diversa istoria comin-
> ciando, cosa poco dilettevole composto havrebbe. Vergilio medesimamente
> dalla poesia d'Omero non si partì, per esser ella già da tutti accettata, & in tutti
> confirmata sì, ch'ogni cosa da lei dissimile, come non poetica, sarebbe stata
> dispregiata da ogn'uno.

[Given that Boiardo's subject matter was already familiar to readers, and so implanted in their minds that, had he not continued it, but, instead, begun a different story, he would have composed something not very pleasant. Virgil similarly chose not to depart from Homer's poetry, given that it was already so accepted and approved by all that anything different from it would have been disdained by everyone as unpoetic.]

So keen was Valgrisi (or was it Ruscelli?) to bring out parallels between Ariosto's and Virgil's careers that, in an addition to Pigna's "Life," first made in the 1560 Valgrisi edition (and not to be found in the original version of Pigna's biography in *I romanzi*), an analogy was drawn between Ariosto's progression from the "umiltà" of his comedies to the "mediocrità" of his satires to the "altezza" of the *Furioso* and the famous progression from pastoral to georgic to epic that characterized Virgil's career.[25]

In *I romanzi* Pigna drew a number of other parallels between Ariosto's and Virgil's poems. These were omitted in the "Life" prefacing the Valgrisi edition because they were not biographical considerations, but also because the editor Ruscelli wanted to indicate these parallels in his own "Annotationi" that followed the poem. Actually, most of the commentary Ruscelli appended to make readers appreciate Ariosto's direct relation to the ancient epic poets was not his own. The first of these "Annotationi," a summary of resemblances between the *Furioso* and the epics of Homer and Virgil, was composed by Tullio Fausto da Longiano as early as 1540, and published originally in the Bindoni and Pasini edition of the poem in 1542. But this very early account of Homeric and Virgilian parallels was not reprinted again, nor did it gain considerable dissemination, until it was appropriated by Ruscelli for the Valgrisi editions.

Fausto da Longiano had defended both Boiardo's and Ariosto's Orlando poems by drawing parallels between them and the epics of antiquity. However, when Ruscelli incorporated this list of parallels in his "Annotationi," he omitted references to Boiardo's poem, and made it look as though Fausto da Longiano had indicated similarities only between Ariosto and the ancient epic poets. The first parallels with the *Iliad* are broad and soon become rather strained. Ariosto, writes Ruscelli,

> fu diligente imitatore de i poeti antichi, Greci & Latini, e massime de i supremi due, Omero, & Virgilio; né da loro si dilunga molto. Il poeta greco, & il Latino, presero un medesimo soggetto, che fu della guerra Troiana, l'Ariosto ad imitatione loro formò un'altra quasi consimile guerra. . . . La causa della guerra Troiana fu la rapina d'Elena, onde per rihaverla, et per vendicarsi dell'oltraggio ricevuto Menelao, & Agamennone fratelli, congregarono tutta la Grecia a quella fattione in suo favore. La causa della guerra di Francia, fu la morte di Troiano, che Agramante per desiderio di vendetta del padre, fece

uno sforzo di tutte le genti d'Africa, che poteron portar' arme, et convocò tutti gli agenti, et s'aggiunse a Marsilio, il quale era già venuto con tutta la Spagna a danni di Francia. Come la guerra Troiana non poteva spedirsi senza Ulisse, così la Francese non devea farsi senza Brunello. . . . Achille era stato preveduto, che havea a morir in quella impresa Troiana, giovane. Ruggiero devea finir sua vita in Francia, giovane. . . .

[was a diligent imitator of the ancient Greek and Latin poets, and especially the two supreme ones, Homer and Virgil; nor does he depart from them much. The Greek and the Latin poet treated a similar subject, which was the Trojan War. Ariosto, imitating them, devised another somewhat similar war. . . . The cause of the Trojan War was the rape of Helen. In order to regain her, and to avenge the insult suffered by the brothers Menelaus and Agamemnon, all of Greece gathered together to fight on their behalf. The cause of the war of France was Troiano's death, after which Agramante, eager to avenge his father's death, put together an army consisting of all the Africans who could bear arms. He convened all the forces, and joined Marsilio, who had already come with all of Spain to the detriment of France. As the Trojan War could not proceed without Odysseus, so the French one could not get under way without Brunello. . . . Achilles was forewarned that he would die young in this Trojan struggle. Ruggiero was to end his life prematurely in France. . . .]

But the list becomes more convincing when it focuses on similarities between the protagonists in the *Furioso* and their counterparts in the *Aeneid*: "Per Carlo Re di Francia, ritrasse Latino; . . . per Rodomonte, Mezentio; per Marfisa, & Bradamante, Pantesilea, & Camilla; per Alcina, Circe; per Cloridano, & Medoro, Niso, & Eurialo; . . . per Melissa, Iuturna. . . ." Ruscelli actually enlarges the original list of parallels by indicating ancient analogues to some of the more fantastic episodes in Ariosto's poem. "Non solo s'è accomodato de i nomi," Ruscelli writes, as he adds to Fausto da Longiano's comments,

ma di molte cose ancora; come Angelica isposta al monstro liberato da Ruggiero su l'Ippogrifo rappresenta Andromeda esposta al monstro liberata da Perseo su'l cavallo Pegaseo; Olimpia lasciata da Bireno nell'isola, Ariadna lasciata da Teseo; le trasformationi de gli huomini in diverse forme nell'isola d'Alcina, quelle di Circe; la novella del Re de' Nubi, et dell'Arpie, la cosa di Fineo; la novella dell'orco, la favola di Polifemo; . . . per lo sterpo in cui era convertito Astolfo, lamentandosi con Ruggiero, lo sterpo di Polidoro, dolendosi con Enea.

[He not only borrowed names but many things besides; as Angelica exposed to the monster freed by Ruggiero on the Hippogryph reproduces Andromeda

exposed to the monster freed by Perseus on the horse Pegasus; Olimpia abandoned by Bireno on the island, Ariadne abandoned by Theseus; the transformations of men into various shapes on Alcina's island, those of Circe; the story
of the king of the Nubians and the Harpies reproduces the story of Phineus;
the story of the Orco, that of Polyphemus; the bush into which Astolfo was
transformed as he complains to Ruggiero, Polydorus as a bush lamenting to
Aeneas.]

These additions are not accidentally devoted to the more fantastic episodes
in the *Furioso*. Pigna, it will be recalled, had pointed out in his letter to
Giraldi that critics objected to the frequency of supernatural occurrences in
the poem. And in book 2 of *I romanzi*—in the course of his biography of
the poet—he countered this criticism by invoking Virgilian and other classical precedents of some of the magical and fantastic events in the *Furioso*. It
is likely that Ruscelli was following Pigna's example. In any case, like Pigna,
he made these fantastic episodes more legitimate by similarly establishing
their venerable ancient precedence.

Ruscelli appropriated even more commentary from rival editions to establish the Italian poem's ancient pedigree. One of the paratexts also included in the appendix of the Valgrisi edition was a "Raccolto di molti
luoghi, tolti, et felicemente imitati in più autori, dall'Ariosto nel Furioso."
Ruscelli announces at the beginning of this "Raccolto" that he is indebted
to previous commentary on Ariosto's imitations, but that he has added to
and revised this earlier scholarship. In fact, after elaborating on Dolce's
preliminary remarks on canto 1, Ruscelli lifted all of Dolce's "Brieve dimostratione" from the Giolito edition and passed it off as his own. Clearly,
once he realized that he could not improve upon Dolce's commentary, he
simply appropriated it. It made a useful addition to his "Annotationi"
given that the general aim of this appendix was to reveal as many resemblances as could be drawn between the *Furioso* and the epic poems of antiquity. Actually, when one counts its surreptitious inclusion in the Valgrisi
editions, it becomes obvious that Dolce's commentary did more than any
other text in the middle of the cinquecento to link the *Furioso* to the
Aeneid. Just between 1542 and 1565 (counting its appearance in seven
Valgrisi editions) the "Brieve dimostratione" appeared in nearly forty
editions.

The main effect of the promotional efforts of editors such as Ruscelli and
Dolce, and of the publishers who employed them, was to make the reading
public connect Ariosto's poem to the epics of antiquity. What else did their
promotion achieve? By endowing *Orlando Furioso* with an epic ancestry,
by simplifying as well as enhancing its origins, by reducing its meanings to a
series of moral commonplaces, they stabilized the text and anchored it to a
canonical heritage. Also, by leading readers to believe that they could gain

from Ariosto's poem whatever edification Homer's and Virgil's poems had provided, these promoters caused readers to perceive the *Furioso* as a serious poem—that is to say, to perceive it in terms of what they thought was serious about poetry.

Legitimacy was also conferred on the modern poem by publishing it in large illustrated editions, supplemented by commentaries and various paratexts—in a format, that is, usually reserved for the major ancient authors. Aside from the fact that the demand for editions rose dramatically from the late 1540s to the end of the 1560s, other indications suggest that the promotional efforts of the Venetian publishing industry were successful. One sign that the poem gained canonical respectability after the midcentury was that it was increasingly referred to or presented as a model for imitation. Not only was it considered similar to the great poems of antiquity in terms of its didactic value, like those poems it was also deemed exemplary as a poetic and rhetorical work of art. So, for example, by 1574, when Toscanella published his *Bellezze del Furioso*—a canto-by-canto commentary on the stylistic highlights of the poem—he assumed that the poem's canonical status was sufficiently established to systematize its function as a guide and storehouse of rhetorical examples for all would-be writers and orators. To be sure, the publication of the *Bellezze* served in itself to consolidate the process of Ariosto's canonization. Still, it was owing to the Venetian promotion of the poem during the previous two decades that Toscanella could unhesitatingly proclaim that Ariosto was the modern equal of the most revered poets of antiquity, and that, like theirs, his work could serve as an encyclopedic fount of poetic art and eloquence.[26]

By the 1560s, however, while the effects of the Venetian promotion of the poem continue to be felt, one also notices that propaganda about Ariosto as the new Virgil abates, as does the assimilation of the *Furioso* to Homer's and Virgil's epics. This change can be attributed partly to the impact of Aristotle's *Poetics* on Italian criticism and literary taste. As the *Poetics* became more widely known and, by the 1560s, more authoritative, it became increasingly apparent that the formal norms Aristotle was taken to have established for the epic poem simply did not apply to Ariosto's romance, despite efforts to find such a congruence.[27] Moreover, a growing number of neoclassical critics exploited Aristotle's authority to discredit the artistic shortcomings of chivalric romance by stressing its deviation from the narrative structure of ancient epic. Despite its great popularity, the *Furioso* was included in this attack, and Ariosto's poem equally condemned for its disregard of unity and continuity. In other words, objections against the poem that were only reported secondhand by Fornari and Pigna around 1550 began to appear in print by the 1560s.

A representative example of this new criticism is Minturno's *Arte poetica* (1563), specifically its first section on heroic poetry, which includes a critique of the modern romanzo, and of Ariosto's decision to write one. Minturno, contrary to an apologist like Giraldi, does not consider the romanzo a separate and legitimate poetic genre, but rather a transgression of various unchanging principles—for example, unity of action—that define heroic poetry. When questioned by his interlocutor (the discussion is presented as a dialogue) on what distinguishes Homer's poetic procedure from that of a *romanzatore*, Minturno makes it clear that the fundamental difference is the unity and coherence of Homer's plots versus the disordered multiplicity of chivalric romance. Ariosto is then singled out and reproached for having failed to follow Homer's example, something he could easily have done, according to Minturno, by focusing on "l'amoroso furor di Orlando, e tutto quel, che segui dopo quella pazzia," instead of bringing in all the other separate actions that confuse his narrative order.[28] Minturno acknowledges Ariosto's great talent, and is even ready to excuse his "abuse" of the rules of heroic poetry on the grounds that he did it to please the multitude. Nonetheless, the main thrust of his critique is to show that he departed altogether from the unchanging principles of ancient epic structure, and, despite Bembo's attempt to make him revise the *Furioso* into a proper epic, chose to leave his poem in the form of a vile and lowly romanzo.

Another of these neo-Aristotelian critics, Filippo Sassetti, begins his "Discorso contro l'Ariosto" (ca. 1575) by defying the currently held opinion that the *Furioso* is a "quasi Iliade novella," and proceeds to refute the various midcentury analogies drawn between Ariosto's poem and the epics of Homer and Virgil. Although Sassetti does not name him, Pigna is clearly one of his targets, and in a section of the "Discorso" he specifically refutes various resemblances that Pigna had drawn in book 2 of *I romanzi*: the parallel between Ariosto's decision to continue Boiardo's *Innamorato* and Virgil's continuation of Homer's Trojan matter; the resemblance between the quarrel over Angelica at the start of the *Furioso* and the quarrel over Briseis at the beginning of the *Iliad*; the similarity of the duel between Ruggiero and Rodomonte closing the *Furioso* and the concluding duel of the *Aeneid*. Sassetti refutes this last parallel (which had been made by others besides Pigna) by pointing out that, unlike the Virgilian ending, Ariosto's closing episode is unconnected to the plot it supposedly concludes:

> Quello che è stato detto che in ciò è il Furioso simile all'Eneide è ben cosa di poco momento: peroché il conquisto di Latio e di Lavinia e la morte di Turno sono in tal maniera intra di loro incatenati che se l'una cosa non accade, l'altra non succeda; ma quale impedimento arrecava il Re pagano a Ruggiero nell'ottener Bradamante? anzi egli ottenuta l'haveva, onde più gagliardo degli altri ne fu riputato giostrando la notte e 'l giorno; che se pure Rodomonte fusse comparso come interessato in quella donna, la cosa sarebbe andata con qualche similitudine.[29]

[What has been said, namely, that in this regard the *Furioso* resembles the
Aeneid, is certainly a matter of small significance; because the conquest of
Latium and of Lavinia and the death of Turnus are so interlinked that if one
event does not take place, the other does not follow; whereas what obstacle
did the pagan king pose to prevent Ruggiero from obtaining Bradamante?
Moreover, he had obtained her because in jousting day and night he was
deemed worthier than the others; if, however, Rodomonte had been shown
to be attracted to this woman, then there could have been some similarity.]

As more formal distinctions of this sort were drawn, one can understand
how unconvincing it became to insist on the parallels between Ariosto's
poem and Homer's and Virgil's epics. If anything, the new Aristotelians
were making it progressively harder to deny that Ariosto had failed to ad-
here to Homeric and Virgilian practice. We saw that in the early stages of
the neo-Aristotelian attack on the *Furioso*, critics such as Fornari still argued that Ariosto conformed in basic ways to the requisites for epic set
forth in the *Poetics*. And Pigna, although he recognized that the *romanzi*
and the ancient epics were formally different, still tried his utmost to relate
the *Furioso* to Homer's and Virgil's poems. His letter to Giraldi, with
which this chapter began, acknowledged the neo-Aristotelian hostility that
was already building up against Ariosto, but he still felt that he could
counter the charges of the classicists by drawing as many resemblances as
he could between the *Furioso* and the canonical poems of antiquity. He did
not think it was yet necessary to assume Giraldi's modernist position,
namely, that the romanzo was a kind of poetry different from the ancient
epic, more amenable to contemporaries, and that, since it was constructed
according to different rules, it was not to be judged by Horatian or Aristotelian criteria. By the 1560s, however, the champions of ancient epic and of
Aristotelian theory had sufficiently undermined claims for the *Furioso*'s
epic ancestry that Giraldi's counterargument became a more viable justification of the poem.

Lodovico Dolce, for example, who in the 1540s had been so instrumental in establishing the Virgilian parentage of the *Furioso*, was by 1560 praising Bernardo Tasso for choosing, like Ariosto, to write a narrative poem
that departed from ancient epic practice. It is in his dedicatory epistle prefacing Bernardo Tasso's *Amadigi* (1560) that Dolce's manifesto on behalf
of the moderns appears. "Dico, adunque," he writes,

> che se coloro che tengono sempre in mano le bilancie d'Aristotile, & hanno
> tutto dì in bocca gli esempi di Virgilio e di Homero, considerassero la qualità
> de' tempi presenti, e la diversità delle lingue, e vedessero ch'a la prudenza del
> Poeta si conviene l'accomodarsi alla dilettatione, & all'uso del secolo nel quale
> egli scrive, non sarebbono d'opinione, che si dovesse scriver sempre ad un
> modo.

[I say, therefore, that if those who are always holding the scales of Aristotle, and cite the examples of Virgil and Homer every day, considered the nature of present times, the diversity of the languages, and recognized that prudence calls upon the poet to accommodate himself to delight, and to the usage of the age in which he writes, they would no longer believe that one must always write in a single manner.]

Changing times, as Giraldi had previously maintained, demand changes in poetic forms and conventions. Even Virgil himself had to be different from Homer, since he lived in a different age. Dolce points out that efforts in the present era to follow "le strade tenute da Virgilio, e da Homero" result in poems that give no pleasure and go unread. (He was probably referring to Trissino's unsuccessful *Italia liberata dai Goti*.) Nobody would have read Ariosto, claims Dolce, had he chosen to follow in the footsteps of Homer and Virgil. It bears recalling that this is proclaimed by the same man whose commentary on Ariosto's imitations did more than perhaps any other text to link the *Furioso* to Virgil's epic. True, nearly twenty years had passed since Dolce's "Brieve dimostratione" was originally published, a period during which more editions of *Orlando Furioso* were issued in Italy than of any other poem. As Dolce does not fail to remark in the same preface to the *Amadigi*, Ariosto's poem, unclassical though it was, "andava per le mani di ciascuno con lode e grido universale." Was it not the extraordinary success of the poem as much as the neo-Aristotelian attack against it that prompted its supporters to defend it progressively rather than conservatively? Whichever cause was more instrumental, the *Furioso* was the best-selling work of modern poetry at the same time that its departures from ancient epic practice were being exposed by hostile critics. This coincidence could not but encourage the legitimation of the poem on other grounds than its resemblance to traditional epic poetry.

It is not that Ariosto's supporters ceased to claim that the *Furioso* was an epic or stopped maintaining that it conformed to Aristotelian practice. As will be shown in Chapter 6, the more conservative impulse to associate the new poem with the ancient classics was to persist until the end of the century. Still, by the 1560s the features of the poem more frequently prized were those that gave pleasure to a contemporary audience: its modern ethos, its *varietà*, its rhyme, and other unclassical features. The poem became valued as a modern counterpart rather than as a replication of ancient epic. No less than the effort to affiliate it to classical epic, this more progressive tendency to legitimize the *Furioso* was fiercely contested by the exponents of neoclassical orthodoxy. The very fact, however, that neoclassical opponents began to make a more concerted effort to decenter Ariosto's poem, and to deny it the status of a modern classic that its champions conferred on it, suggests in itself that the poem was attaining such status.

Chapter Three

COMMENTARIES ON IMITATIONS IN
ORLANDO FURIOSO

Midcentury Venetian publishers and editors played a vital role, as the last chapter showed, in promoting the *Furioso* as the modern equivalent of the ancient epics. In their efforts to bestow the status of a classic on Ariosto's poem, they presented it in large, annotated, and illustrated editions—in a format, that is, that had been reserved for editions of canonical ancient authors. The text of the poem was supplemented with prefaces, biographies, allegorizations, glossaries, and commentaries designed to enhance the value of the work, mainly by associating it with the great poems of antiquity. Among these various "paratexts" the ones that served to establish most specifically the poem's links to ancient poetry were the commentaries on Ariosto's imitations and borrowings.

There were basically three such commentaries (not counting Ruscelli's plagiarized one) that accompanied sixteenth-century editions of the poem: Tullio Fausto da Longiano's, originally published in 1542; Lodovico Dolce's, also first published in 1542 (it was the one plagiarized by Girolamo Ruscelli in 1556) and then amplified in 1566; and Alberto Lavezuola's, which appeared in 1584. Despite their protophilological appearance, these commentaries served largely honorific ends: they advertised the impressive pedigree of the *Furioso*. That is why they deserve a chapter in this study: not as early records of Ariosto's imitative procedures but as efforts to secure more legitimacy for the poem. To be sure, these commentaries tell us which of Ariosto's imitations their authors chose to recognize, and, over time, one notices that they identify more fully the wide range of precursors that Ariosto alluded to or imitated. But this should not be taken as an index of a progressive appreciation of the poem's rich intertextuality. With the possible exception of Lavezuola's "Osservationi" of 1584, these commentaries did not intend to elucidate that intertextuality as much as to affiliate the poem with the prestigious heroic poetry of antiquity. Dolce's first commentary (as I already indicated in the last chapter) was composed to make the *Aeneid* appear to be the predominant model of the *Furioso*. It was so frequently republished (by the end of the century it was appended to more than forty-five editions) that it played a vital role in making the reading public connect Ariosto's poem to Virgil's. In fact, Dolce's simplistic and honorific account of the Virgilian parentage of Ariosto's borrowings became so accepted that his commentary virtually could not be displaced. As will be shown, publishers and readers continued to prefer Dolce's commentary even after its bias and inadequacy were exposed by Lavezuola's more accurate "Osservationi."

The first commentary on Ariosto's imitations, Tullio Fausto da Longiano's, accompanied the 1542 edition of the *Furioso* published in Venice by Bindoni and Pasini. Fausto's annotations must have been composed several years earlier, because his prefatory remarks are dated 12 March 1540. Actually, his observations on Ariosto's imitations were not contained in a separate commentary but dispersed among various *annotazioni* at the beginning and at the end of the Bindoni edition.[1] His first general observations, which are part of his preface, indicate Ariosto's debt to Boiardo's *Orlando Innamorato* and then go on to establish the high pedigree of both Orlando poems by pointing out their similarities to Homer's and Virgil's epics, particularly the resemblances among their various heroic protagonists. The resemblances initially refer to both Boiardo's and Ariosto's poems. The emperor Charles, we are told, reproduces Latinus; Agramante, Turnus; Rodomonte is a redoing of Mezentius. But the list soon becomes a series of parallels (which do not need to be translated) between the *Furioso* and the *Aeneid*:

> Per Marfisa e per Bradamante, Penthesilea, e Camilla. Per Alcina Circe. Per Cloridano e Medoro Niso et Eurialo. Per l'Orco ne la novella di Norandino Polifemo. Per Melissa Iuturna. Per Bardino Acete. . . . Per Ruggiero e Rodomonte combattenti nel fine de l'opera, e morte di Rodomonte: Enea, e Turno combattenti, e morte di Turno in ultimo de la Eneide. Per Brandimarte morto e sue essequie: l'essequie e la morte di Palante. . . . Per il sterpo in cui era convertito Astolpho lamentantesi di Ruggiero, il sterpo di Polidoro dolentesi con Enea. Per Draghinazzo formato da Malagigi in Gradasso saltante in nave per ingannar Rinaldo, la nuvola trasformata in Enea da Iunone per levar Turno de la battaglia. . . . Per la genealogia di Ruggiero, quella d'Enea.

Cursory though it may be, this list of parallels does begin to identify many of Ariosto's imitations of Virgil in the *Furioso*.

Fausto da Longiano's more specific comments about these and other imitations, however, are interspersed in the notes appended to the poem. In these more specific annotations he cites further parallels with the *Aeneid*. For example, in canto 7, referring to Melissa's arrival in Alcina's realm to extricate Ruggiero from her, Fausto notes at 7.53 (he quotes the first line of the octave but indicates neither number nor canto, referring only to the page on which it appears in this edition): "Usurpato in parte da Virg. quando Giove mandó Mercurio a Carthagine ad ammonire Enea che partisse." He then cites *Aeneid* 4.259–67, and, again, at 7.60 he cites

Aeneid 4.272–76 to show how closely Ariosto echoes Virgil's text; again, he does not provide specific references to book and lines in the Virgil. At 18.50–51 he indicates that Dardinello's rallying speech to his troops imitates Pallas's similar exhortation to the Arcadians in *Aeneid* 10.369ff. Some of his comments focus on the imitations he had listed in the preface. For instance, about the depiction of Cloridano and Medoro he notes at 18.165: "Il ritratto di Niso e d'Eurialo, e le sentenze istesse." He then traces in some detail Ariosto's imitation of Virgil's account of Nisus and Euryalus in *Aeneid* 9. He comments in similar detail on a few of Ariosto's more conspicuous imitations of Ovid. For example, his notes on 10.96, 99, 100, and 103 reveal how closely Ruggiero's rescue of Angelica is modeled on Perseus's rescue of Andromeda in *Metamorphoses* 4.663ff. Fausto focuses as well on the epic similes that Ariosto borrowed from the two ancient poems, and in the course of providing other glosses and notes he occasionally singles out one of these and indicates its Virgilian model (for example, at 17.11 and 18.153).

Although Fausto's treatment may initially seem unsystematic and rapid, more careful inspection of his scattered comments reveals that he identified most of Ariosto's imitations of the *Aeneid*, many of the similes borrowed from Virgil, and a number of the episodes modeled on the *Metamorphoses*. Considering the range and accuracy of these annotations, and the fact that Ariosto's ancient models had never before been so precisely identified, one is surprised that this commentary was not reprinted in Venice for well over a decade. One reason may have been that its format was impractical. Readers could not easily locate the observations on particular imitations, interspersed as they were among other notes and glosses. The more important reason was that for a decade after 1542, the year Fausto's "Annotazioni" first appeared, the publishing of *Orlando Furioso* became increasingly monopolized by the house of Gabriel Giolito, and one of the features of the Giolito editions was a commentary by Lodovico Dolce entitled "Brieve dimostratione di molte comparationi et sentenze dell'Ariosto in diversi autori imitate." This commentary immediately eclipsed Fausto da Longiano's despite the fact that Dolce did not identify very many more imitations. It is even likely that Dolce derived his observations from Fausto's earlier commentary (see note 6). Unlike Fausto's dispersed annotations, however, Dolce's "Brieve dimostratione" (sometimes entitled "Brieve dimostramento") was a separate commentary entirely devoted to Ariosto's borrowings.

Dolce's was to become the most frequently reprinted commentary on Ariosto's imitations in the cinquecento. Not only was it appended to the twenty-eight Giolito editions published between 1542 and 1560 (including the 1553 edition in Spanish), it also appeared in contemporary editions published in Rome and Lyon, and from the late 1560s until the end of the century it was being reprinted steadily by other Venetian publishers (see note 19). It was even appropriated by Ruscelli and appeared as part of his annotations in the numerous Valgrisi editions published after 1556.

Dolce aimed primarily to identify the ancient models of Ariosto's extended similes since he realized that this was the most convenient way of demonstrating the epic pedigree of the Italian poem. Focusing on the origins of the epic similes also allowed him to highlight the poem's Virgilian ancestry; almost all of the nearly thirty similes he selects are shown to be modeled on ones in the *Aeneid*.

Fausto da Longiano had already indicated where in Virgil Ariosto had borrowed a number of his similes. But Dolce tried to be more exhaustive, and the format of his commentary was more practical. Whereas Fausto, in the course of other notes and glosses, cited only the first line of one of Ariosto's similes and then quoted the Virgilian model, Dolce provided Ariosto's entire simile as well as its model, permitting his readers easy comparison of both full texts. For example, at 8.71 he cites the simile that describes Orlando's restless thoughts, as he tosses in his bed worrying about the fate of Angelica while the rest of besieged Paris is asleep:

> Qual d'acqua chiara il tremolante lume,
> dal sol percossa o da' notturni rai,
> per gli ampli tetti van con lungo salto
> a destra e a sinistra, e basso et alto.

He then observes:

> Comparatione felicemente tolta da Virgilio nel principio dell'ottavo [*Aeneid* 8.20–25]: dove egli così dice:

> > Sicut aquae tremulum labris ubi lumen ahemis
> > Sole repercussum aut radiantis imagine lunae
> > Omnia pervolitat late loca iamque sub auras
> > Erigitur summique ferit laquearia tecti.[2]

Usually Dolce points to the models for Ariosto's similes in the *Aeneid* without any observations at all (for example, at 11.20, 17.11, 40.31). On a few occasions, however, he comments on Ariosto's improvement of a Virgilian simile. For instance, he recognizes that the fatal duel between the young Saracen prince Dardinello and the stronger Rinaldo in canto 18 is modeled on the duel between Pallas and Turnus in *Aeneid* 10. The simile used to describe the clash between Rinaldo and Dardinello reads:

> Come vider Rinaldo, che se mosse
> Con tanta rabbia incontra quel Signore:
> Con quanta andria un Leon, ch'al prato havesse
> Visto un Torel, ch'ancor non senta amore.

(18.151)

Dolce then refers to the model in *Aeneid* 10.454–56, where Virgil compares Turnus's attack on Pallas to a lion attacking a bull:

> Utque Leo, Specula cum vidit ab alta
> Stare procul campis meditantem praelia Taurum,
> Advolat: haud alia est Turni venientis imago.

He goes on to observe that whereas Virgil's comparison was to a lion attacking a bull, Ariosto compares Rinaldo's attack on Dardinello to that of a lion assaulting an immature bull. Dolce does not yet recognize (as he will in his revised commentary of 1566) that Ariosto's change is due to his imitation of Statius's adaptation of Virgil's simile in *Thebaid* 7.670–73, but he appreciates that the reference to a young bull conveys more appropriately the "imbecillità del morto giovane Dardinello."[3]

Dolce also comments on longer imitative episodes in the poem. As with the similes, he chooses to cite primarily the passages that can be shown to be modeled on the *Aeneid*. In fact, after identifying the Virgilian models for similes, Dolce occasionally points to their larger surrounding contexts in the *Aeneid*, when these are also imitated by Ariosto. Before commenting on the simile describing the clash between Rinaldo and Dardinello, Dolce points to several other parallels between Dardinello's exploits in canto 18 and Pallas's in *Aeneid* 10. Again, at 18.22 Dolce shows that the simile describing Rodomonte's slaughter of the Parisians as he retreats from the city is modeled on the one used to describe Turnus's single stand against the Trojans at the end of *Aeneid* 9 (792–96). He points out as well that the entire account of Rodomonte's forced exit from Paris imitates that of Turnus from the Trojan camp. Other, more extensive imitations of the *Aeneid* in the Italian poem are also identified. In 7.53ff., when Melissa comes to retrieve Ruggiero from Alcina's clutches, Dolce notes the parallels with Mercury's mission in *Aeneid* 4 to make Aeneas abandon Dido and Carthage. And at the start of the night expedition undertaken by Cloridano and Medoro (18.115) he states: "Questa è la medesima inventione nel sovradetto di Virgilio [that is, *Aeneid* 9] nella persona di Eurialo & Niso." At the start of canto 39, about Melissa disguising herself as Rodomonte to break the temporary pact between the Christians and the Saracens, Dolce notes: "Si come nel sovradetto libro [that is, *Aeneid* 12] Iuturna sorella di Turno sotto la forma di Camerto [sic] disturba i patti giurati tra il Re Latino & Enea: così parimente l'Ariosto a imitatione di quello fa Melissa con falsa apparenza di Rodomonte rompe i patti tra Carlo & Agramante."

Dolce seeks to identify every major imitation of the *Aeneid* in the *Furioso* and as many of the similes borrowed from it as he can. He even adduces Virgilian sources for similes not borrowed from Virgil (for example, at 14.120). He cites the *Aeneid* as a model so often that the reader is led to believe that Ariosto imitated Virgil almost as extensively as Virgil had imitated Homer. Dolce creates this impression not simply by making the *Aeneid* the predominant model; he makes Virgil appear to be the most influential precursor by always positing a dyadic relation between the texts of the *Aeneid* and the *Furioso*. Dolce ignores texts other than Virgil's that served concurrently as models for certain of these imitations. In such instances—when Ariosto imitated ancient and vernacular poets as well as Virgil—Dolce points to the *Aeneid* exclusively. As previously mentioned, both Statius's *Thebaid* (7.670–73) and Virgil are models for the comparison of Rinaldo's attack on Dardinello to that of a lion attacking a young bull (18.151). Yet Dolce disregards the Statian model despite his appreciation of Ariosto's notable departure from Virgil's simile. Again, when commenting on the encounter in canto 6 between Ruggiero and the metamorphosed Astolfo, he notes, "la inventione di Astolfo trasformato in Mirto è tolta dal Polydoro di Virgilio [*Aeneid* 3.19–56]"; he then proposes that in this episode Ariosto actually surpasses Virgil. But he quite overlooks (although he must have perceived) that, in addition to the Polydorus episode, Ariosto was imitating the encounter between Dante and Pier della Vigna metamorphosed into a plant in canto 13 of the *Inferno*.

Dolce does refer to classical texts other than the *Aeneid* imitated by Ariosto, but the only model that he cites with any frequency is Ovid's *Metamorphoses*. The imitations of Ovid's poetry he selects, however, serve again to bring out the epic aspects of the *Furioso*. For example, he comments at some length on the parallels between Ruggiero's liberation of Angelica in canto 10 and Perseus's heroic rescue of Andromeda in *Metamorphoses* 4, especially the combat with the sea monster. Later in his commentary he pays close attention to the similarities between Ariosto's description of the "epic" tempest that nearly drowns Ruggiero at the start of canto 41 and its model in *Metamorphoses* 11 (with a few references to *Aeneid* 1). In general, however, Dolce tends to disregard the amatory matter in the *Metamorphoses* imitated by Ariosto, and his commentary makes virtually no references to Ovid's *Heroides* despite the fact that Ariosto frequently imitated them as well.[4] By assuming the *Aeneid* and the *Metamorphoses* to be dominant models, and then focusing only on Ariosto's imitations of the similes and "epic" features of Ovid's poem, Dolce makes it evident that he aims to establish the *Furioso*'s links to Latin epic, and to Virgil's above all.

In the course of the twenty-five years after it first appeared in 1542, Dolce's "Brieve dimostratione" became the most frequently reprinted commentary on Ariosto's imitations. Its inclusion in the Giolito editions alone meant that it was reprinted twenty-seven times between 1542 and 1560. It was virtually unrivaled in the middle of the century. When in 1553 G. A. Valvassori decided to publish an edition of the *Furioso* to compete with

Giolito's, the commentary he appended was a version of Fausto da Longiano's "Annotationi" as they had been modified by Pietro Ulivi for the sole Giunta edition of the *Furioso* published in Florence in 1544.[5] Ulivi had extracted Fausto's comments on Ariosto's borrowed similes and amplified them in a separate commentary entitled "Dimostratione delle comparationi . . . con le citationi de luoghi da l'autore imitati." Obviously, this was an attempt to replicate the format of Dolce's commentary. This resemblance must have prompted Valvassori to append it along with the rest of Fausto da Longiano's annotations (but without acknowledging Fausto's authorship) to the six editions of the *Furioso* he published between 1553 and 1563.

Still, Dolce's "Brieve dimostratione" remained the most widely read commentary. A clear sign of its appeal was its appropriation by Girolamo Ruscelli in the edition of the *Furioso* published by Valgrisi that first appeared in 1556. Considering the literary rivalry between Dolce and Ruscelli (each had already annotated rival editions of Boccaccio's *Decamerone*), and the critical attack Ruscelli had leveled at Dolce's work in his *Tre discorsi* (1553), it is surprising that Ruscelli felt no compunction about appropriating virtually all of Dolce's "Brieve dimostratione" and retitling it in his endnotes to the Valgrisi edition as a "Raccolto di molti luoghi, tolti, e felicemente imitati in più autori, dall'Ariosto nel Furioso." Ruscelli does point out at the beginning of this "Raccolto" that he is indebted to previous commentary on Ariosto's imitations, but he never names Dolce. And although he claims to have revised and amplified the commentary, except for elaborating Dolce's first two remarks on imitations in canto 1, he simply lifts all of Dolce's subsequent commentary and passes it off as his revised version.[6] There were at least seven Valgrisi editions of the *Furioso* between 1556 and 1565 containing this pirated version of Dolce's commentary. If one adds them to the editions published by Giolito and to the several non-Venetian editions that also included it, this means that Dolce's "Brieve dimostratione" was reprinted at least forty times between 1542 and 1565.

Despite its popularity, Dolce revised and enlarged his original commentary, possibly because he was encouraged to do so by the publisher G. A. Valvassori. Whatever the reason, his modified version first appeared in the amplified 1566 Valvassori edition of the *Furioso*, which now appended Dolce's and other commentaries to the end of each canto.[7] Dolce's basic change was to indicate more imitative passages in each canto, and to refer to more ancient poetic texts as models. His emphasis remains on Ariosto's borrowed similes, but one soon notices that, aside from citing additional similes from Virgil and Ovid, Dolce now refers occasionally to passages in Catullus, Horace, Lucan, and Seneca, and in a few instances he even points to imitations of Dante and Petrarch. But the new author who looms largest in Dolce's "Imitazioni" is Statius. Virtually ignored in the original commentary, Statius's *Thebaid* now becomes second only to the *Aeneid* as a model for Ariosto's imitations.

The first extensive comment on Ariosto's debt to Statius occurs in the notes to canto 14 when Dolce remarks that the description of the House of Sleep (14.92–94) is partly modeled on Statius's account of the House of Sleep in *Thebaid* 10.84ff. In his earlier commentary Dolce had noted that the passage beginning at 14.92, "Giace in Arabia una valletta amena," imitated Ovid's description of the House of Sleep in *Metamorphoses* 11.592ff., remarking that in this description "Ovidio è alquanto più copioso." In the new commentary, however, he adds, "Nel descriver questa casa del Sonno il virtuosissimo e magnanimo Signor Erasmo de' Signori di Valvasone tien per risoluto, ed io aderisco a lui, che l'Ariosto abbia imitato Stazio, ma con alquanto più di copia e leggiadria [The most virtuous and magnanimous Signor Erasmo de' Signori di Valvasone holds for certain, and I support him, that Ariosto imitated Statius in describing this House of Sleep, but with a good deal more copiousness and elegance]."[8] Dolce goes on to note the similarities between the account in *Thebaid* 10.84ff. and Ariosto's in stanzas 92–94 and 101. As he first suggests in this comment, he owes his new appreciation of Ariosto's use of Statius to Erasmo di Valvasone. Although no lectures or writings by Erasmo on Ariosto and Statius are known, his translation of Statius's poem in ottava rima, published in Venice in 1570, attests to his intimate knowledge of the *Thebaid*.[9] Dolce's numerous acknowledgments to this fellow man of letters suggest that Erasmo communicated directly his views of Ariosto's imitations of Statius. However he obtained them, Dolce was probably prompted to enlarge his original commentary by Erasmo's observations. Certainly Dolce's recognition of the *Thebaid* as an important model for the *Furioso* constitutes the most significant difference between his revised and his original commentary.

The new prominence Dolce gives the *Thebaid* as a subtext is particularly evident in cantos 14–19, the segment of the poem that describes the siege of Paris. Immediately noticeable is how this recognition of Statius as a model complements his earlier comments on the Virgilian echoes and imitations in this epic segment of the poem. For instance, while Dolce amplifies his comments in cantos 16 and 18 on the parallels between Rodomonte and Turnus fighting single-handedly against their respective foes, his observations are now complemented by his new appreciation of the similarities between Rodomonte's battle and Capaneus's solitary assault on Thebes. Again, Dolce prefaces his observations on these parallels with an acknowledgment to Erasmo di Valvasone, and concurs that "nel Furioso

veramente per lo danno che fa Rodomonte dentro Parigi s'ha la simili-
tudine di quel che fa Capaneo dentro Tebe [indeed the harm done by
Rodomonte inside Paris is similar to that done by Capaneus inside
Thebes]." But, he adds, "in molto parti da questo luogo l'Ariosto non
meno allude a Turno, introdotto da Virgilio a fare il medesimo nello stec-
cato de'Trojani [in many parts of this episode Ariosto alludes as well to
Turnus, brought in by Virgil to do the same inside the Trojan camp]."
Then, basing himself on indications provided by Erasmo, he cites passages
from *Thebaid* 10 to illustrate how Ariosto imitates them in 16.24, 25,
and 26.

Dolce's revised commentary on the start of canto 17 is particularly interesting. In the earlier "Dimostratione" he noted that Rodomonte's assault
on the royal palace after getting into Paris, and his fierce combat in the
gran corte, were modeled on the assault and destruction of Priam's palace
as narrated in Aeneas's account of Troy's destruction (*Aeneid* 2.438ff.). In
this episode, therefore, Rodomonte was modeled not on Turnus but on
Pyrrhus. Dolce pointed out that the comparison of the fierce Rodomonte
in his shining armor to a snake in his new skin (17.11) was the same simile
Virgil used to describe Pyrrhus at the entrance of Priam's palace (*Aeneid*
2.469–75). In the new commentary, however, he establishes from the start
of the episode that *Thebaid* 10, specifically the account of the havoc caused
by Capaneus inside Thebes, is as important a model as the *Aeneid*. Dolce
observes that Ariosto's description of the populace throwing down turrets,
timber, and slabs on Rodomonte (see 17.10 and 12) imitates Statius's similar account of the Thebans' attempt to drive off Capaneus by hurling down
on him pillars, beams, and even war machines (see *Thebaid* 10.856–59).
Yet Dolce also notes a similar action in Virgil "nel 2 dell'Eneide dove parla
di Pirro," and he cites *Aeneid* 2.445–49. The intimation that Statius was
imitating Virgil and that Ariosto was imitating both becomes almost explicit in Dolce's next observation. Pointing out, as he had in his original
commentary, the Virgilian model for the simile of Rodomonte as a snake in
his new skin, he now adds that this simile was also "imitato da Stazio," and
he quotes *Thebaid* 4.95–98 to show that Ariosto may have sought to imitate Statius's imitation of Virgil.

These comments reveal Dolce's awareness that not only was Ariosto
imitating two models, but the two models were themselves affiliated by a
history of imitation. Yet he is so set on positing a dyadic relation between
the imitative text and its model that even when he perceives that there is
more than one model being imitated, he beckons the reader to choose the
one that seems most fitting. This refusal to posit the presence of several
models is particularly apparent in his revised observations about the simile
in canto 18 that describes Rinaldo's furious and fatal assault on the
younger Dardinello:

> Con tanta rabbia incontra quel signore
> Con quanta andria un leon ch'al prato avesse
> visto un torel ch'ancor non senta amore.

(18.151)

In his earlier commentary Dolce cited as a model the simile of a lion attacking a bull that Virgil used to describe Turnus closing in on young Pallas (*Aeneid* 10.454–56). He then remarked that Ariosto had changed Virgil's image of a bull to the more appropriate one of a *torel* or bullock to describe the younger, less experienced Dardinello. In his revised commentary he observes that this change can be attributed to Ariosto's imitation of another model, namely, a simile in the *Thebaid* that refers to a lion and a bullock, rather than to a mature bull. He acknowledges that Statius may have provided the model for the simile:

> Ma quantunque ciò sia veramente imitato da Virgilio, nondimeno più m'accosto al parer del mio valorosissimo e virtuosissimo Sig. Erasmo di Valvasone: il quale tiene, che per la differenzia che si vede fra Virgilio e l'Ariosto; questa comparazion sia più tosto presa da Statio nel lib. 7. della Tebaide; poichè fra l'uno e l'altro è pochissimo o di niun momento.

> [However true it may be that this is imitated from Virgil, nonetheless I agree more with the opinion of the most valorous and virtuous Erasmo di Valvasone, who maintains that, from the difference one can note between Virgil and Ariosto, it is more likely that this simile is taken from book 7 of Statius's *Thebaid* since there is virtually no difference between one and the other.]

And he quotes *Thebaid* 7.670–73:

> Qualis ubi primam leo mane cubilibus altis
> Erexit rabiem et saevo speculatur ab antro . . .
> Aut cervum, aut nondum bellantem fronte iuvencum.

The reader is not denied the possibility of choosing Virgil as the model but is encouraged to opt for Statius's simile on the grounds that it is literally closer to Ariosto's. Dolce can contemplate the possibility of two models, but he feels that the reader must make a choice between them. He cannot assert that the origin of the simile is ambivalent, presumably because this would work against his overall effort to establish clear, unilateral affiliations between Ariosto's text and its Roman models.

It is notable that Dolce fails to observe that Statius's simile was itself an imitation of Virgil's. Actually, aside from his brief observation about the Rodomonte-as-snake simile, Dolce never points out that many of the Statian passages he identifies as models are themselves imitations of the passages in the *Aeneid* upon which Ariosto also modeled himself. This oversight could come from Dolce's relative unfamiliarity with the *Thebaid*. More likely it is related to his refusal to contemplate Ariosto's habit of imitating prior imitative poetry and models at the same time. Nonetheless, as Dolce proceeds to identify the simultaneous presence of Virgil and Statius in the narrative devoted to the siege of Paris, the reader becomes increasingly aware that Ariosto was consciously imitating two models, one of which was modeled on the other. This is particularly apparent in the episode that allows Dolce to illustrate most amply Ariosto's imitation of Statius as well as of Virgil: the fatal night expedition undertaken by Cloridano and Medoro to retrieve the body of their young ruler Dardinello (18.165–19.16).

In his original commentary Dolce had cited only Virgil's account of Nisus and Euryalus as the model for the exploits of Cloridano and Medoro. In the revised commentary he recognizes that Statius's account of the similar night sortie of Dymas and Hopleus (*Thebaid* 10.347ff.) is at least as important a model. He points out correctly that in both Statius's and Ariosto's stories, but not in Virgil's, the young warriors act out of love and duty to their dead masters. Dolce is keen to make his readers aware that certain passages that may have seemed to be imitations of Virgil, as he had proposed in his earlier commentary, are closer to passages in Statius's account of the night expedition. For example, when commenting on Medoro's prayer to the moon to shed light on the battlefield (18.184), he had originally observed that it was modeled on but was a "più bella & più piena Apostropha" than Nisus's prayer to the moon when he sees his companion Euryalus surrounded by the enemy (*Aeneid* 9.403–9). In the new commentary he maintains that, more likely, Ariosto modeled his text on Dymas's prayer to the goddess of the moon in *Thebaid* 10, given that the immediate context of this prayer is more similar:

> Ma chi dicesse, che questa conversione, o orazione fosse più tosto presa da Stazio, che da Virgilio non errerebbe punto a mio parere, poichè quello che segue nell'altre stanze, è simile a versi di Stazio: ed acciocche si veggano amendue questi paragoni, io gli sottoscriverò, lasciandone il giudicio a' belli ingegni.

> [Whoever might claim that this oration was taken from Statius rather than Virgil would not be at all wrong in my opinion, because what follows in the other stanzas resembles Statius's lines: and so that both comparisons can be seen, I will provide them below, leaving the judgment to fine wits.]

He then cites Dymas's prayer to Cynthia to shed light on the battlefield (*Thebaid* 10.365–70).

Dolce does not eliminate the reference to Nisus's prayer in the *Aeneid* as a possible model despite his new claim that Ariosto's imitation was more indebted to the *Thebaid*. He asks the "belli ingegni" reading his commentary to judge which of the two passages served as the model, and although he wants them to share his recognition that Statius's is the specific subtext, the record of his own changing views allows them to realize what he refuses to acknowledge: that Ariosto may have wanted to evoke both passages. The similarities between the two subtexts may have also reminded these readers, if they needed such reminding, that Statius's night expedition was an imitation of Virgil's. Dolce himself was surely aware that the night sortie of Hopleus and Dymas was one of the most successful imitations of the *Aeneid* in the *Thebaid*; Statius makes his debt explicit at the end of the episode, when he expresses the hope that Nisus and Euryalus will befriend the ghosts of Hopleus and Dymas. Yet Dolce again refuses to comment on the Virgilian origin of Statius's episode or on the likelihood that Ariosto chose to imitate it as well as Virgil's precisely because it was an imitation of the *Aeneid*.

Despite his perception that Ariosto's imitations of Statius complement his imitations of Virgil, Dolce was unable to modify his assumption that Ariosto's imitative practice was unilateral. One might have thought that once he recognized that similes from both the *Thebaid* and the *Aeneid* served as models for a particular Ariostean simile (as he noted at 18.151), he would notice that Ariosto had drawn on several affiliated models for other borrowed similes. But Dolce continues to maintain that Ariosto's borrowed similes entail unilateral imitation. This is partly due to his neglect of Ariosto's vernacular models, in particular, his imitations of prior chivalric romances. Such texts as Pulci's *Morgante* and Boiardo's *Innamorato* provide Ariosto with models for similes that are also partly modeled on classical precedents.[10] But even discounting Dolce's neglect of vernacular models, and aside from his comments on the presence of both Statius and Virgil as subtexts, he virtually never indicates other instances when Ariosto simultaneously imitates two or more ancient models that are related by a history of imitation.[11]

That Dolce's appreciation of Ariosto's combinatory imitation of Statius and Virgil does not extend to the poet's similar use of several affiliated models elsewhere suggests that the prime objective of the revised commentary was to demonstrate the importance of the *Thebaid* as a model in the *Furioso*. One is led to conclude that Dolce's motivation here was the same as when he gave such prominence to the *Aeneid* as a model, and also the *Metamorphoses* as models: to establish the ancient epic ancestry of Ariosto's poem. It is even arguable that by identifying Ariosto's imitations of the *Thebaid*, Dolce fulfilled his intent to anchor the *Furioso* in the epic tradition more effectively than he could by establishing Ariosto's debt to the *Metamorphoses*, given the questionable generic identity of Ovid's narrative poem.[12] Had Dolce been more aware of Ariosto's borrowings from Statius in 1542, he doubtless would have highlighted these borrowings in his original commentary. Still, as late as the 1560s he obviously felt that his long-standing efforts to establish the epic pedigree of the *Furioso* could be effectively reinforced by a proper acknowledgment of the poem's links to a work that was, after all, one of the major post-Virgilian achievements in heroic poetry.

This is not to say that the only added value of the revised commentary was to make readers more aware of Ariosto's imitations of the *Thebaid*. As a result of this basic revision, the new commentary makes the presence of the *Aeneid* as a model less monolithic than it had been in the "Brieve dimostratione." In general, the commentary is more sensitive to Ariosto's wide repertory of ancient models. It even begins to acknowledge some of Ariosto's allusions to Dante and Petrarch. Moreover, Dolce's comments on imitations that mingled Statius and Virgil served, however unintentionally, to make readers aware that Ariosto's imitations were not always unilateral and did not simply involve a dyadic relation to a single prior model. While Dolce himself did not extend his insights, most likely some of his readers, especially the "belli ingegni," perceived Ariosto's habit of imitating several models that were themselves affiliated through imitation. It took the next and last major commentary of the century, however, to make readers fully aware of this frequent imitative practice as well as of Ariosto's more complex intertextual strategies.

The last Renaissance commentary on Ariosto's imitations was Alberto Lavezuola's "Osservationi sopra il Furioso . . . nelle quali si mostrano tutti i luoghi imitati dall'autore nel suo poema." Paginated and signed separately, it was issued with the lavish edition published by Francesco dei Franceschi in Venice in 1584. Its accuracy and range of references make it the first commentary to do justice to the *Furioso*'s intertextuality. In fact, not until they were scrutinized by late nineteenth century philologists were Ariosto's imitations and borrowings more precisely identified. Lavezuola was conscious of prior commentaries, especially Dolce's; he reveals from the start his intent to identify poems and texts that Dolce had overlooked. Moreover, one of his general aims is to show that although Dolce and others had singled out the *Aeneid* as a model, other poems were more likely sources for Ariosto's imitations. Thus, the first notable simile in the poem,

> Timida pastorella mai si presta
> non volse piede inanzi a serpe crudo
> come Angelica tosto il freno torse,

(1.11)

is not, as Dolce had proposed, an imitation of *Aeneid* 2.379–81 but rather an imitation of Ovid's simile in *Fasti* 2.341–42:

Attonitusque metu rediit, ceu saepe viator,
Turbatum viso retulit angue pedem.

To support this initial correction of Dolce's gloss, Lavezuola goes on to say that Ariosto did indeed imitate Virgil's simile at *Aeneid* 2.379, but that the imitation occurs much later, at 39.32, and not here in canto 1.

Although Lavezuola generally tends to reduce the predominant role Dolce granted the *Aeneid* as a model, he still enjoys identifying, now and then, significant imitations of Virgil's epic overlooked by Dolce.[13] He is also fond of pointing to imitations of Virgil's shorter poems that his predecessor ignored. For example, in his remarks on canto 14 Lavezuola cites the simile that compares Mandricardo's destroying Doralice's escort of guards to a raging fire in a field of dry stubble (14.48). He proposes that this simile is inspired by Virgil's account in the *Georgics* (1.84–85) of the usefulness of burning stubble in fallow fields, and he substantiates his claim by showing precise verbal parallels between Ariosto's and Virgil's lines. He then indicates that Ovid also used the simile when comparing Apollo's love for Daphne to burning stubble at *Metamorphoses* 1.492ff.

These remarks reveal one of the major differences between his commentary and Dolce's. Lavezuola does more than adduce other models for Ariostean similes; he is ready to entertain the possibility that Ariosto had several models in mind for some of his similes. Lavezuola's familiarity with Roman poetry and its imitative character make him recall, much as Ariosto could recall, not only the recurrence of particular similes in the works of different poets but more generally when and where each Roman poet borrowed from or rewrote the poetry of predecessors. A striking example of his readiness to see a multiplicity of versions as models is his remarks on Ariosto's short simile describing the blushing of Angelica when, naked, chained to a rock, and about to be devoured by the sea monster, she is addressed by her rescuer Ruggiero: "Forza è ch'a quel parlare ella divegna / quale è di grana un bianco avorio asperso" (11.98). Dolce had cited *Aeneid* 12.67–69 as the model for this simile: "Indum sanguineo veluti violaverit ostro / Si quis ebur." Lavezuola corrects this claim:

Questa comparatione oltre che possa esser tolta come tutto hanno detto di Vergilio [and he cites the lines above]. Può esser anco dal quarto delle Trasformationi

> Hic color aprica pendetibus arbore pomis
> Aut ebore tincto est
>
> [*Metamorphoses* 4.331–32]

Usò primiero tal comparatione nel 6. dell'Odissea Homero [actually Homer uses it at *Iliad* 4.141], l'usò Statio nel 1. dell'Achilleide.

Lactea Massagite veluti cum pocula fuscant
Sanguine puniceo, vel ebur corrumpit ostro
[*Achilleid* 10.307–8]

Usolla Claudiano nel primo del Rapimento di Proserpina

Non sic decus ardet eburnum
Lydia Sydonia quod femina tinxerat ostro.

This remarkable genealogy of Ariosto's simile is not provided simply to display the commentator's erudition. Lavezuola is the first to appreciate Ariosto's predilection for models that have such genealogies or that are themselves part of a history of prior imitations. He is also the first commentator to recognize that when Ariosto imitated a text that was itself imitative, he often alluded to the model(s) of his model in his imitation. Consider his comments on the two similes used to describe Dardinello's death, after the Saracen prince is felled by the mightier Rinaldo:

Come purpureo fior languendo muore,
che 'l vomere al passar tagliato lassa;
o come carco di superchio umore
il papaver ne l'orto il capo abbassa:
così, giù de la faccia ogni colore
cadendo, Dardinel di vita passa.

(18.153)

Whereas all previous commentators had cited as a model the famous similes Virgil used to describe the death of Euryalus at *Aeneid* 9.434–37, Lavezuola cites Virgil's own models:

La comparatione del papavero fu presa da Virgilio in Homero, & la maniera con che l'Ariosto la descrive, è più somigliante all'Homerica, che alla Virgiliana. Porremo quella d'Homero, la quale è nell'8 dell'Iliade, poiché da altri quella di Virgilio è stata notata, ponendovi l'Ariosto, ne l'horto, che Virgilio lo tralascia. [And he cites *Iliad* 8.306–8 in a Latin version:]

Papaver aut in alteram partem caput inflexit,
Quod in horto fructu gravatum est, humiditatisque vernis.

After pointing out how Ariosto's "ne l'orto" specifically alludes to Homer's text, he discusses the origins of the second simile:

La comparatione poi del fiore tagliato del vomere fu prima usata da Catullo, il quale così vagamente l'espresse in quel saffico scritto a Furio, & Aurelio.

velut prati
Ultimi flos praetereunte postquam
Tactus aratro est.

[Catullus 11.22–24]

Ove non è dubbio, che l'Ar. non habbia altresi imitato quel (praetereunte autem) col verso: che 'l vomere al passar tagliato lassa.

Lavezuola's careful and accurate analysis makes his observations particularly convincing. But it is his knowledge of Virgil's own imitative practice and, most important, his awareness that Ariosto habitually imitated imitative texts that enable him to trace the presence of Virgil's precursors in addition to that of Virgil in this particular simile.

Lavezuola does not limit himself to epic similes in order to reveal this recurring imitative practice. He is aware that imitations on a larger scale exhibit similar receding genealogies. Consider his observations on the episode of Olimpia *abbandonata* at the start of canto 10. Dolce had identified the tenth epistle of Ovid's *Heroides*, Ariadne's complaint to Theseus, as the primary model for the episode. In his revised commentary he noted resemblances between some of Ariosto's verses and those in Catullus's account of Ariadne in Poem 64, but he did not specify the debts. Partly to be novel, Lavezuola plays down the primacy of Ovid's verse epistle and highlights the echoes of Catullus 64 in the episode. By showing, quite correctly, that those parts of Olimpia's lament (for example, 10.28–33) thought to have been simply imitations of Ovid are simultaneously echoing Catullus's anterior treatment of Ariadne, he makes an educated reader aware of the receding history of imitation embodied in Ariosto's text. To make sure, however, that a less well informed reader will not overlook the fact that in *Heroides* 10 Ovid was himself imitating Catullus's poem, he makes it clear when commenting on 10.34: "Tratto da Ovidio nella sua Arianna fatta da lui parimente di quella di Catullo." Although Lavezuola plays down the presence of *Heroides* 10 in this episode (it had already been indicated by Dolce and others), in general his commentary is the first to recognize Ariosto's frequent borrowings from Ovid's verse epistles. He identifies both sizable imitations of the *Heroides*—as when he shows that Bradamante's anxious waiting for Ruggiero in canto 32 is partly modeled on Phillis's waiting in *Heroides* 2—and Ariosto's borrowings on a smaller scale.[14]

One might presume that imitations of Statius imitating Virgil would have offered Lavezuola further opportunities to reveal the poetic genealogies that so often make up Ariosto's imitations of several models at once. But the fact that Dolce's revised commentary had paid so much attention to their simultaneous presence made Lavezuola disregard Ariosto's imitations of the *Thebaid*. He does occasionally point to the Statian origins of similes overlooked by Dolce, and when he can, he likes to point to imitations of the *Achilleid*. Yet when he comments on the Cloridano and Medoro episode, he does not even refer to *Thebaid* 10, and he points to only one specific imitation of *Aeneid* 9 (the description of Euryalus's beauty at lines 176–81), presumably because it was one of the few left unidentified by Dolce.

Lavezuola sometimes identifies a number of subtexts in an episode with-out explicitly noting that they themselves are linked by *imitatio*. Nonethe-less, on the basis of his perceptive comments, readers can reconstruct the links and eventually recognize the genealogy embodied within these imita-tions. Consider his comments in canto 6 on the encounter between Rug-giero and Astolfo transformed into a myrtle bush (6.23–53). Dolce had observed—as had Fausto da Longiano—that this episode imitated Aeneas's encounter with Polydorus also transformed into a plant (*Aeneid* 3.19–56). Lavezuola disregards the Polydorus episode when he comments on Ruggiero's exchange with Astolfo-as-myrtle, beginning rather by identi-fying the Dantean source of the simile Ariosto uses to describe the voice that hisses from the wounded plant. Ariosto's comparison is as follows:

> Come ceppo talor, che le medolle
> rare e vote abbia, e posto al fuoco sia,
> poi che per gran calor quell'aria molle
> resta consunta ch'in mezzo l'empia,
> dentro risuona, e con strepito bolle
> tanto che quel furor truovi la via;
> così murmura e stride e si coruccia
> quel mirto offeso, e al fine apre la buccia.
>
> (6.27)

"La comparatione della predetta stanza," writes Lavezuola, "è cavata da Dante nel canto 13 dell'Inferno dicendo:

> Come d'un stizzo verde, ch'arso sia
> Da l'un de'lati, che da l'altro geme
> E cigola per vento che va via."
>
> (*Inferno* 13.40–42)

He praises Ariosto for outshining Dante and goes on to mention two other treatments of similar metamorphosis—by Ovid and by Boccaccio—that were also being alluded to by the poet:

> La favola poi del Mirto che stride, e si coruccia per l'offesa fattagli allude alla quercia, ch'Erisittone appresso Ovidio nell'ottavo delle Trasformationi tagliò nel bosco di Cerere.
> Contremuit, gemitumque; dedit decidua quercus
> Et poi
> Editus & medio sonus est de robore talis.
> Anchor che, habbia poi più evidentemente, inquanto al servirsi delle parole, e delle forme del dire imitato il Boccacio nel 6 del Filocopo [sic], nel descrivere la fonte di Fileno, che si tramutò in quella.

The deliberate omission of Virgil's Polydorus episode is conspicuous, and in contrast to Dolce's almost exclusive references to Ariosto's Latin models, Lavezuola's inclusion of Dante and Boccaccio is striking. Indeed, his appreciation of Ariosto's imitations of Dante, Boccaccio, and other Italian poets is one of the prominent novelties of his commentary. His recognition of the imitation of *Inferno* 13 is not unprecedented (Fornari had noted it in 1550 in his *Spositione sopra l'Orlando Furioso*), but Lavezuola is the first commentator to recognize Boccaccio's *Filocolo* as one of the subtexts of this episode. Actually, the account of Fileno transformed into a fountain is one of two episodes in the *Filocolo* specifically alluded to at 6.28ff. The other is the episode of Idalagos transformed into a pine (5.6.3), who, like Astolfo, speaks out after being wounded inadvertently by Filocolo. As Ariosto was well aware, in both episodes Boccaccio was imitating Dante's account of Pier della Vigna in *Inferno* 13, and in the second story he compared Idalagos to Virgil's Polydorus. Although Lavezuola does not point out that Boccaccio was consciously imitating Dante imitating Virgil, his perceptive comments allow the reader to begin to reconstruct this elaborate genealogy. That is to say, if the reader is aware that Virgil's Polydorus episode is the initial subtext in Ariosto's account, Lavezuola's commentary can help him recognize that, in addition to Virgil, Ariosto imitates Ovid and Dante imitating Virgil, as well as Boccaccio imitating Virgil and Dante.

Sometimes Ariosto did not incorporate the model(s) of his model in an imitation of a well-known imitation, but left the reader to infer that his model derived from one or more prior texts. In such instances, Lavezuola makes the implicit genealogy explicit. A notable example is the passage in canto 18 describing Rodomonte's forced exit from Paris after he has single-handedly slaughtered the population. Finding himself outnumbered and driven back by his Christian foes, Rodomonte is compelled to dive into the Seine to escape sure death (18.21–25). The episode is modeled closely on that of Turnus's forced exit from the Trojan camp in *Aeneid* 9.789ff. In his "Brieve dimostratione" Dolce had recognized that the epic simile describing Rodomonte pursued by his foes (18.22) imitated the description of the retreating but ever-proud Turnus (*Aeneid* 9.792–96). When Lavezuola comments on Rodomonte's retreat, he gives a fuller account of Ariosto's imitation by showing specific parallels with *Aeneid* 9.812–13 and 9.797–99. But he also points out—revealing again how alert he is to this characteristic in Ariosto's models—that Virgil's account of Turnus's defiant exit was itself an imitation of the tribune Caelius's lone stand against the Istrians in Ennius's *Annales* 15. "Nè Virgilio fu auttore d'un cotal pugna," he reminds readers, "havendolasi pigliata dal quintodecimo libro d'Ennio, come pone Macrobio." Indeed, Macrobius cites the passage from Ennius (itself an imitation of *Iliad* 16.102–11) as the model for *Aeneid* 9.806ff. to illustrate how "certain passages in Virgil which he is believed to have borrowed from Homer . . . [are] in fact taken from Latin authors who had previously transferred them from Homer to use in their own poems" (*Saturnalia* 6.3). Lavezuola points out that Ariosto did not actually allude, as was often his wont, to the model of his model. Presumably the poet expected his literate readers, at least those who had read Macrobius, to recognize the genealogy that Lavezuola indicates explicitly.

As did his comments on the "Virgilian" simile describing the death of Dardinello (18.125) and the encounter between Ruggiero and the metamorphosed Astolfo, these remarks on Rodomonte's forced exit from Paris reveal that Lavezuola's appreciation of Ariosto's complex imitations grew from an effort to show that Ariosto was not simply imitating Virgil—as Dolce had persistently maintained—and that when he was, he drew from the Roman poet's own imitations as well. I do not mean to suggest that Lavezuola identified a genealogy of subtexts in a simile or an episode only when he wanted to show that Virgil was not the exclusive model. He was aware that, in general, Ariosto's imitations were rarely unilateral; and some imitations whose several related models he identifies had nothing to do with Virgil's epic.[15] Still, I believe that it was Lavezuola's reaction to Dolce's insistence on the *Aeneid* as the dominant and only object of Ariosto's imitations that made him alert to the poet's habit of embodying or referring to several prior versions of what he was rewriting. One of the striking and original contributions of Lavezuola's commentary is its identification of prior Italian poets alluded to or imitated by Ariosto: primarily Dante, Boccaccio, and Petrarch (in that order of frequency), but also Poliziano, Sannazaro, and Bembo. Especially notable are Lavezuola's numerous references to Dante. He perceives correctly that most of Ariosto's borrowings from Dante are lexical and prosodic. Although he points to a few imitations of scenes from the *Commedia*, most of his references are to borrowed phrases and expressions (for example, at 2.5, 31.34, 34.54); rhymes and half-lines (for example, 5.26, 6.78, 13.57, 28.15); and similes (for example, at 1.62, 6.27, 13.16, 18.36, 24.96, 33.84). Sensitive though he is to Ariosto's use of Dante, Lavezuola considers Dante's poetic art relatively crude and primitive; on several occasions, he points out that Ariosto in his imitation always refines and improves on the *Commedia* (see his comment at 9.23). He is less condescending about Petrarch's poetry, which he recognizes as a subtext in various parts of the *Furioso*, but his references to the *Rime* and the *Trionfi* (for example, 24.87, 25.14, 31.93) are less frequent than those to Dante. In fact, he seems to pay closer attention to borrowings from Poliziano (primarily the *Stanze*) than to those from Petrarch.[16]

Despite his appreciation of Ariosto's use of the major trecento poets, Lavezuola overlooks his debt to medieval chivalric romance. Given the contempt of sixteenth-century humanists toward these early tales of adventure, such an omission is hardly surprising. Yet his disregard is not due to ignorance; at least twice he refers to Ariosto's borrowings from a *Tristano* "d'un certo Romanzatore antico," references accompanied by disparaging remarks characteristic of the hostile attitude of sixteenth-century literati.[17]

Lavezuola knew some of the early Italian chivalric romances, but seems to have been unfamiliar with (or not to have had access to) their French predecessors. On one occasion (at 17.68) he points out correctly that the story of Grifone's betrayal by Orrigille and Martano is drawn from the story of King Meliadus in a French romance, but comments that he knows only the Italian translation of this tale from *Palamedes*. In view of the total disregard of such romance sources by prior commentators it is quite remarkable that Lavezuola goes to the trouble of providing this reference. The example Lavezuola gives shows that Ariosto imitated mostly plots and episodic situations from the early prose and verse romances and not the surface of their texts. Given that Lavezuola focuses on the verbal and stylistic analogues between Ariosto's poetry and his models, his lack of attention to Ariosto's borrowings from medieval romances is somewhat understandable. Nonetheless, he could have devoted more attention to Ariosto's extensive debt to Boiardo's *Orlando Innamorato*. He acknowledges that the personalities of certain protagonists in the *Furioso* (for example, Brunello and Rodomonte) are Boiardo's inventions, but he fails or rather refuses to recognize the extent to which Ariosto imitated Boiardo's poetic language—both his similes and his imitations of the classical poets.[18]

This relative neglect of Ariosto's debt to chivalric romances notwithstanding, when compared to Dolce's commentary Lavezuola's seems infinitely more attentive to Ariosto's allusions to Italian poets and vernacular sources. It is also generally more comprehensive and more precise than Dolce's commentary, especially in its recognition of the complex commingling of sources in Ariosto's imitations. From a modern point of view, Lavezuola's commentary provides the first adequate account of the poet's imitative procedures. This commentary, however, enjoyed nothing like the publishing success of Dolce's "Brieve dimostratione." It originally appeared in the sumptuous 1584 edition (considered by some the most lavish) of the *Furioso* published by Francesco dei Franceschi. But the "Osservationi" were not republished in the sixteenth century. In fact, the commentary was not published again until 1730, when it appeared along with many other early commentaries in the great Orlandini edition. On the other hand, Dolce's "Brieve dimostratione" was printed about forty times between 1542 and 1566, and even after his enlarged version was published in 1566, the original commentary continued to be reissued. After 1584, when one might have thought that Lavezuola's commentary would have quite superseded it, Dolce's original commentary was reprinted at least five times before the end of the century.[19]

Modern readers may find Lavezuola's "Osservationi" more intelligent and generally more adequate, but Dolce's first commentary was far more appealing to readers in the cinquecento. Clearly, commercial motives determined to some extent the fact that Lavezuola's commentary was appended to one *Orlando Furioso* in the sixteenth century and Dolce's to more than fifty, but why did no Venetian publisher choose to reprint Lavezuola's commentary again? Why was it considered unprofitable? Had Dolce's "Brieve dimostratione" not continued to appear quite regularly after 1584, one might assume that Lavezuola's was not reprinted because demand for such commentaries was declining altogether, as was the demand for Ariosto's poem generally. But there had to be other reasons, because Dolce's original commentary did continue to be reissued.

Lavezuola's commentary radically modified an account of Ariosto's imitations that had become normative and thereby virtually unimpeachable. Dolce's account achieved this normative status because, by establishing the Virgilian, epic parentage of the *Furioso*, it satisfied a need to anchor the modern Italian poem in a respectable—that is, an ancient—tradition. Beginning with Giolito, Venetian printers realized that Dolce's legitimating commentary added to the poem's prestige, enhanced the appeal of their product, and therefore contributed to the commercial success of the poem. Dolce's unambiguous affiliation of *Orlando Furioso* and Virgil's epic accounts for the ongoing popularity of his commentary. Late sixteenth century readers were more disposed to entertain the unilateral ties between Ariosto and Virgil posited by Dolce than the complex and sometimes indeterminate derivation of Ariosto's imitations proposed by Lavezuola. This preference can be explained partly by the critical attitudes about the *Furioso* prevailing in 1584.

Lavezuola's "Osservationi" was published in 1584, the same year as Camillo Pellegrino's *Il Carrafa*, the dialogue that championed Tasso's *Gerusalemme Liberata* (first published in 1581) at the expense of the *Furioso* and sparked the critical war between the Tassisti and the Ariostisti. The ensuing quarrel, which lasted until the end of the century, revolved around which of the two poets had, as Pellegrino put it, "achieved a greater degree of honor in epic poetry." This is hardly the occasion to consider the debate in any detail (I discuss it at length in Chapter 6).[20] What must be kept in mind, however, are some of the objections leveled against the *Furioso* by Tasso and his supporters. Foremost among these was the poem's failure to conform to classical epic norms, particularly its refusal to organize itself around a single action and a single protagonist. Moreover, the multiplicity of plots and the absence of any hierarchy among them supposedly produced only confusion in the minds of its readers. Related to this criticism of the romanzo's confusing multiplicity was the complaint that Ariosto's poem defied decorum, political and religious as well as social and literary.

If one considers the implications of Lavezuola's account of Ariosto's imitative procedures, it is apparent that his comments could lend support to these accusations, especially those about the poem's flouting of decorum and of hierarchy. After all, Lavezuola shows that, contrary to Dolce's claims, Ariosto does not imitate only the *Aeneid* in a given passage, but

Ovidian or Catullan elegy, or Dante's terza rima, or an episode from one of Boccaccio's prose romances as well. This mixture of classical and modern precursors, or of models from different poetic genres, can be seen as homologous to the multiplicity of tones and registers, the mixture of styles often found in Ariosto's octaves and attacked by the poet's detractors as indecorous. Besides, the question may be asked whether the genealogies of texts that Lavezuola identifies in certain complex imitations, extending back to Virgil or his precursors and forward to quite recent Italian poets, do not reduce all precursors to equal rank and thereby defy the hierarchy of status that distinguishes ancient from modern poets and epic poems from lesser genres. To the extent that Lavezuola's commentary was exposing, however unwittingly, Ariosto's refusal to make such distinctions among his precursors, it provided further proof of Ariosto's lack of decorum. More broadly, by revealing that the origins and the models of Ariosto's imitations were multiple, mixed, and often even indeterminate because of their commingling, Lavezuola was providing evidence that the *Furioso* was a confused, synarchic text on all levels. Critical opponents had already identified such confusion and lack of discrimination in terms of plot structure, character portrayal, and diction. Now Lavezuola provided a commentary that supported these damaging accusations even with respect to Ariosto's eclectic imitative procedures.

Considering the critical climate, a publisher who thought of including a commentary on imitations in a late sixteenth century edition of the *Furioso* would have done better commercially by sticking with Dolce's "Brieve dimostratione." Despite the fact that Dolce's effort to affiliate the poem to Roman epic was being countered by Ariosto's neoclassical enemies, at least his commentary enhanced the poem's status and was unambiguous about its Virgilian ancestry. This feature—Dolce's provision of a single, unambivalent, and honorific (since usually Virgilian) precedent in each imitative case—goes far to explain the popularity of his commentary in the cinquecento. As observed in the last chapter, all the editorial apparatus and commentary that accompanied the numerous editions of the *Furioso* from 1540 on—allegorizations, inventories of *sentenze*, glosses, prefaces, and commentaries advertising the poem's epic bloodlines—aimed either to place the poem in a prestigious tradition or to stabilize it by domesticating its erratic, ambivalent meanings. The success of the "Brieve dimostratione" can be attributed to its combination of these two desired modes of providing legitimacy: it gave the modern text a respectable ancestry, and it ascribed single unequivocal sources for its imitations. That Dolce's reductive assessment of the parentage of Ariosto's imitations was belied by Lavezuola in 1584 does not seem to have mattered. Readers preferred not to have to contemplate Ariosto's tendency to destabilize and complicate their assumptions that poets derived their imitations from single unambiguous origins.

The problem with Lavezuola's "Osservationi" was that its extraordinary account of the text's eclectic and ambivalent origins clearly brought out this subversive aspect of Ariosto's imitative technique. The commentary had to be ignored or forgotten lest it jeopardize, even in a limited way, more than forty years of effort on the part of curators to stabilize and legitimize the *Furioso*. The fact that Lavezuola's remarkable elucidation has remained virtually forgotten makes one wonder whether the preference does not persist for commentaries that suppress or at least ignore the ambivalence and multiplicity of Ariosto's masterpiece.

Chapter Four

AFFILIATIONS WITH OVID'S
METAMORPHOSES

WHILE the main trend among Ariosto's midcentury promoters was to affiliate his poem to Virgil's epic, by the 1560s one finds that the *Furioso* is increasingly associated with another Latin poem, in many ways more closely kindred: Ovid's *Metamorphoses*. The features shared by the two poems, especially the multiplicity and the variety of their narratives, are often invoked in contrast with the unity of Homeric and Virgilian epic. In fact, by the last third of the century, efforts to dissociate Ariosto's poem from classical epic may well have been reinforced by the kinship increasingly perceived between it and the *Metamorphoses*. Yet even as the genealogical descent from the *Aeneid* previously ascribed to the *Furioso* lost some credibility, its affiliation to the *Metamorphoses* endowed the modern poem with a different but no less honorific pedigree.

Links between Ovid's and Ariosto's poems were already being made before the middle of the century. In the previous chapter I mentioned that the first commentaries on Ariosto's imitations, published in the early 1540s, identified some of his borrowings from the *Metamorphoses*. However, since the main objective of these commentaries was to emphasize the Virgilian or else the general epic ancestry of the *Furioso*, they focused on the martial or heroic events of the Italian poem. As a result they belittled Ariosto's debt to Ovid by disregarding a number of important amatory episodes that Ariosto had modeled on episodes in the *Metamorphoses*. Moreover, since these commentaries served to identify classical sources of the *Furioso*'s subject matter and were concerned therefore with material rather than formal imitation, they overlooked some of the compositional similarities between the *Furioso* and the *Metamorphoses*. The formal ties between the two poems became more recognized when champions of the romanzo, seeking prestigious antecedents of the non-Aristotelian features of chivalric romance, found them in Ovid's poem.

G. B. Giraldi is the first of these critics to establish connections between the romanzo and the *Metamorphoses*. When Giraldi affirms the rights of modern *romanzatori* to depart from classical epic norms he cites the example of the *Metamorphoses* as a precedent, maintaining that Ovid disregarded Virgilian practice as well as Aristotelian and Horatian rules because he realized that they did not apply to his type of composition. Yet, far from being reproached by critics for "avere tralasciati gli ordini di Virgilio e di Omero," Ovid was and continues to be acclaimed for his poetic achievement. The romance poet, Giraldi then proposes, must similarly be able to recognize that the rules observed by Virgil and Homer are inapplicable and must be disregarded when composing poems of many actions.[1] Giraldi does not dwell on the similarities between the modern romanzo and the *Metamorphoses*, but he justifies the multiplicity and the *varietà* of the romanzo by citing the precedence of such features in the *Metamorphoses*. Following is a passage where he associates the copious digressions of the romanzo and of the *Metamorphoses*, in contrast to Virgil's and Homer's less errant narratives.

> E quivi è da por mente che in queste digressioni che contengono giostre, tornei, amori, bellezze, passioni del'animo, campo, edifici e simili altre cose, è molto più largo lo scrittore dei romanzi che non è stato ne Virgilio, ne Omero. E in queste parti è piu simile ad Ovidio (parlo delle sue Mutazioni) che non è ad alcuno altro poeta.[2]

> [Here one needs to bear in mind that in these digressions, which contain jousts, tourneys, love affairs, beauties, passions of the mind, battlefields, buildings, and other such things, the writer of romances is much more copious than either Virgil or Homer. In this respect he is more like Ovid (I speak of his *Metamorphoses*) than any other poet.]

Even from this observation one can see that Giraldi was aware of the "unclassicist" way in which Ovid composed the *Metamorphoses*. It was precisely because he could appreciate its departures from traditional epic form that Ovid's major poem served him as the best and virtually the only ancient example to validate the romanzo's similar disregard of Aristotelian and Horatian norms of epic structure.

Giraldi's comments helped midcentury readers recognize the un-Aristotelian aspects shared by the *Furioso* and the *Metamorphoses*. But an awareness of the kinship between the two poems was brought about less by commentary of this sort than by a remarkable literary phenomenon which, itself, reflects the prominent status attained by Ariosto's poem: the decisive influence that the *Furioso* and its commercial success had on the two major Italian translations of the *Metamorphoses* published in the cinquecento. It should be said at the outset that Ariosto's poem influenced more than new versions of Ovid in Italian. In the wake of its tremendous success, almost all midcentury narrative poetry produced in ottava rima imitated the "maniera ariostesca": from the "rifacimenti" of Boiardo's *Innamorato*, to the various sequels of the *Furioso*, to other rhymed translations of ancient narrative poems (for example, the *Iliad*, the *Aeneid*, and, later, the *Thebaid*). However, the degree to which Ariosto's poem marked and shaped translations of the *Metamorphoses* was especially pronounced. Moreover, none of the other narrative poems done in the "maniera ariostesca" enjoyed anything like the success of these Ovids in ottava rima.

The two translations of Ovid's poem I refer to were Lodovico Dolce's *Trasformationi*, first published in Venice in 1553, and Giovanni dell'Anguillara's *Metamorfosi*, first published in complete form in 1561. Anguillara's translation was particularly successful. Although a full count remains to be made, more than twenty-five editions of it were published between 1561 and 1590, and it continued to be printed steadily well into the seventeenth century. Dolce's translation was also published repeatedly until it was replaced by Anguillara's. Altogether there were eight editions of Dolce's *Trasformationi* between 1553 and 1570.[3] That the first six of these were published by Gabriel Giolito is not surprising since Dolce served as reader, editor, and general consultant for this important Venetian publisher who specialized in vernacular Italian literature and *volgariz- zamenti* of the classics.

Dolce's close association with Giolito has significant bearing on my topic since Giolito was the most important publisher of *Orlando Furioso* in the mid–sixteenth century. Moreover, Dolce, it will be recalled, was the editor of the Giolito *Furioso*, and it is in editions of the poem published by Giolito that we find the first advertisements of Dolce's forthcoming translation of the *Metamorphoses*. In an "Avviso" to the readers appended to the 1550 edition of the *Furioso*, Giolito announces the future publication of Ariosto's additional *Cinque canti*, adding, "speriamo di darvi similmente fra pochi mesi le dilettevoli Trasformationi d'Ovidio tradotti del . . . Dolce in questa ottava rima." This announcement can be found again in the 1551 and 1552 editions of the *Furioso*, but in the latter edition Giolito's advertisement is modified as follows:

> Di molte opere da me più volte promesse, tra pochi mesi o giorni vi si daranno le Trasformazioni d'Ovidio le quali per aventura saranno di qualità, che ad alcuni pedanti, o Simie si leveranno le occasioni (se essi havranno giudicio) di affatticarsi (il che sia detto senza offendere alcuni) in perder carte.[4]
>
> [Of the many works more often promised by me, in a few months or days you will be given Ovid's *Metamorphoses*, which perchance will be of such quality that it will deter certain pedants, or Apes (if they have any judgment) from working hard at wasting paper (which is said without offense to anyone).]

Dolce's translation of Ovid did not actually appear in print until 1553. It seems that one of the motives for this premature publicity, or at least for the slur about rival translators, was to discourage Anguillara, who had already begun his translation of the *Metamorphoses* and was circulating his version of the first book(s) among Venetian literati.[5] More interesting, how-

Plate 1. *Le Trasformationi di M. Lodovico Dolce* (Venice: G. Giolito, 1555). By permission of the Houghton Library, Harvard University.

ever, than the competitive motives prompting these advance notices of Dolce's *Trasformationi* is the fact that they appear in several editions of the *Furioso*. For this already suggests that when Giolito commissioned Dolce to do the translation in or before 1548 (when the Venetian Senate granted Giolito a ten-year privilege to publish "il Metamorfoseo d'Ovidio tradotto dal Dolce in ottava rima") he did so, in large part, to capitalize on the growing success of the *Furioso*. At any rate, when Giolito decided to advertise Dolce's forthcoming *Trasformationi* in editions of the *Furioso*, he did so presumably because he assumed that devotees of Ariosto's romanzo would prove likely buyers of the *Metamorphoses* in Italian, especially if rendered in ottava rima.

Why the publication of Dolce's *Trasformationi* was announced to readers of the Giolito *Furioso* becomes even more apparent as soon as one looks at any copy of Dolce's translation published by Giolito. The format and typographical layout of the *Trasformationi* are virtually indistinguishable from the *Furiosos* in quarto published by Giolito in the 1550s. The two texts are not only of the same size, but of the same type, with two columns of octaves on each page (see the openings from both books reproduced in plates 1 and 2). Both texts are even adorned by similar engravings, although there are more illustrations per canto in Dolce's translation.

Plate 2. Lodovico Ariosto, *Orlando Furioso* (Venice: G. Giolito, 1551). By permission of the Houghton Library, Harvard University.

Dolce's fundamental alteration, of course, was to convert Ovid's unrhymed hexameters into octaves of hendecasyllabic lines. Hence, like the *Furioso*, Ovid's poem in Italian appears in ottava rima.[6] Like Ariosto's poem, moreover, Dolce's translation is divided into cantos: Ovid's original fifteen books are split up into thirty cantos in the *Trasformationi*. Dolce also imitates Ariosto's characteristic manner of beginning cantos with *exordia* of varying lengths in which the narrator comments on or draws *sententiae* from events in the preceding canto. He even brings up, as Ariosto occasionally did, contemporary Italian issues in these *exordia* (see, as an example, the beginning of the sixth canto reproduced in plate 1). If one examines Dolce's translation to see where he divided each of Ovid's books to produce twice the number of cantos, one is struck by another feature borrowed from Ariosto: canto ends. Dolce imitates the tantalizing interruptions of narrative that characterize canto ends in the *Furioso* by often finishing his cantos in the midst or at the start of one of Ovid's stories.[7] And he also imitates Ariosto's technique of making each canto end with a narratorial address to the audience fictitiously presumed to be listening to the *romanzatore* reciting his poem.

Dolce's *exordia* at the start of his cantos, and his interruption of narra-

tive at their close, already show that the translator tried to adopt as many
aspects of Ariosto's canto structure as a relatively faithful rendering of
Ovid's narrative would allow. However, Ovid's narrative design within
each book—basically a chain of separate stories usually involving a changing cast of protagonists for each story—did not permit Dolce to imitate
Ariosto's characteristic technique of suspension and eventual resumption
of major plot lines within cantos. The aesthetic principle and desirability of
varietà motivating this technique in the *Furioso* was satisfied, nonetheless,
by the sheer number of different stories provided in each book of the *Metamorphoses.*

One might presuppose that Dolce's transformation of the *Metamorphoses* into a *romanzo all'Ariosto* would so alter Ovid's original work as to
make it an altogether different kind of poem. Yet despite Dolce's remarkable formal alterations of the Latin poem, one is struck by how much of
Ovid's matter and manner are preserved in the *Trasformationi.* One is
struck, that is, by how readily the *Metamorphoses* lends itself to becoming
an Italian romanzo. Surely one reason Dolce chose to translate Ovid's
poem into a romanzo was that, like Giraldi, he recognized some of the
formal affinities shared by the *Metamorphoses* and Ariosto's romanzo.[8]

But it was not simply because he perceived affinities between Ovid's and
Ariosto's poems that Dolce transformed the *Metamorphoses* into its most
kindred modern genre. Probably a more important factor that led Dolce to
recast the *Metamorphoses* into ottava rima, and that prompted Giolito to
commission it, was economic as well as literary: namely, the great commercial success of *Orlando Furioso* in the late 1540s and 1550s. As I indicated
at the start of this study, the ceaseless reprinting of Ariosto's poem from
1545 to 1570 confirms that Italian readers of the time found it the most
appealing work of modern literature. It was largely in order to cater to their
literary taste that Giolito published a *volgarizzamento* of Ovid *all'Ariosto.*
Presumably that is also why Dolce eventually produced translations of
Homer's and Virgil's epics in ottava rima. He seems to have translated two
versions of the *Aeneid* in ottava rima which appeared right after his death:
L'Enea di M. Lodovico Dolce tratto di Virgilio (Venice: G. Varisco, 1568)
was the first. The other version was conflated with a "rifacimento" of the
Iliad and published in 1570 by Giolito's house as *L'Achille e l'Enea di M.
Lodovico Dolce.*[9] In 1573 Giolito also published *L'Ulisse di M. Lodovico
Dolce da lui . . . ridotto in ottava rima.* In addition to Homer and Virgil,
there also appeared in 1570 *La Thebaide di Statio ridotta del Sig. Erasmo di
Valvassone in ottava rima.* While the tremendous vogue of the *Furioso*
stimulated this trend to present ancient epics in ottava rima, it was also the
publishing success of the *Metamorphoses* recast as modern romance (both
Dolce's and Anguillara's versions were being reprinted steadily in the

1560s) that inspired publishers to try the same with the other great poems of antiquity. But the ancient epics in the verse form of romances did not appeal to the reading public nearly as much as the *Metamorphoses*. For example, Dolce's first translation of the *Aeneid* in ottava rima (1568) was never reprinted again, nor was his translation of the *Odyssey*. His massive transformation of both the *Iliad* and the *Aeneid* was reprinted twice (1571, 1572) but disappeared thereafter. Similarly, an earlier version of the *Aeneid* in ottava rima, Aldobrandi Cerretani's *Eneide toscana*, was not reissued after its original 1560 publication in Florence. Despite the reading public's appreciation of *Orlando Furioso* and also of Ovid in ottava rima, it seems to have been more discriminating than Giolito and Dolce had anticipated. Readers not knowing Latin who sought the *Aeneid* in Italian eventually preferred to read it in *verso sciolto* (the meter that most closely corresponds to the heroic Latin hexameter). By the 1570s, even before Annibale Caro's translation of the *Aeneid* in *verso sciolto* (it was first published in 1581, but completed and already known by 1566) became the most popular Italian version, prevailing literary taste discouraged further attempts to translate Virgil's epic in ottava rima. Anguillara himself, whose translation of the *Metamorphoses* was to supplant Dolce's, began in 1561 a translation of the *Aeneid* in ottava rima, but he was not inspired—presumably for lack of positive response—to complete more than two books of the poem.[10]

The failure of several translators of Virgil to capitalize on a demand in this period for classics in ottava rima suggests that Italian readers did not find the *Aeneid* and the verse form of romance very compatible. On the other hand, they clearly appreciated and continued to enjoy Ovid's *Metamorphoses* recast as romance. By 1570, Anguillara's *Metamorfosi* in ottava rima was already establishing itself as the most popular Italian translation of Ovid's poem in the sixteenth century. Five editions were published between 1561 and 1570, and twenty more were to appear between 1570 and 1590.

This translation of Ovid was also decisively influenced by *Orlando Furioso*. Familiar as Anguillara was with Ariosto's poem (he composed the *argomenti* summarizing each canto of the *Furioso* in the 1563 edition published by Giorgio Varisco), he could hardly avoid being influenced by Ariosto's verses and rhymes when, like Dolce, he converted Ovid's hexameters into ottava rima. However, aside from the verse form, his *Metamorfosi* exhibits less structural similarity to Ariosto's poem than does Dolce's *Trasformationi*. To begin with, even though the *Metamorfosi* is at least three times as long as Ovid's Latin poem, it is not redivided into cantos but retains the original structure of fifteen books. Consequently, the imitations of Ariosto's canto structure previously observed in Dolce's translation are not to be found in Anguillara's. More apparent than structural similarities

between the *Metamorfosi* and the *Furioso* are the editorial and typographical similarities between them. Editions of Anguillara's translation progressively acquired more and more of the trappings that were added to editions
of the *Furioso* after the midcentury: *argomenti* in verse summarizing the
contents of each book, *allegorie*, engraved illustrations, and, most telling,
by 1563, "annotationi" (by Giuseppe Orologgi) appended to each book,
much in the same way that moral and historical commentaries came to be
appended to each canto of the *Furioso*.

Although the verse form and the editorial presentation of the *Metamorfosi* already reveal the influence of Ariosto's *Furioso*, that influence manifests itself even more clearly in the Italian translation itself. For Anguillara
did not hesitate to imitate, borrow from, and allude to the actual matter
and language of the *Furioso*. Before briefly examining some of these imitations, I should point out that Anguillara's translation is very free and, compared to Dolce's, considerably less faithful to Ovid's original text.[11] The
amplification of Ovid's stories and episodes is the most noticeable of Anguillara's licenses as a translator. Perhaps the most striking instance of such
amplification is his *rifacimento* of the story of Pyramus and Thisbe: 111
hexameters in Ovid's poem (4.55–166) are expanded into a tale of 912
lines in the *Metamorfosi* (4, oct. 31–145). In this case as well as in less
extreme cases of Anguillara's amplification one can also perceive the influence of *Orlando Furioso*. For such enlargements and elaborations of Ovid's
relatively brief stories display the translator's recurring impulse to provide
novelle in verse of the sort Ariosto frequently wove into his complex plot
(see, among many examples, the story of Ginevra, Ariodante, and Po-
linesso in *Orlando Furioso*, canto 5; or that of Ricciardetto and Fiordispina
in canto 25, or that of Giocondo and Astolfo in canto 28).

Some stories in Ovid's *Metamorphoses* were already similar enough to
novelle that they called for less amplification on Anguillara's part. Consider, for example, Ovid's story of Cephalus and Procris (*Metamorphoses*
7.690–862). Although it took Anguillara eighty octaves to "translate" it
(*Metamorfosi 7*, oct. 251–332), this story required much less enlargement
than did that of Pyramus and Thisbe to become the *novelle* in rhyme that
Anguillara desired. How easily Ovid's story of Cephalus and Procris could
be transformed into an Ariostean *novella* is revealed, of course, in the *Furioso* itself since Ovid's story had already served as one of the principal
sources for one of Ariosto's own *novelle*: the calamitous tale that Rinaldo's
Mantuan host tells about his own lack of faith in his wife's fidelity (*OF*
43.11–46). Not only was Anguillara fully aware of Ariosto's imitation of
Ovid's story; upon closer examination of his translation of Cephalus's tale,
one notices that it is actually *contaminated* by Ariosto's story of the Mantuan host.[12] In other words, Anguillara's version of Cephalus and Procris is

a translation of Ovid's story contaminated by a narrative in the *Furioso* which is itself an imitation of the same story in the *Metamorphoses*. Such imitation of Ariosto's own imitation of Ovid is far from unusual in the *Metamorfosi*. In fact, virtually every imitation of the *Metamorphoses* in the *Furioso* is imitated in turn by Anguillara when he translates, or rather transforms, the particular episode or passage in Ovid's poem that had previously served as a model for Ariosto.

This imitation of Ariosto's own imitation of Ovid is particularly apparent in Anguillara's rendering of Perseus's rescue of Andromeda (*Metamorfosi* 4, oct. 412–41). Ariosto, as the first readers of the *Furioso* already recognized, had modeled Ruggiero's rescue of Angelica from the Orca (*OF* 10.91–115) on Ovid's account of Perseus's rescue of Andromeda (*Metamorphoses* 4.663–774). However, one of the most noticeable differences between Ariosto's and Ovid's rescues is that Ruggiero flies in on the winged Hippogryph to save Angelica while Perseus is propelled by winged sandals. Medieval accounts and representations of Perseus's exploit had already altered Ovid's in this way by depicting winged Pegasus as Perseus's means of transport when he rescues Andromeda from the monster.[13] When Anguillara translates Ovid's story at the end of book 4 he disregards the winged sandals propelling Ovid's Perseus but instead mounts the hero "sul Pegaseo veloce" (*Metamorfosi* 4, oct. 411). But it is not simply in order to perpetuate a medieval tradition that Anguillara provides a flying horse for Perseus. He does so, it soon becomes clear, to make more recognizable his imitation of Ariosto's own emulation of Ovid in canto 10 of the *Furioso*. One has only to compare Ovid's original narrative (*Metamorphoses* 4.663–774), Anguillara's rendering of it (*Metamorfosi* 4, oct. 412–41), and Ariosto's account of Ruggiero's rescue of Angelica (*OF* 10.91–115) to recognize how extensively Ariosto's episode contaminates Anguillara's translation.[14]

Readers of the *Metamorfosi* who failed to appreciate Anguillara's emulations of Ariosto found his rival imitations pointed out in Giuseppe Orologgi's "Annotationi," which began to accompany the translation in the 1563 edition. For instance, in his "Annotationi" to book 4 of the *Metamorfosi*, Orologgi makes this final observation after commenting on the episode of Perseus and Andromeda: "Ha quivi l'Anguillara fatto molto concorrenza all'Ariosto." In book 8 Anguillara enlarges Ovid's very brief reference to the plight of Ariadne abandoned on Naxos (*Metamorphoses* 8.174–79) to thirty-five octaves that fully describe her pathetic situation and her lament upon finding herself so abandoned by the faithless Theseus (*Metamorfosi* 8, oct. 105–41). Commenting on Anguillara's account of Ariadne's lament, Orologgi correctly observes that here, again, the translator was emulating Ariosto: "Se in luogo alcuno l'Anguillara si è affaticato

con l'ingegno di concorrere con l'Ariosto si è affaticato in questa descrit-
tione del lamento di Arianna, fatto da quel gran poeta in persona di Olimpia [If Anguillara strived to match wits with Ariosto anywhere, it was in
this description of Ariadne's lament, which that great poet had Olimpia
utter]." Ariosto's description of Olimpia abandoned by Bireno, and especially her ensuing lament (*OF* 10.10–34), were modeled on Ovid's similar
description of Ariadne abandoned by Theseus as well as Catullus's account
of Ariadne's flight in Poem 64. However, in this instance, Ariosto's Ovidian source was not the *Metamorphoses* but *Heroides* 10. Anguillara also relied on Ovid's tenth epistle in the *Heroides* when he took the liberty to
enlarge the account of Ariadne's abandonment briefly mentioned in the
Metamorphoses. But he took that liberty primarily because he could not
resist the opportunity to emulate one of the most moving of several pathetic monologues in Ariosto's poem. Anguillara not only elaborates but
often intensifies the pitiable laments, usually in the form of monologues,
voiced by the many women in the *Metamorphoses* who have been betrayed
or unrequited in love. As in the case of Arianna's lament, these pathetic
monologues regularly betray the language and rhetoric used by Ariosto in
the monologues that so often accompany his descriptions of *donne ab-
bandonate* or of female protagonists whose passions remain unfulfilled.[15]
Such emulation in Anguillara's translation of certain passages in the *Metamorphoses* of Ariosto's prior imitations of these passages is a recurring practice in the *Metamorfosi*. While this practice attests to the influence of the
Furioso on the *Metamorfosi*, it also served to make more evident, at the
time that Anguillara's translation first appeared, Ariosto's extensive debt
to Ovid. In fact, Anguillara emphasized Ariosto's Ovidianism almost dis-
proportionately, since whenever he imitated Ariosto's poem he evoked
only those parts of it that were modeled on or inspired by Ovid's poem.
   Both Dolce's and Anguillara's recastings of the *Metamorphoses* reveal
how important a position in the literary system the *Furioso* had already won
for itself by the 1550s and 1560s. Had Ariosto's poem remained marginal
and not become so exemplary a modern poetic achievement, Dolce's
Trasformationi would not have imitated its prosodic and formal features,
nor would Anguillara have felt the need to emulate Ariosto in his version of
the Latin poem. As I mentioned earlier, it was not only the *volgarizzamenti*
of the *Metamorphoses* that imitated formal and substantial features of the
Furioso. Other classical epics were also domesticated by being recast as
romanzi all'Ariosto. That the *Odyssey* and the *Thebaid* and the *Aeneid* were
also "ridotti in ottava rima" further confirms the ascendance Ariosto's
poem enjoyed in the literary system. Still, the most frequently reprinted
and widely disseminated of these translations in ottava rima remained the
versions of the *Metamorphoses* discussed above. This dissemination pro-

duced a wider recognition of the kinship between Ovid's and Ariosto's poems.

We saw that, at about the same time that Dolce's *Trasformationi* first appeared, resemblances between the modern romanzo and Ovid's *Metamorphoses* were already being drawn by Giraldi. Whether or not the affiliation Giraldi made between the two poems had any bearing on Dolce's *Trasformationi*, one can discern that after the repeated publication of the *Trasformationi*, and then of Anguillara's translation, the resemblances between the *Furioso*, or, more generally, the modern romanzo, and the *Metamorphoses* are more frequently asserted. Such affiliation tends to be found in the critical discourse generated by the debate between the moderns and ancients over the merits and defects of the contemporary romanzo in contrast to the ancient epic. Given that more of the hostile than the supportive criticism of the romanzo survives from this debate (even after 1585, when the debate turned into a quarrel between champions of Tasso and defenders of Ariosto), the linkage made between Ovid's poem and the romanzo is often brought up in a disparaging context. For example, in the course of his negative critique of the romanzo in the first book of *L'arte poetica* (1564) Antonio Minturno links the *romanzatori* and Ovid by defining their poems as "Historie favolose" and by emphasizing the un-epic and un-Aristotelian narrative arrangement that their poems share.[16] Neo-Aristotelians writing after Minturno almost automatically group together the *Metamorphoses* and the *romanzi* when they think of narrative poems made out of multiple plots. So, when Jason Denores disparages poems whose multiplicity of actions "rendono il poema confuso & non lasciano tempo a comprederle tutte in un tratto [jumble up the poem and do not leave time to understand them all at once]," he cites as examples "l'Achileide di Statio, & le trasformationi di Ovidio & molti de Romanzi de'nostri tempi."[17] And in his commentary on Aristotle's *Poetics* Castelvetro links the *Furioso* and the *Metamorphoses* even more specifically when he disparages plots based on the many actions of many protagonists:

> E tanto meno potremo ricevere per favola ben fatta quella che non solamente più azzioni d'una persona, o una azzione di più persone, ma insieme contiene più azzioni di più persone, come contiene il poema delle *Trasformationi* d'Ovidio; e questo vizio è ancora riconosciuto nell'*Orlando Furioso* di Lodovico Ariosto, narrando l'uno e l'altro più azzioni di più persone.[18]

> [And all the less could we consider a plot well made that not only contains many actions of one person, or the single action of many persons, but contains many actions of many people, as does Ovid's *Metamorphoses*; and this defect is also perceived in Ludovico Ariosto's *Orlando Furioso*. Both poets narrate the many actions of many persons.]

On the other hand, among the champions of the romanzo, the modern genre, specifically the *Furioso*, is legitimized by invoking the precedence of Ovid's major poem. For instance, at one point in Giovanni de' Bardi's "In difesa dell'Ariosto" (1583), one finds that the author counters objections about Ariosto's mixture of high and low styles in the *Furioso* by citing Ovid's poem as a classical example that contains and serves to justify such a mixture.

> Non si è ancora abbassato assai Ovidio nelle sue Metamorfosi, il quale, invece di cantar le lodi delli Dii, ha cantato lor adulterj, e rapimenti di fanciulli? . . . Merita adunque biasimo l'Ariosto per aver mescolato fra azioni tanto magnifiche, e grandi alcuna cosa varia, e piacevole? No di vero. . . .[19]

> [Didn't Ovid lower himself a great deal in his *Metamorphoses* when, instead of praising the gods, he sang about their adulteries and their rapes of little boys? . . . Does Ariosto deserve to be blamed then for mixing together with such great and magnificent actions something varied and pleasant? Surely not. . . .]

As de' Bardi's remarks already demonstrate, a positive effect of the affiliation forged between the *Furioso* and the *Metamorphoses* was the artistic legitimation of such formal features in the *Furioso* as its copiousness, its variety, its multiplicity, and its mixture of high and low styles. Despite the hostile criticism that Ovid's style had provoked at least since Quintilian, the *Metamorphoses* held a secure place in the canon, and, however its artistic features were judged, there was no doubt that it was one of the important achievements of Roman poetry. Against those who viewed as inartistic flaws the *Furioso*'s episodic structure and its multiplicity of plots and characters, the precedence of such features in an acknowledged work of art like the *Metamorphoses* served as a legitimizing counterargument. At the end of Chapter 2 I mentioned that by the 1560s and 1570s one finds abated the earlier tendency to associate the *Furioso* with the *Aeneid*, as well as with Homer's epics; I then proposed that it was largely the influence of Aristotle's *Poetics* on Italian thinking about poetry that made the affiliation between the *Aeneid* and the *Furioso* more difficult to uphold. Clearly, in conjunction with Aristotle's influence, the kinship increasingly perceived between the *Furioso* and Ovid's un-Virgilian *Metamorphoses* must have reinforced the trend to dissociate Ariosto's poem from Virgil's epic. Yet even as the claims of the *Furioso*'s Virgilian ancestry were losing credibility, Ariosto's poem acquired a new affiliation to ancient poetry, one just as honorific, at least for those who admired Ovid's artistic achievement.

The critical view of Ovid's poem also changed as a result of being associated with the *Furioso*, and it is with some remarks about the changing perception of the ancient poem that I wish to conclude this chapter. Between 1553 and 1590 there were, counting both Dolce's and Anguillara's translations, thirty-three editions of the *Metamorphoses* published in ottava rima. The continuing publication of humanist editions of the Latin poem notwithstanding, the overall effect of these widely available vernacular versions was to make critics and readers associate Ovid's poem with the modern romanzo, above all Ariosto's. This association, occurring at the same time that the quarrel between the ancients and the moderns began, could not but alter the critical perception of the *Metamorphoses*, especially of its relationship to other canonical works of Latin and Greek poetry. One must recall that it was almost precisely between 1553 and 1590 that the debate over the merits of the modern romanzo versus classical epic became one of the central literary disputes in Italy. This literary dispute, as Bernard Weinberg has shown, was part of a larger quarrel between the "ancients" and the "moderns." He sums up the arguments of the opposing sides as follows:

> Homer and Virgil practised narrative poetry in the guise of the epic, Aristotle and Horace solidified its rules in the name of the epic, all future narrative poets must adopt the form of the epic; thus the "ancients." Adopting the epic form means, first and foremost, committing oneself to a single action, illustrious in nature and performed by a great hero, unified according to Aristotle's recommendations. It means, also, excluding all materials of a "lower" sort and observing strictly the decorum of the noble style. None of these conditions is acceptable to the "moderns." They regard the romance as that narrative form most amenable to the tastes of their contemporaries, the one which the "times" demand. If the romance has rules at all, they are definitely not those of the epic. For it admits a multiple plot, requires no unity of action, permits a free breaking up and intertwining of episodes, glories in the mixture of every possible level and kind of matter. It is a "free" form, thus in contrast to the rigid "regulation" of the epic. Because he practised it so well, because indeed he excelled all other writers of narrative poetry (Homer and Virgil not excluded), Ariosto in his turn may be taken as the model for those who, in the future, may wish to succeed in the genre.[20]

Throughout the course of this debate between proponents and opponents of literary classicism, Dolce's and Anguillara's *volgarizzamenti* of the *Metamorphoses* were continually published. These popular translations of Ovid's poem in romanzo form, appearing just when the merits of the modern romanzo were being disputed, could not but make readers more aware of the "modernity" of the *Metamorphoses*. Moreover, by forcing Italian readers to link Ovid's poem with the unclassical romanzo, these translations served to intensify the historical awareness that Virgilian norms of epic, disregarded by the modern romanzo, had already gone unobserved, to no loss, by the *Metamorphoses* almost as soon as they had been established by the *Aeneid*.

Today we almost take it for granted that Ovid's *Metamorphoses* is very different, even defiantly different, from Virgil's epic.[21] More broadly, we distinguish various and often antithetical styles and outlooks among ancient writers. We can perceive that Roman literature, to say nothing of the Greco-Roman legacy, does not consist of a homogeneous body of classical authority but displays in its own development the revisionary dynamics of literary history in general. In an illuminating essay on what he calls the "counter-classical" sensibility in ancient poetry, W. R. Johnson writes that "it was only rather recently, perhaps about the time our modern Homer was devised, or about the time Romanticism arose, that modern critics began to do rather methodically what the ancients had no difficulty in doing: distinguishing among ancient writers wide varieties of sensibilities and world-views and so firmly denying the existence of a persistent, unalterable Graeco-Roman sensibility."[22] I would maintain that "counter-classical" strains in ancient poetry, Ovid's in particular, began to be appreciated earlier, but not much before the end of the sixteenth century in Italy. To be sure, brief and often derogatory commonplaces about Ovid's rhetoric (derived from Seneca and Quintilian) were continually invoked by medieval and Renaissance scholiasts to distinguish Ovid's style from that of other Latin poets. But before the legitimacy of the modern Italian romanzo is asserted in the 1550s one can rarely find any sympathetic commentary on Ovid's different kind of narrative poem, or on his refusal to observe the epic norms established by Homer and Virgil. As mentioned earlier, when G. B. Giraldi defended Italian romances in his *Discorso* of 1554, he cited Ovid's conscious departure from classical epic norms as an ancient precedent for the same phenomenon in the contemporary romanzo. Such new and perceptive observations began to make Ovid's difference more apparent, but it was, I contend, largely due to the continuous publication of Dolce's and Anguillara's *Metamorphoses* in ottava rima that Ovid's challenges to classicism from within became more broadly recognized. In fact, by translating the *Metamorphoses* in the ways and at the time they did, Dolce and Anguillara served to reveal Ovid's defiance of classical epic structure more effectively than could any contemporary critic.

How this new perception of the *Metamorphoses* affected Ovid's subsequent legacy in the late sixteenth and seventeenth centuries still remains to be investigated. What I wish to emphasize is the seminal role played by *Orlando Furioso* in generating this perception. For if the "counter-classical" aspects of Ovid's poetry began to be more widely perceived in the latter half of the cinquecento as a result of the debate about the romanzo and because of the steady publication of Dolce's and Anguillara's *Metamorphoses* in ottava rima, this was owing originally to the tremendous popularity of *Orlando Furioso*. Obviously, the debate about the legitimacy of the romanzo and the critical perceptions it stimulated would not have occurred had it not been for the acclaim won by the *Furioso*. And, as I have demonstrated, neither Dolce nor Anguillara would have translated Ovid in the ways they did had it not been for the broad appeal of Ariosto's prior achievement.

Chapter Five

CRITICAL RESPONSES TO NARRATIVE DISCONTINUITY IN *ORLANDO FURIOSO*

I INDICATED at the start of this book that, from the midcentury on, critics perceived that the *Furioso* violated several of the basic Horatian-Aristotelian principles that were being established as requisites for heroic poetry and that they attacked the poem for these transgressions. As early as 1548, G. B. Pigna had reported, as we saw, that objections were being voiced about the poem's title not corresponding to its main subject, its many and confusing actions, its lack of continuity, its excessive dependence on magic and the supernatural, and its author's failure to observe decorum. Forty years later one finds Ariosto's hostile critics making more or less the same complaints. At the beginning of Gioseppe Malatesta's *Della nuova poesia* (1589), a spirited defense of the *Furioso*'s modernity that will be examined in a later chapter, a speaker in the dialogue who is critical of the poem and its author quickly lists what are considered its chief defects:

> il far il Poema suo non d'una atione d'un solo, ma di molte di molti: il segnar le materie, che narra intempestivamente, & quando il lettore aspetta ogn'altra cosa, che di vedersele togliere dinanti, il denominar l'opera da Orlando; e far tuttavia, che Ruggiero sia il personaggio principalmente inteso in essa: il cominciar la narratione da una facenda straniera al soggetto del Poema. Il non porre invocatione nel principio del suo cantare: oltre a diversi errori commessi parte intorno al decoro, parte circa il costume nella formatione de i suoi cavalieri; i qualitutti errori con altri, che non dico, o controvengono per diritto nell'observazione degli approvati heroici, come è l'Ulisia, l'Iliade, e l'Eneade particolarmente, o si oppongono a gli stessi precetti, che l'arte della poesia ha già stabiliti, & fermati intorno all'epico Poema.[1]

[for making his poem not one action of a single protagonist, but many of many; announcing subjects that he presents at untimely moments, and when the reader expects something quite other than to have what is in front of him taken away; for naming the work after Orlando but, nonetheless, making Ruggiero its principal protagonist; for beginning his narrative with an event foreign to the subject of the poem. For not having an invocation at the beginning, as well as various other faults, some having to do with decorum, some regarding the behavior of the characters he depicts. All of which defects, and more that I omit, either flout the rules of approved epic poems such as the

Odyssey, the *Iliad,* and especially the *Aeneid,* or counter the precepts that the art of poetry has established and fixed for the epic poem.]

The two defects of the poem that head this list of complaints were the ones most frequently brought up by neo-Aristotelian critics in the second half of the sixteenth century: the poem's lack of unity and the poet's disregard of narrative continuity. In this chapter I wish to focus on the criticism of the *Furioso*'s discontinuity, not only because it was voiced repeatedly, but because this particular animus can best serve to represent the general neoclassical bias against the poem. Moreover, the effects of this criticism— as they manifest themselves in the narrative practices of later cinquecento poets—also serve to illustrate the extent to which Aristotelian poetics affected Italian poetry after 1550.

The narrative of the *Furioso* is, indeed, discontinuous. By considering why it had to be so, and also why Ariosto exaggerated this characteristic of the romanzo, we can appreciate more fully the critical responses of sixteenth-century readers to the discontinuity of his poem. One has to bear in mind that the many actions, characters, and various adventures of chivalric romance required multiple plot lines that had to be interrupted constantly in order for each of them to progress more or less simultaneously. Thus, when Ariosto chose to make his *Orlando Furioso* a sequel to Boiardo's *Orlando Innamorato,* he opted for a discontinuous narrative. Moreover, the technique of *entrelacement,* or interweaving, which allowed the narrator to advance his various plots by shifting back and forth among them, invited—in fact, had built into it—authorial intrusion. Whenever Ariosto has to abandon one of his plot lines, he intervenes as narrator to announce that it is time to leave a protagonist or a situation in order to take up or return to another. Examples can be found in almost every canto:

> Ma perché varie file a varie tele
> uopo mi son, che tutte ordire intendo,
> lascio Rinaldo e l'agitata prua,
> e torno a dir di Bradamante sua.
>
> (2.30)

[But as I have need of a number of warps and a variety of threads if I am to complete the whole of my tapestry, I shall leave Rinaldo and his pitching prow and return to the tale of his sister Bradamante.][2]

Occasionally the narrator will justify these transitions by claiming that he makes them for the sake of *varietà* and for the pleasure such variety produces:

Ma perché non convien che sempre io dica,
né ch'io vi occupi sempre in una cosa,
io lascerò Ruggiero in questo caldo,
e girò in Scozia a ritrovar Rinaldo.

$(8.21)^3$

[Now as I should do wrong to keep you ever attending to the same tale, I shall leave Ruggiero to bake and make off to Scotland to find Rinaldo.]

It becomes evident, too, that since Ariosto likes to unite separate story lines, if only temporarily, he cannot do so until events in one have caught up with the events in another. For example, after Orlando goes mad in the middle of the poem, we follow his wanderings until he reaches the bridge built by Rodomonte (24.14). But this bridge has yet to be built—something that will take place only after Isabella has died, an event that itself will result after the infatuated Rodomonte tries to possess her in canto 29. Obviously, Ariosto must suspend his account of Orlando at Rodomonte's bridge until all these events have occurred.

When Ariosto interrupts a plot line yet briefly anticipates its sequel, he reminds us that, unlike his characters or his first-time readers, he knows the final outcome of his poem. It is possible that he offers readers a glimpse of the future to arouse their curiosity; but he has other motives for letting a plot line get ahead of itself. Consider, as another example, the interruption that occurs at 12.65 when he takes leave of Angelica, who, fleeing pursuers as is her wont, comes upon the body of a young man lying wounded in the forest. Ariosto leaves her in this frozen stance beholding the young soldier, who remains unidentified for seven entire cantos. The poet knows, of course, what will be revealed to the reader only at canto 19—namely, that the young man is Medoro. After being wounded and nearly killed in a night expedition during the siege of Paris he is left lying in the way of the fleeing Angelica, who will restore him back to health and, in the process, fall in love with him. While it may be true that the suspension at canto 12 leaves us curious to find out the identity of the mysterious young man Angelica has stumbled upon, the curiosity quickly dissipates as we get distracted by new adventures. More significantly, by this glancing forward before interrupting, the poet effectively reveals the omniscient purview he commands of his plot's future outcome and thereby affirms the control he exerts over his complex narrative. The poet wants the narrative to appear erratic and wayward, and he exploits the discontinuous character of the romance plot in order to achieve that effect. But it becomes progressively clear that he breaks his plot lines very deliberately and precisely at the point that he wants to.

The kind of interruptions discussed so far tend to leave the reader curious but not overly frustrated by the suspension of the narrative. Frequently, however, Ariosto's interruptions are sudden, premature, and quite disconcerting. They can regularly be found at the end of cantos, since a recurring tactic of the poet is to defy the expectation of closure at the end of a canto by terminating it at the start or at the height of a dramatic episode. As frustrating as it may be to be left hanging at the end of a canto, the reader who continues reading is not deprived of continuity for very long, since, after an authorial intervention at the start of the next canto, the episode that was cut off is resumed again. Although the reader comes to expect that the story broken off at the end of one canto will be resumed very soon in the following one, it should not be overlooked that the authorial judgments and comments that begin every canto are themselves interruptive. Whether long or short, these *proemi*, as they were called, obviously contribute to the poem's discontinuity by disengaging the reader from the narrative whose sequel he or she usually yearns to discover after the suspenseful break of the previous canto. As I shall point out later, the *proemi* were criticized increasingly by sixteenth-century readers who found the authorial intrusions in the *Furioso* as disruptive as its narrative shifts.

More disconcerting than the unexpected interruptions at the ends of cantos are those that occur within cantos. When Ariosto shifts from one plot to another, he tends to interrupt the story suddenly and prematurely, and always when he is sure that the reader is totally captivated by the action taking place. Among the many examples that could be cited, a typical one occurs in canto 11. Near the beginning of this canto, Ruggiero, left unrequited by Angelica, who has just managed to escape his sexual assault after he rescues her from the Orca, is eventually distracted by the noise of a duel between a giant and a knight. As he watches the giant overcome the knight and unlace his helmet for the kill, Ruggiero realizes that the victim is none other than Bradamante, and he rushes to assist her. The giant seizes the stunned Bradamante, slings her over his shoulder, and runs away, furiously pursued by Ruggiero. Just as the chase reaches a crescendo, the narrator interrupts it abruptly and shifts to Orlando's adventures, which had been left in abeyance for more than a canto:

> Così correndo l'uno, e seguitando
> l'altro, per un sentiero ombroso e fosco,
> che sempre si venia più dilatando,
> in un gran prato uscir fuor di quel bosco.
> Non più di questo; ch'io ritorno a Orlando,
> che 'l fulgur che porto già il re Cimosco,
> avea gittato in mar nel maggior fondo,
> accio mai più non si trovasse al mondo.

(11.21)

[The giant ran off and Ruggiero pursued him down a path through the deep shade; the path gradually broadened out until it took them clear of the wood into a broad meadow. But enough of these two for now: I am returning to

Orlando; he had taken King Cimosco's thunder-machine and thrown it into
the depths of the sea, so as to obliterate every last trace of it.]

The acceleration of the tempo, the heightening of tension before the unexpected shift, the defiance of formal expectation by making the break in
mid-octave: these tactics regularly characterize Ariosto's sudden transitions. And, as in this example, the poet almost always chooses to interrupt
the action at a dramatic moment when the reader's engagement has been
fully secured yet before the action reaches any satisfying conclusion. To be
sure, the multiple plot structure of his romance required repeated narrative
shifts; however, they did not have to be as sudden and as premature as he
liked to make them. Why, then, did he suspend his narrative so abruptly in
this way?

The usual but inadequate explanation is that these interruptions serve to
create suspense and therefore prompt the reader to read on in order to
discover the outcome of the action left unresolved. Already in the very first
defenses of the modern romanzo that appeared in the middle of the sixteenth century the interruptions were justified on these grounds. Here, for
example, is what G. B. Giraldi had to say on this matter in his *Discorso* on
the composition of romances, published in 1554:

> Perché avendosi gli scrittori de' romanzi prese le azioni di molti da principio,
> non hanno potuto continuare di canto in canto una materia, essendo elle tutte
> insieme congiunte. Ma è stato lor mestieri, per condur l'opera al fine, poiché
> hanno detto d'un lor personaggio, frapporvi l'altro e rompere la prima mate-
> ria ed entrare nei fatti d'un altro, e con questo ordine continuare le materie
> insino al fine dell'opera: la qual cosa hanno fatto con maraviglioso artificio.
> Perocché in questo lor troncar le cose, conducono il lettore a tal termine,
> prima che le tronchino, che gli lasciano nell'animo un ardente desiderio di
> tornare a ritrovarla: il che è cagione che tutto il poema loro sia letto, rima-
> nendo sempre le principali materie imperfette insino al compimento dell'
> opera.[4]

[Since the writers of romances have taken the actions of many from the beginning, they have not been able to continue one matter from canto to canto,
seeing that they are all connected together. In order to lead their work to the
end it has rather been their practice to speak first of one person, then to
interpose another and interrupt the first subject and take up the deeds of the
other, and by such succession continue the matters to the end of the work.
This they have done with marvelous art, because in their interruptions they
lead the reader to such a point before they break off the narrative that they
leave in his mind an ardent desire to return to it. Their whole poem is read
as a result since the principal matters are not concluded until the work is
completed.]

While Giraldi's views were challenged by critics in his own time, many modern commentators have shared his opinion that the function of Ariosto's interruptions was to arouse suspense and thereby keep readers engaged and curious to read on.

Ariosto's sudden interruptions definitely produce suspense, but readers usually find that so much else occurs to engross them in the narrative between the interruption and the resumption of a story that they tend to forget or to cease being interested in the earlier situation when it is eventually resumed. They may recall the aggravation of being deprived of knowing the outcome earlier, but none of the suspense and curiosity aroused at that previous moment remains. Numerous instances of such frustrating breaks and their deferred but ungratifying sequels can be found in the segment of the poem that runs from canto 15 to canto 19 where the narrative constantly shifts from the epic conflict in and around Paris under siege to the adventures of Astolfo and Grifone in the Middle East.[5] As readers move from one of these transitions to another they come to realize that, unlike the interruptions at canto ends, which leave them briefly deprived, the interruptions within cantos leave them unrequited but without the prospect of gratification.[6]

The interruptions in Ariosto's poem that I have begun to describe met with increasing hostility in the latter half of the cinquecento. As can be gathered from the list of objections in Malatesta's *Della nuova poesia* (1589) cited initially, the *Furioso*'s discontinuity was as commonly criticized by the end of the century as its lack of unity, its misleading title, and the indecorous conduct of its chief protagonists. Actually, the objections to Ariosto's interruptions began to be voiced several decades earlier. One can infer that already in the 1550s Ariosto's sudden shifts provoked unfavorable reactions. The first telling signs are to be found in the margins of different Venetian editions of the poem, starting with the Valgrisi edition of 1556. At those places within cantos where the narrative is suspended, marginal notes indicate where, later in the poem, the reader can find the suspended plot line continued. Presumably this was meant to allow readers to skip the intervening narrative and go straight to the sequel instead of being left frustrated by the break.

Even more telling evidence that the sudden transitions irritated readers is that G. B. Giraldi and G. B. Pigna, the first defenders of the romanzo as a modern genre, made a point of justifying them. These critics not only showed that the multiple actions of the romanzo required that the narrator suspend one plot so that he could resume another, they sought to justify these suspensions on the grounds that such premature breaks aroused the desire to read on. Pigna, in his treatise on *I romanzi* of 1554, actually distinguishes between timely interruptions and premature ones, and it is clear from the instances of the latter kind that he cites that it is Ariosto's interruptions he has in mind. When the *romanzatore* suspends his narrative, Pigna explains,

> tralascia o quando il tempo dà che s'interponga, o quando nol dà. Quando il dà, l'anima di chi legge, quieto rimane. dal che ha contentezza, & perciò piacere: restando egli con una cosa compiuta. come se un naufragio è finito, o una singolar battaglia, o un fatto d'arme, o una peregrinatione, o cose simiglianti. Quando nol dà, l'animo resta sospeso. & ne nasce perciò un desiderio che fa diletto: essendo che un certo ardore è causato, che è di dover la fine della cosa sentire. come in sul bello d'una tempesta ritirarsi, o nel tempo che due sono per menar le mani, o che una guerra si prepari, o da un luogo levar uno & a mezza strada & anche prima abbandonarlo, & far altre cose così fatte. Et ciò più s'usa che il primo modo: conciosia che il compositore di farne sempre più innanzi andare s'ingegna.[7]

[he suspends the narrative either when the time presents itself, or when it does not. When it does, the mind of the reader remains at rest, from which he derives satisfaction and therefore pleasure, remaining as he does with something completed. As when a shipwreck is over, or a particular battle, or a feat of arms, or a wandering, or similar matters. When the time does not present itself, the mind remains in suspense, from which there arises a desire which produces pleasure. A certain eagerness is produced, namely, to find out the end of the matter, as when one is drawn away at the height of a storm, or at the moment when two fighters are about to lay hands on each other, or when a war is in the offing, or when someone is abandoned halfway to his destination or earlier, and other things of this sort. And this [untimely] suspension is used more than the first, since the writer strives to make the reader always go on.]

In romances premature breaks are more usual, Pigna explains, because they fulfill the *romanzatore*'s design to leave us in suspense and thereby make us read on. I mentioned earlier that Giraldi, whose *Discorso* on composing romances appeared the same year as Pigna's treatise, also maintained that the romanzo's necessary interruptions were artfully exploited to arouse a desire to continue reading. But, unlike Pigna, Giraldi expresses misgivings about the dislocating effects of such interruptions. Immediately after rationalizing them on the grounds that they make the reader go on, Giraldi maintains that it would be preferable, because less disruptive, to organize the romance plot around the many actions of a single hero rather than the many actions of many heros. "Egli è vero," he writes, "che s'altri si desse a comporre le azioni di un uomo solo, si potrebbe continuare un canto con l'altro senza rompere le materie e' tralasciarle per ripigliarle poi e seguirle di novo [It is true that if anyone set about composing the actions of only one man, he would be able to continue one canto after another without breaking the subject matter, and without leaving it off and then resuming and continuing it anew]."[8] Such a plot structure would avoid the discontinuities of the traditional romanzo without forfeiting its pleasurable variety. Anyone familiar with Giraldi's own effort at writing a romanzo—his unfinished *Ercole* (1557), based, as the title suggests, on the many exploits of Hercules—will realize that these prescriptions for a superior romance plot were meant, in fact, to justify his own departures from Ariosto and Boiardo. His choice of a plot that dealt with the many actions of one rather than of many protagonists aimed, as his theory suggests, to achieve greater continuity than had prior *romanzatori*. Giraldi did not make this choice out of some neoclassical impulse (Aristotle, it will be recalled, disapproved of plots organized around the many actions of one hero) but rather, it would seem, to preempt the growing criticism being leveled at the discontinuities of the romanzo, and of Ariosto's in particular.

That such criticism began to affect the composition of narrative poetry around the middle of the century is confirmed by one of Giraldi's contemporaries, Bernardo Tasso, the father of Torquato. In 1556 and 1557 Bernardo actually exchanged a number of important letters with Giraldi on their different notions of the romanzo as these are embodied in the *Ercole* and the *Amadigi*, respectively. However, it is especially in his letters to Vincenzo Laureo, Sperone Speroni, and Girolamo Molino that one can see how the objections (voiced by the first two of these correspondents, among others) to the discontinuities of the romanzo affected Bernardo's composition of his *Amadigi*.[9] The modern predilection for *varietà* and the other pleasures of chivalric romance led Bernardo to write a romanzo of many actions rather than a poem with a single plot (which is what he initially composed), but it becomes clear from his letters that he was pressured by literary colleagues to make his *Amadigi* more similar to classical epic than previous *romanzi*. From his comments in these letters it also becomes evident that what provoked particular criticism from Sperone Speroni and Vincenzo Laureo were characteristic factors of discontinuity in his romanzo: the narratorial comments and interventions at the beginning and end of cantos, and also within cantos when plot lines have to be shifted. It is not unreasonable to infer that these judges must have objected even more to such features in *Orlando Furioso* since Ariosto's interventions were more pronounced and frequent than Bernardo's in the *Amadigi*. Actually, one is not simply just left to infer such objections. Among the few surviving records of Sperone Speroni's attacks against the *Furioso* is the criticism of Ariosto's interruptive addresses to the reader that he voices in a fragment entitled "De' romanzi," probably written soon after Tasso's *Amadigi* appeared in 1560 (in the fragment itself Speroni mentions his unsuccessful attempt to get Tasso to reduce his many actions to just one). Here, for instance, are Speroni's complaints about the authorial *proemi* that characterize the beginnings of cantos in all *romanzi*, but that are particularly notable in the *Furioso*:

> Far poi in ogni canto proemio, o ricercar, come dice il Giraldo [sic] è grandissima inezia, perche *non erat [h]is locus* [Horace, *Ars poetica*, 19]. . . . Però dico, siano belli quanto si vuole i principii de' canti dell'Ariosto, son sempre inetti, e molte volte non catenati e congiunti alla cosa del poema.[10]

> [And to start each canto with a proem, or "ricercar," as Giraldi calls it, is most inappropriate, because "it was not the place for these." I say therefore that, however beautiful the beginnings of Ariosto's cantos may be, they are always inappropriate, and many times unlinked and unrelated to the matter of the poem.]

In anticipation of such objections, Bernardo Tasso had originally substituted the various kinds of addresses to the readers and *moralità* one finds in Ariosto's *proemi* with varied descriptions of dawn at the beginnings of his cantos. Each canto ended, moreover, with a description of night falling before the narrator announced briefly that it was time to bring the canto to a close. These recurring sunrises and sunsets framing each canto suggest what care Tasso took to make his pauses and shifts as timely as possible. In order to avoid being accused of making premature or gratuitous breaks in his narrative *all'Ariosto*, he tried to make as many of the narrative shifts as possible coincide with the start of cantos. Nonetheless, his neoclassical colleagues still objected. In a letter to Girolamo Molino of 1558 he writes that these "judicious" colleagues

> m'hanno persuaso a discostarmi dalla maniera de'Romanzi, quanto sia possibile; e alzandomi in ogni sua parte, quanto si può, alla Eroica dignità, a ridurlo in Libri, levandone tutti i principii, e fini de' Canti, i quali erano tutti con una descrizion di notte, e di giorno.

> [have persuaded me to depart as much as possible from the manner of romances; and raising myself, whenever possible, to heroic dignity, to convert the poem to books, removing from it all the beginnings and ends of cantos, which all consisted of descriptions of night[fall] and of day[break].]

Tasso was reluctant to give in to these pressures, since he did not feel that the romanzo's particular features ought to be subjected to the different laws of epic. He did eventually eliminate in the first fifty cantos of his poem most of the descriptions of nightfall at canto ends, and a good number of the sunrises, but, still, although his canto openings rarely consisted of moralizing *proemi*, he continued to address his audience at the start and end of cantos. The same judges, he tells Molino, also wanted him to remove the authorial interventions that in Ariosto's and other *romanzi* occur when shifts have to be made from one plot line to another, but he did not altogether heed their advice.[11] Bernardo realized that his *Amadigi* could not accommodate such neoclassical strictures without confusing his readers and thereby depriving them of pleasure, the chief goal of his poetic effort. Given the narrative conventions of the romanzo, he had to shift from one plot to another and to inform his audience when he did so. Again, he had to warn his auditors when he brought a canto to an end, and to address them before resuming the narrative in the next one. Nonetheless, what one notices about Bernardo's practice, in comparison to Ariosto's, is how much briefer and less obtrusive his interventions are in the *Amadigi*, and how much less frustrating his suspensions. His effort to make his narrative seem less fragmented than Ariosto's is apparent at every shift and pause in his poem. He may have resisted the radical suggestions of his neoclassical correspondents, but it is clear that their dislike of the romanzo's endemic discontinuity made him attenuate it as much as he could in his contribution to the genre.

One must recall that it was also in the 1550s—when Giraldi's and Pigna's defenses of the romanzo appeared, and Bernardo Tasso wrote his *Amadigi*—that Aristotle's *Poetics* was being assimilated in Italy, having been rediscovered and made available in the previous decade. As it gained currency and influence, Aristotle's theory lent its authority to the growing number of neoclassical critics who were keen to discredit the artistic shortcomings of chivalric romance as compared to the ancient epic norms they were championing. Despite its great popularity, *Orlando Furioso* was included in this attack against the romanzo. As the objections of Speroni, cited above, begin to indicate, these critics were quick to condemn Ariosto's disregard for narrative continuity, and in opposition to Giraldi's and Pigna's justifications, they denied that his interruptive technique had any positive function whatsoever.

Representative of the new Aristotelianism that began to dominate Italian literary criticism is Antonio Minturno's *Arte poetica* (1563), which, in the section devoted to heroic poetry, includes a sustained critique of the modern romanzo and of Ariosto's decision to write one. Minturno, contrary to the apologists of the new genre, did not consider the romance a legitimate form of poetry but rather a transgression of various unchanging principles—for example, unity of action—that define heroic poetry. The way in which the *romanzatore* dismembers his actions particularly offends Minturno. He therefore singles out the shifts and interruptions characteristic of the romanzo as principal defects. His condemnation includes a distinction, like Pigna's, between timely and untimely interruptions. Timely interruptions are associated with proper epic practice, whereas untimely ones, as the following statement indicates, are characteristic of the *roman-zatori* (the general examples given bring Ariosto's practice immediately to mind).

> Ma non concede [il tempo] che impresa una battaglia, o cominciata una tem-pesta, o qualunque altra cosa, nel meglio s'interrompa, e quando più se n'at-tende il fine, si tralasci per trattar d'alcuna altra facenda, la quale ad altre persone, in altra parte, nel medesimo processo di tempo avvenuta sia; com' hanno propriamente in costume i romanzatori senza riguardo di ciò, che 'l tempo ricusa, e del desiderio, che lascian ne gli animi degli ascoltanti anzi molesto, che dilettevole.

> [But time does not allow that when a battle is under way, or a storm or some other thing has started, it should be interrupted in the middle, and when the end is most eagerly awaited to abandon it in order to deal with another event which has occurred simultaneously to other persons in other places; as is the peculiar custom of writers of romance who pay no attention to what the time requires nor to [the audience's] desire and thereby annoy rather than please their listeners.]

After echoing Pigna's distinctions to make it clear that he is responding to this prior defense of the romanzo, Minturno refutes Pigna's claim that untimely interruptions can produce pleasure by stimulating a desire to read on. "Percioché," he goes on,

> a niuno ragionevolmente dee piacere, che alcuna cosa interrotta gli sia, quanto più gli diletta. Nè truovo esser vero, che l'attenzione più se n'accenda: ma più tosto se ne spenga. Conciosia, ch'ella se n'infiammi col desio d'intenderne il fine, non quando si tralascia la cominciata narrazione per un'altra: ma quando per molti accidenti a quella istessa materia appertenenti s'indugia la finale essecutione.[12]

> [Because it cannot reasonably please anyone that a thing should be inter-rupted at the moment when it most delights him. Nor do I find it to be true that the attention is kindled, but rather that it is extinguished [by such inter-ruption]. Because it is inflamed with the desire to hear the end of the story, not when the narrative already begun is abandoned for another; but when the outcome is delayed by many accidents that pertain to the same subject.]

Minturno condones episodic digressions from a central action, and even a suspension of it, as long as the intervening narrative remains linked to that central action. But the *romanzatori* have no regard for such coherence; they drop a plot line at will, to shift or to return to another in a completely disorderly fashion. Refusing to acknowledge that any narrative that fails to conform to ancient norms of unity and continuity can be satisfying, Min-turno is unable to see the *Furioso*'s interruptions as anything but proof of the romanzo's structural defectiveness in comparison with classical epic. Nonetheless, he is correct to maintain that, far from being pleasurable, premature interruptions of the sort Ariosto inflicts on his readers can only frustrate or annoy them.

Such perceptive but unsympathetic criticism can also be found in what is perhaps the most interesting attack of the period against the *Furioso*: Filippo Sassetti's "Discorso contro l'Ariosto," composed about 1575–1576, but never published by the author. Sassetti's objections to the discontinuity of the *Furioso* arise when he points out that the poet is compelled to suspend his various plots precisely because he is burdened with more than one of them, and has to keep all of them progressing forward. Sassetti refuses to grant the romanzo a legitimate and separate generic identity— for him the romance is merely an epic badly put together. As a result, he does not acknowledge, as had the apologists of the new genre, that the necessary interruption of the several plot lines is a structural norm. As Minturno before him, he considers Ariosto's interruptions structural flaws inherent in an episodic narrative that refuses to observe classical norms of unity and continuity. When he attacks Ariosto's narrative technique he does not even distinguish between timely and untimely breaks in the narrative, but suggests that all the shifts flout temporal consideration. Ariosto is constrained, he writes,

> a tralasciare le incominciate materie; et hora indietro rivolgersi, hora passare avanti senza avere alcun riguardo alla continuatione del tempo et appunto quando egli comincia a muovere come se a sommo studio 'e volesse privare chi legge a ascolta di quel diletto: egli lascia la narratione incominciata saltando in un'altra materia quanto si voglia diversa da quella che egli aveva prima alle mani.

> [to interrupt materials that he has begun; and now to turn backward, now to pass forward, without paying any attention to the continuation of time; and precisely when he begins to shift, as if with the greatest deliberation he wished to deprive the reader or the listener of that pleasure, he abandons the narrative that he has begun, jumping into another matter that can be altogether different from the one he was first treating.]

The effect of these transitions, Sassetti maintains, is a "raffreddamento dell'affetto già a muoversi incominciato [cooling of the passion which has already begun to be aroused]." He goes on to describe the frustration that the interruptions provoke in the reader with a vivid analogy:

> In questi tralasciamenti che sono nel Furioso pare che si senta il medesimo diletto che gusterebbe colui che con fretta andandosene colà dove egli desiderasse di ritrovarsi fusse da alcuno a viva forza ritenuto, per lasciarlo poi andare quando l'occasione fusse di già passata.

[It seems that from these interruptions in the *Furioso* one derives the same pleasure as would someone who, hastening to reach his desired destination, was very firmly held by someone, and then allowed to go on when the opportunity was already over.]

Sassetti's account of the reader's response is quite accurate. As I observed earlier, the sensation often caused by Ariosto's interruption and resumption is not the pleasure of deferred gratification, but the aggravation of being stopped short, or being drawn into narratives only to be pulled out of them and left deprived. Although Sassetti comes close to recognizing that these annoying effects may have been intentional, he cannot finally accept the possibility that such alienating effects are anything but the product of artistic *errore*, and of a flawed poetic structure. Still, his observations are precious because they attest how aggravating the interruptions in the *Furioso* were to some cinquecento readers. After describing the unpleasantness Ariosto's reader experiences when deprived of continuity, he remarks on the current editorial attempts to alleviate these frustrations. I stated earlier that, beginning in the 1550s, different Venetian publishers of the *Furioso* provided marginal indications to alert readers to where in the poem interrupted episodes were subsequently resumed. Sassetti's remarks on these "paratextual" aids make it clear that they were designed to remedy what he calls the "inconvenience" of Ariosto's discontinuous narrative:

> I rivenditori delle stampe hanno bene essi cognosciuto quanto ciò [the premature interruptions] conturbi l'animo di chi legge o di chi ascolta, e per rimediare a questo inconveniente hanno, laddove le materie si troncano, segnato il numero delle carte e delle stanze dove si ripiglia la tralasciata narratione.[13]

[Book publishers have well recognized how much the interruptions disturb the mind of a reader or of a listener, and to remedy this inconvenience, wherever the narratives are interrupted, they have indicated the page numbers and the stanzas where these are subsequently resumed.]

The *Furioso*'s lack of continuity prompts Sassetti to criticize another of Ariosto's narrative procedures: his authorial comments and intrusions, including, of course, the *exordia* or *proemi* at the start of each canto. When one recalls that the ends of cantos in the *Furioso* always consist of suspenseful breaks in the action, not resumed until the next canto and then continued only after the narrator has intervened with a preliminary comment, judgment, or address to the reader, one can well understand why these *proemi* were also singled out by Ariosto's critics as factors contributing to discontinuity. Sassetti was hardly the first to object to these *proemi* or to the other authorial interventions in the poem. I noted earlier how criticism of such interventions by Speroni and others affected Bernardo Tasso's handling of canto beginnings and ends in his *Amadigi*. Sassetti, however, makes more explicit the Aristotelian grounds of his objections. He begins his criticism of Ariosto's interventions by referring to Aristotle's praise of Homer's self-effacement as a speaker in his epics. The passage he has in mind can be found in chapter 24 of the *Poetics* (1460a5–10). In a recent English rendering it reads as follows:

> In addition to the many other reasons why Homer deserves admiration, there is this in particular, that he alone among the epic poets has not failed to understand the part the poet himself should take in his poem. The poet should, in fact, speak as little as possible in his own person, since in what he himself says he is not an imitator. Now the other poets are themselves on the scene throughout their poems, and their moments of imitation are few and far between, but Homer, after a few introductory words, at once brings on a man or a woman or some other personage, and not one of them characterless, but each with a character of his own.[14]

After alluding to this passage, Sassetti remarks that Aristotle would have little to praise in the *Furioso* given the many "discorsi" that the poem contains. By "discorsi" the critic means, presumably, the various comments and moral judgments on the action that Ariosto makes in his own voice, and that regularly occur at the beginnings of cantos. For example, in the proem of canto 10, the narrator, looking back at the account of Olimpia's exceptional devotion to Bireno, proposes that Olimpia deserves first prize among the faithful lovers of history. The narrator's judgment of his characters is just as often negative. Gabrina's perversity, for instance, makes him so indignant that in the proem of canto 22 he has to explain to his lady readers that her exceptional evil does not blind him to the virtues of the fair sex. And to reassure these same readers of his sympathy for them, at the start of canto 29 the narrator voices his anger at Rodomonte's generic condemnation of women and promises that he is going to make his character pay dearly for his misogyny. Sassetti actually cites this last *proemio* as an example of Ariosto's objectionable intrusions and then maintains, with Aristotle and contemporary Aristotelians to support him, that such observations and opinions are not part of the imitated action in the work, but belong to the audience that judges the action from outside. These authorial interventions, he goes on to say, jeopardize the poem's credibility, presumably because, by drawing the reader out of its imaginative world, they disrupt his or her involvement in it.

This criticism of Ariosto's authorial interventions, immediately following, as it does, the attack against his premature interruptions, suggests that sixteenth-century critics considered both these narrative features sources of discontinuity. Although Sassetti's attack against Ariosto was never published, it is representative of the hostile criticism leveled at the *Furioso* in the 1570s and 1580s. As I mentioned above, his was hardly the sole or the first voice objecting to Ariosto's authorial intrusions. Nor, it turns out, was Sassetti the only critic to derive these objections from Aristotle's praise of Homer's self-effacement. Before him, both Torquato Tasso and Castelvetro had already associated their critique of Ariosto's *exordia* and other interventions with the same passage in chapter 24 of the *Poetics*.

Tasso had criticized the *proemi* in the *Furioso* as early as 1562 in the preface to the *Rinaldo*, his youthful effort to write a romanzo that heeded what was taken to be Aristotle's demand to minimize the presence of the narrator. In this preface to the readers, Tasso proclaims that he does not want his work to be judged either by militant Aristotelians or by the enthusiastic fans of Ariosto, since he can anticipate their respective objections. "I troppo affezionati de l'Ariosto," he writes,

> mi riprenderanno che non usi ne' principi de' canti quelle moralità, e que' proemi ch'usa sempre l'Ariosto e tanto più che mio padre . . . anch'ei talvolta da questa usanza s'è lasciato trasportare [though Bernardo, as we saw, was also persuaded to remove such *proemi*]. Benche, d'altra parte, né il principe dei poeti Virgilio, né Omero, né gli altri antichi gli abbiano usati, ed Aristotile chiaramente dica nella sua *Poetica* . . . che tanto il poeta è migliore, quanto imita più, e tanto imita più quanto men egli come poeta parla e più introduce altri a parlare: il qual precetto ha benissimo servato il Danese, in un suo poema composto ad imitazione de gli antichi, e secondo la strada ch'insegna Aristotile. . . . Ma non l'han giá servato coloro che tutte le moralità e le sentenze dicono in persona del poeta; né solo in persona del poeta, ma sempre nel principio de' canti: ch'oltre che ciò facendo non imitino, pare che siano talmente privi d'invenzione, che non sappiano tai cose in altra parte locare che nel principio del canto.[15]

[Those too devoted to Ariosto will reproach me for not employing at the start of cantos those moralities and proems that Ariosto always uses, and the more so because my father also sometimes let himself get carried away with this practice. Even though, on the other hand, neither Virgil, the prince of poets, nor Homer, nor the other ancient poets used them, and Aristotle clearly states in his *Poetics* that the better the poet is, the more he imitates, and the more he imitates, the less he speaks as a poet, and the more he introduces others to do the speaking. [Cataneo] Danese observed this precept extremely well in the poem he composed in imitation of the ancients, and along the path indicated by Aristotle. . . . But it was not observed by those who state all moral opinions and judgments in the person of the poet; and not only in the person of the poet, but always at the beginning of cantos; besides the fact that, by doing this, they are not imitating, they seem to so lack invention that they do not know how to place such matters anywhere else but at the beginning of a canto.]

Tasso acknowledges here the influence that Aristotle's preference for unmediated *mimesis* had, and would continue to have, on his narrative poetry. In the *Gerusalemme Liberata* he even sought to imitate the Homeric practice praised by Aristotle by limiting the appearance of the narrator to a preliminary invocation and a few very brief addresses to characters in the action. But more than for the Aristotelianism it displays, I find the above passage interesting because it links Ariosto's intrusive *proemi* and Aristotle's comments in chapter 24 of the *Poetics*. Like Sassetti after him, when Tasso thought of Ariosto's authorial intrusions, he thought of the way they transgressed Aristotle's call for a minimal use of the poet's own voice.

The same association is to be found in Castelvetro's commentary on Aristotle's *Poetics*, first published in 1570, some five years before Sassetti's "Discorso." Castelvetro makes several critical remarks about Ariosto in his commentary, and one of the occasions on which he cannot resist disparaging the *Furioso* occurs during his discussion of Aristotle's praise of Homer's self-effacement (at 1460a). According to Aristotle, Castelvetro maintains, a poet should avoid speaking in his own person if he wishes to fulfill his proper duty as an imitator (Castelvetro's term is *rassomigliatore*). Yet, as undesirable as it is for the poet to narrate events or to describe them too often in his own voice, it is much worse for the poet to comment personally on various actions narrated.

> Se il poeta, in quella parte dell'epopea nella quale narra solamente e racconta l'azzione e non introduce persona a favellare, non è rassomigliatore, secondo Aristotele, e per conseguente non è poeta, che diremo noi del poeta, in quella parte dell'epopea nella quale egli né narra azzione né introduce persona a favellare, ma giudica le cose narrate, o riprendendole, o lodandole, or tirandole a utilità comune e ad insegnamenti civili e del ben vivere? Certo non altro se non che egli non è rassomigliatore. . . . Ora se egli non è rassomigliatore né per cagione del modo né per cagione della materia, seguita che ancora non sia in questa parte poeta. Il che non è errore da stimare poco, prima per quella parte, poi per l'altre parti ancora nelle quali è rassomigliatore e poeta, conciosia cosa che giudicandole e parlandone come che sia, si mostri persona passionata e la quale v'abbia interesse, e perciò si toglia a se stesso la fede e si renda sospetto a' lettori d'esser poco veritiere narratore. Senza che non si fa poco odioso altrui, scoprendo certa superbia e confidanza di bontà, quando, posposto l'ufficio di narratore che era suo proprio, imprenda l'ufficio di predicatore e di corregitore de' costumi fuori di tempo; nel quale errore non cade mai Omero, ma sì Virgilio alcuna volta, . . . [several examples of authorial interjections in the *Aeneid* are provided]. E più spesso di lui vi caggiono quelli poeti che sono meno buoni di lui, e massimamente Lucano . . . ; e più spesso di tutti Lodovico Ariosto nel suo *Orlando Furioso*.[16]

[If in that part of an epic poem in which he does nothing but narrate and describe the action, and does not represent a character speaking, the poet, according to Aristotle, is not an imitator and consequently not a poet, what shall we say of the poet in that part of the epic in which he neither recounts an action nor represents a character speaking, but passes judgment on the subjects narrated, dealing out either praise or blame, or drawing from them benefits for the commonwealth and lessons about politics and the good life? Certainly that he is no imitator. . . . And if he is not an imitator either in the mode of his imitation or in its matter, in that part, then, he is not a poet. This is an error of no small consequence, not only for that part of the epic, but also for the other parts in which he is an imitator and a poet, because by judging or commenting on the actions, he reveals himself to be passionate and partial and thus forfeits the faith of his readers and makes them suspect him to be a narrator of little veracity. Moreover, by neglecting his proper role of narrator and inappropriately assuming that of a preacher and moral censor, he makes himself odious by revealing a certain pride and self-righteousness. This is an error into which Homer never fell but that Virgil occasionally committed. . . . And more frequently than Virgil it was committed by lesser poets, and especially by Lucan . . . ; and most of all by Ludovico Ariosto in his *Orlando Furioso*.]

It is useful to learn from this passage that among modern poets, Ariosto was considered the greatest offender against Aristotle's demand for minimal authorial presence in epic narrative. Usually, late cinquecento commentators on the *Poetics* do not refer to the practice of vernacular poets, and even rarely of Roman poets. For example, in Alessandro Piccolomini's *Annotationi . . . nel libro della Poetica d'Aristotele* (1575), the next Italian commentary after Castelvetro's, the same passage from chapter 24 is discussed at some length, but one is left to surmise which individual authors Piccolomini has in mind when he castigates poets who intervene personally in their poems. Modifying Castelvetro's and prior interpretations of the passage, Piccolomini claims that Aristotle would allow the poet to speak in his poem as long as he assumes the disinterested voice of an objective narrator. What must be avoided, he argues, is the kind of personal intervention or judgment that occurs

> quando il poeta spogliandosi l'habito di poeta, non come narratore, ma come giudicatore & stimator delle cose narrate, & come (insomma) interessato parla. com'a dir (per essempio) invocando, proponendo, esclamando, consigliando, proferendo qualche sententia sopra le cose dette, inserendo qualche corrolario; l'humana miseria deplorando, la fortuna detestando, qualche virtù secondo l'occasion lodando, o altra . . . cosa facendo, non come poeta, ma come egli stesso.

[when the poet, shedding off his poet's role, speaks not as a narrator but as a judge and assessor of the matters narrated—in short, as someone partial. For example, by invoking, proposing, asserting, recommending, or proffering moral commonplaces about the narrative, and adding some corollary views; deploring human misery, despising fortune, praising some virtue bearing on the occasion, or doing something other, not, however, as a poet, but as himself.]

Piccolomini does not identify the poets who resort to such malpractice, but one can infer that he would share Castelvetro's view that Ariosto was a chief offender since the various admonitions he castigates in the passage above could well serve as an inventory of the kinds of judgments made in the *proemi* of the *Furioso*.

Piccolomini goes on to explain that the poetic representation does not appear "ben fatto" when, as a result of such personal interventions, the poet "si scuopra, come interessato, & adherente più ad un fatto che ad un'altro, & più ad una persona, che ad un'altra, in quel, che narra; & per conseguente deroghi, & nuochi in questa guisa alla credibilità, & alla fede di quel che ei dice [reveals himself as partial, and more supportive of one deed in his narrative than another, or of one character than another. By doing this he limits and jeopardizes the credibility and the trustworthiness of what he says]." Besides jeopardizing the credibility of his poem by making judgments on the action or the characters represented, the author misappropriates a function that belongs to the audience. The poet should forego "il giudicare, il lodare, il biasmare, o altra cosa fare che appartenga a coloro, che leggono: dovendo il poeta apparir, come neutrale, & lasciar libero il giuditio a gli altri sopra le cose, che egli imitando narra [judging, praising, blaming, or other responses that belong to the readers. The poet must appear neutral and leave his readers free to judge the matters that, in the process of imitating, he narrates]."[17] After one reads Piccolomini's general objections, it becomes apparent that Sassetti's subsequent critique of Ariosto's interventions is little more than a specific application of these objections to the *Furioso*. Like Piccolomini, Sassetti maintains that Ariosto's *exordia* belong outside the realm of the poem along with the audience's other subjective responses. He also points out that Ariosto's kind of interventions can only diminish the poem's credibility by breaking whatever continuity the imitation had achieved.

Sassetti's critique of Ariosto's intrusions was far from an isolated reaction. By 1575 the new Aristotelians had virtually made a tradition of attacking his interruptions and his various narratorial interventions. Even the English were aware of their criticism. In the "Briefe Apologie" that prefaces his translation of *Orlando Furioso* (1591), Sir John Harington acknowledges that two "reproofs" were made about the author by Aristotle's followers: "One, that he breaks off narratives verie abruptly. . . . Another fault is that he speaketh so much in his own person by digression which they say also is against the rules of Poetrie because neither Homer nor Vergill did it."[18] Harington's comments attest that the neo-Aristotelian opposition to the *Furioso* was well established and widely known by the end of the sixteenth century. Castelvetro, Piccolomini, and Sassetti shared a dislike of Ariosto's obtrusive presence as a narrator because it was unclassical. They also criticized this procedure because it broke the continuity of his fiction and, as a result, dissolved the illusion achieved by it. The neo-Aristotelians were concerned that the make-believe that the poet sought to achieve by his mimesis could only be jeopardized by Ariosto's sort of narrative interventions and breaks.

But even more objectionable to the neo-Aristotelians was that Ariosto's intrusions made the author's presence and his artificial manipulations too obvious. The sudden transitions had a similar effect: they exposed further the artifice of his fictive construct. Underlying the animus against Ariosto's technique was a neoclassical bias against conspicuous artifice and the attendant belief that the more unrevealed the art, the more perfect it was: *ars est celare artem*. It was, in part, this belief that had prompted all the critics from Speroni to Sassetti to characterize Ariosto's authorial intrusions as inept and inartistic. In general, the neo-Aristotelians valued unity, continuity, and verisimilitude because these features allowed the poet to achieve a closer correspondence between art and nature. Conversely, they sought to exclude from poetic representation all the elements that might make its fictive and artificial character too visible. Among these undesirable elements were multiplicity of plot and the fragmentation of narrative it necessitated, authorial commentary, and, in general, any form of obtrusive mediation between the poetic representation and the audience. No wonder that the *Furioso* became a target of neo-Aristotelian criticism.

Despite the influence of their objections on later cinquecento poets, the neo-Aristotelians were unable to marginalize *Orlando Furioso*. Not that their efforts to discredit the chivalric romance, of which the attack against the *Furioso* was part, were unsuccessful. By the end of the century, they had quite effectively managed to exclude most popular *romanzi* (including Pulci's *Morgante* and even Boiardo's *Orlando Innamorato*) from the poetic canon they were actively establishing. They had also hoped, from the start, to deprive the *Furioso* of the status it had acquired as a modern heroic poem. Their hopes were only fueled by the appearance in 1581 of Tasso's *Gerusalemme Liberata*—a poem which, in their view, represented a far more genuine equivalent of the ancient epic, and which they used to further expose the shortcomings of Ariosto's poem. Yet, even with the *Liberata* to reinforce their claims, the neoclassicists failed to marginalize the *Furioso* in the way that they did the other *romanzi*. The following two chapters, on the defenses of the poem provoked by the neo-Aristotelians in the 1580s, will reveal why its status could no longer be so diminished: the poem had secured for itself so significant a place in the culture that it became a site where men of letters could converse or argue about the latest poetic issues. It had attained, moreover, so firm a place in the culture that its legitimacy was now being exploited by the champions of every form of poetic modernism.

Chapter Six

LIONARDO SALVIATI'S DEFENSE OF
ORLANDO FURIOSO

AT THE END of my account of the preliminary legitimation of *Orlando Furioso*, I pointed out that already by the 1560s the efforts to affiliate the poem to the canonical epics of antiquity were losing ground. Not only were the new Aristotelians making it progressively evident that the norms Aristotle and Horace were taken to have prescribed for the epic were not satisfied by Ariosto's romance; at the same time that these neoclassicists were undermining claims for the *Furioso*'s epic ancestry, Giraldi's progressive argument that it was a modern romanzo composed according to different principles from those characterizing Greek and Roman epic became a more viable justification of the poem. Following Giraldi's lead, defenders of the *Furioso* argued that changing times demanded changes in poetic forms, and that Ariosto's romanzo, because of the features that distinguished it from ancient epic, conformed much more effectively to modern usage and taste, as its success so evidently confirmed. Both the extraordinary success of the poem and the neo-Aristotelian attack based on its failure to meet the norms of the ancient *epos* encouraged its champions to promote it as a modern counterpart rather than as a replication of ancient epic.

This more progressive effort did not, of course, displace attempts to affiliate the poem to the canonical epics of antiquity. Enough sixteenth-century Italians cherished the notion that the *Furioso* was a traditional heroic poem that the idea could not be dislodged. As I will show in this chapter, Lionardo Salviati's *Infarinato secondo* (1588), one of the major defenses of the *Furioso* at the end of the century, still seeks to legitimize the poem by assimilating it to the major epics of antiquity, even though such assimilation now entails a revision of the standardizing interpretation of these ancient poems.

Salviati's defense was first published in an abbreviated version as the response of the Accademia della Crusca to the attack made against the *Furioso* by Camillo Pellegrino in *Il Carrafa o vero della epica poesia*, published in 1584. One cannot therefore fully understand Salviati's counterargument without first taking into account the basic complaints that Pellegrino made about the *Furioso* in this dialogue. Moreover, *Il Carrafa* deserves to be reviewed with some care because it succinctly summarizes the hostile criticism that neo-Aristotelians had been voicing against Ariosto's poem since the 1560s.

Actually, Pellegrino had an advantage over previous opponents of Ariosto. He could measure the *Furioso* not only against ancient epic but also against the latest Italian instance of the genre: Tasso's *Gerusalemme Liberata*, originally published in 1581. In fact, *Il Carrafa* was the first published work to argue that the *Liberata* was superior to the *Furioso* as an epic poem because it conformed more closely to Aristotelian rules and ancient precedents. Debates over the relative merits of the two works had begun almost immediately after the original publication of Tasso's poem, but it was Pellegrino who first brought together the various arguments on both sides into a dialogue, and by clearly championing Tasso over Ariosto he sparked off a critical war between *Ariostisti* and *Tassisti* that endured until the end of the century.[1] Before Attendolo (Pellegrino's spokesman in the dialogue) first proposes that Tasso is the superior poet, he does concede that, in comparison to the vile works of prior *romanzatori*, Ariosto, Bernardo Tasso, and Luigi Alamanni have, in parts of their poems, attained some semblance of heroic dignity even though they lack "la perfezione dovuta ad epico poema." When, a little later, Carrafa (Attendolo's sole interlocutor) asks him why Ariosto and Bernardo Tasso cannot be deemed "poeti del primo grado," Attendolo replies that it is because they failed to unify their poems around a single action, and ignored Aristotle's call for a poem whose body "possa comprendersi in una sola vista [may be perceived in one single view]." Instead, they formed "un mostro di più capi e di diverse membra non ordinate, che l'intelletto si stanca in considerarle [a monster of many heads and various irregular limbs that tires the intellect considering them]."[2] On the other hand, it is because Tasso observed the rule of the single unified action that he achieved the perfection lacking in his father's and in Ariosto's poems.

Carrafa expresses surprise at this demotion of Ariosto, given the great fame his work had already secured "non solo in Italia ma quasi nel mondo tutto." While Attendolo admits that the poet deserves to be called "divino" for his poetic spirit, he laments that he chose to apply his great talent to the making of a vulgar romanzo instead of composing a poem based on Aristotelian precepts. According to Attendolo, Ariosto decided that writing a regular epic would preempt the universal pleasure he wanted to produce. Therefore, he chose rather

> di essere primo fra i poeti compositori di romanzi che secondo o terzo fra gli osservatori delle poetiche leggi, e perciò nella intessitura del suo poema attese solamente alla vaghezza e al diletto, posponendo l'utile che, come sapete et è parere de' migliori, è il fine della poesia, ricercato per mezzo del diletto.
> (p. 318)

[to be first among poets who composed romances than second or third among those who observe the laws of poetry, and therefore in the construction of his poem he devoted himself solely to pleasure and delight, neglecting the profitable, which, as you know, and also in the opinion of the best judges, is the end of poetry, and is sought by means of delight.]

It is important to note here the clear distinction that is being made between the romanzo and legitimate poetry. Earlier, Attendolo had made it clear that Ariosto forfeited the possibility of writing serious poetry when he decided to produce a popular romanzo instead of heeding Bembo's advice to compose a poem of a single action. And near the beginning of the dialogue, when Carrafa first asks why Bernardo Tasso cannot be considered an epic poet, he is told that it is because he chose to base his *Amadigi* on a completely false story, to fill it with numerous digressions completely unconnected to the main action, and imitated, instead, various actions, and of several protagonists. In other words, because the *Amadigi* had all the features of a romanzo, its author could not be deemed an epic poet. Pellegrino seeks to so distinguish the romanzo and establish its inferiority to the epic in order to diminish Ariosto's achievement. But it is also evident that, at this stage, he does not want his differentiation of the two kinds of writing to be taken as a generic distinction. He does not say, in the passage cited above, that by composing a popular romance Ariosto avoided being second- or third-rate among epic writers but rather among "osservatori delle poetiche leggi." Clearly, this suggests that, despite their differences, *romanzi* do not constitute a separate genre from epic but rather an inferior, illegitimate form of writing.

Pellegrino's differentiation of the romanzo and the epic is not original. His observations about the lowly (because popular) chivalric romance reiterate similarly hostile views expressed by Antonio Minturno in his *Arte poetica* twenty years earlier. Pellegrino even acknowledges, in his subsequent debate with Salviati, that some of the distinctions he draws between epic and romance were pointed out before him by Minturno. There is, however, one significant difference in Pellegrino's definition of the romanzo: it is more precise than Minturno's. When Minturno distinguished this lowly and flawed form of writing from epic, he described it in terms of what it lacked (primarily unity and continuity), and therefore did not give it a clear, positive identity. However, when Pellegrino distinguishes the romance from epic to establish its inferiority he singles out several features: its imitation of many actions, and of many protagonists, including wicked and immoral ones; its completely false stories; its lack of gravity; its unconnected digressions; and, in general, its confusing discontinuity. These features are all deemed defective, but they begin to constitute a generic definition nonetheless. Salviati, as we shall see, clearly perceived Pellegrino's distinction between the romanzo and the epic as a generic one, and he vehemently opposed it. Yet Pellegrino, at least in *Il Carrafa*, cannot acknowledge it to be so, because to identify the romanzo as a separate genre would contradict his assumption that there are unchanging and universal poetic laws. When, in fact, Carrafa reminds his interlocutor that some of Ariosto's defenders (he has in mind Giraldi and his followers) deny Attendolo's claim that, in relation to the epic, the romanzo is a *lower* form of writing, and argue instead that it is *another* modern genre of poetry and, as such, exempt from the "leggi della [lingua] greca e della latina," Attendolo simply replies that it is futile to contradict the "regole dell'arte della epica poesia" formulated and observed by the ancients because these rules have acquired the permanent validity of doctrinal principles (pp. 318–19).

At this point in the dialogue, Carrafa, ready to concede that Tasso excels Ariosto in plot organization, doubts that Ariosto has been surpassed in any other way, and he challenges Attendolo to demonstrate in more detail "in che cosa il Tasso sia in bontà poetica superiore all' Ariosto" (p. 320). Attendolo complies by offering to compare their handling of the three parts that, in addition to plot, Aristotle deemed constitutive of epic poetry: *costume*, *sentenza*, and *locuzione*. And, indeed, the rest of the dialogue is devoted primarily to a consideration of the two poets' treatment of these parts.

In his synopsis of *Il Carrafa*, Bernard Weinberg summarizes what Pellegrino has to say about Tasso's superior handling of character, thought, and language:

> *Character.* Tasso's personages are all heroic, worthy of the epic (except when he needs to introduce "some vile or wicked one in order to integrate his plot"), they are all appropriate—this means that decorum is observed in every respect—and this appropriateness extends to the rest of the requisites; they are all "similar" to their historical characters, "consistent" in their words and actions. Finally, they are all "good" within the limits prescribed for the epic; the protagonist (contrary to the case in tragedy) is "supremely good" whereas the others are middling or even bad, as the plot demands. *Sentenza*: Pellegrino includes under this heading the expression of ideas and passions and the development of argument; he thinks that Tasso is less successful here than elsewhere because of a brevity which leads to obscurity and a certain unfamiliar quality. *Language*: here, in the part which constitutes "the major difficulty of the poetic art," Tasso is supreme; for his metaphors, his ways of speaking, his passionate quality, generate wonder and delight in the mind of the reader.[3]

While this summary provides an idea of the issues discussed in the rest of *Il Carrafa*, it does not reveal the specific objections raised against Ariosto's treatment of character and poetic language (perhaps "diction" would be a more appropriate translation of *locuzione* than "language"). Pellegrino's critique of *costume* in the *Furioso* was particularly provocative, and I would like to dwell on it to make more intelligible Salviati's eventual counter-claims.

Pellegrino organizes his comparative evaluation of Ariosto's and Tasso's treatment of *costume* or character according to what he takes Aristotle's four requisites for *ethos* to mean in the *Poetics* (see chap. 15): "la prima è che sia buono [*khrestos*], la seconda che sia convenevole [*harmotton*], la terza che sia simile [*homoios*] e la quarta eguale [*homalos*]" (p. 323).[4] Attendolo first points out that epic requires that its chief protagonists possess and enact the highest form of goodness, not just the middling sort Aristotle prescribes for tragic protagonists. The problem with *Orlando Furioso* in this regard is that, the title notwithstanding, there are no principal protagonists in the poem—or rather, all of the many characters appearing in the poem are no less prominent than Orlando, Ruggiero, Carlo, and Agramante. Moreover, among those that have important roles in the work's many digressions and episodes are "persone sceleratissime, vili, e del tutto indegne, contra gli insegnamenti di Aristotile [vile and most wicked characters, and completely unworthy, contrary to Aristotle's precepts]" (pp. 323–24).

As for "convenevolezza," or the decorum of characters according to their rank, sex, age, and profession, Attendolo cites several violations of this principle. Others, he says, have already complained that it was not appropriate for Ruggiero to stay with Alcina "tanto tempo effeminato." He finds Ricciardetto's tricking and seduction of Fiordispina a worse transgression of decorum, and he charges that the poem is full of such "sconvenevolezze." These may well render a romanzo charming, he avers condescendingly, "ma sono del tutto indegne d'un poema eroico" (p. 324).

The third requisite is that characters be "similar" to their historical or traditional representation. How readily sixteenth-century critics conflated Horatian and Aristotelian precepts is revealed here when Attendolo cites the *Ars poetica* (119–24) to illustrate Aristotle's notion of *to homoion* or similarity. Horace, he says, conforming with Aristotle, demands that when a poet treats a "persona nota per fama d'istoria o di favola, dee fingerla tale quale dalla fama della istoria o della favola sara divulgata [character well known because of historical or fictional fame, he must depict him or her in the same way that history or fiction has made that character famous]" (p. 325). Ariosto, he goes on to say, violates this principle in his depiction of Orlando because, Boiardo's poem notwithstanding, this knight was celebrated as "castissimo e saggio" in earlier history and fiction. On the other hand, Tasso, even though he invents Rinaldo, faithfully observes the principle of similarity by making Goffredo, Raimondo, and Tancredi conform to their historical portrayals.

Finally, Ariosto is accused of not making his characters consistent or "eguali," the fourth Aristotelian requisite of *costume*, once again defined by another quotation from Horace:

> Siquid inexpertum scaenae commitis et audes
> personam formare novam, servetur ad imum
> qualis ab incoepto processerit, et sibi constet.
>
> (*Ars poetica* 125–27)

Rodomonte is singled out as a character whose behavior, on several occasions in the poem, is inconsistent with the "temerità e fierezza" that is supposed to characterize him from the start.[5] Such "incostanza di costumi" is not to be found in *Gerusalemme Liberata*. Tasso's Argante, for example, who possesses several of Rodomonte's initial attributes, is depicted from beginning to end as bold, fierce, and implacable (p. 327). Similarly consistent are the portrayals of Erminia, Clorinda, and Tasso's other invented characters. Attendolo cannot but conclude that Tasso surpasses Ariosto in his handling of all four aspects of characterization.

However, when he moves on to consider *sentenza*, which includes thought and the depiction of emotions and passions, Attendolo concedes that Ariosto was very gifted in this respect, and more successful than Tasso given that the latter was prone to use expressions quite remote from common usage and was therefore less clear than Ariosto. But in *locuzione*, or poetic diction, the fourth constitutive part of poetry, which Pellegrino considers the "maggior difficultà dell'arte poetica" (p. 329), Tasso clearly surpassed his predecessor. Much of Attendolo's discussion of diction consists of the comparison of specific passages from the two works in order to demonstrate how Tasso's "locuzioni più artificiose" and his more metaphorical use of language warrant his claim.[6] He goes on to point out that, more than for its beauties, Tasso's diction deserves praise because it dispelled the mistaken assumption that, owing to inherent weakness, the Italian language "non era atta a sostenere il peso della eroica dignità" (p. 339). By endowing the vulgar tongue with the weight and dignity that contemporaries had thought possible only in Greek and Latin, Tasso confirmed that Italians could equal and even excel the ancients not only in lyric and elegiac poetry but in epic as well.

After championing Tasso over Ariosto, Attendolo ends the dialogue doubting that his preference for Tasso will be shared by his contemporaries. Ariosto's fame has so taken root that his reputation may well last as long as the Italian tongue remains alive. Yet, should it eventually die, as Latin did, then Ariosto's "dolcezza" will no longer delight the ears of the multitude. At that future point in time the flaws of the poem that Attendolo has exposed will become all too apparent, and then finally "della *Gier-*

usalem liberata, come corpo più perfetto et ordinato secondo l'arte, si farebbe stima maggiore che dello *Orlando furioso*" (p. 343).

These final qualifications failed to appease Ariosto's champions, who saw in *Il Carrafa* a concerted attempt to demote the *Furioso* now, not in some hypothetical future. These supporters quickly produced defenses of the poem to offset the charges brought against it by Pellegrino. Among the first were Francesco Patrizi's *Parere in difesa dell'Ariosto*, and Orazio Ariosto's (the poet's grandnephew) *Difese dell'Orlando Furioso*, which appeared in 1585. They were followed, in the same year, by the first of Lionardo Salviati's replies, presented as a collective response from the newly founded Accademia della Crusca and entitled *Degli Accademici della Crusca difesa dell'Orlando Furioso dell Ariosto contra l'Dialogo dell'epica poesia di Camillo Pellegrino. Stacciata prima.* I do not intend to review the entire quarrel that Pellegrino's dialogue and these responses subsequently provoked, since this prolonged dispute between the respective champions of Ariosto and Tasso has been surveyed adequately by Bernard Weinberg.[7] My aim is to dwell rather on the major defense of the *Furioso* in this dispute, namely, Salviati's responses to Pellegrino, which began with the defense just cited, subsequently referred to as the *Stacciata prima* ("the first sifting"). In response to this initial counterattack Pellegrino defended and elaborated his position in a *Replica* that also appeared in 1585. Subsequently, after he had responded to Tasso's *Apologia in difesa della sua Gierusalemme liberata*, Salviati continued his debate with Pellegrino in *Lo 'Nfarinato secondo ovvero dello 'Nfarinato Accademico della Crusca, risposta al libro initolato Replica di Camillo Pellegrino*, which, owing to publishing delays, did not appear until 1588. The *Infarinato secondo* contained a record of the entire debate between Salviati and Pellegrino—that is, it reprinted *Il Carrafa* (albeit in segments), the Cruscans' (i.e., Salviati's) response to it in the *Stacciata prima*, Pellegrino's *Replica*, and finally Salviati's counterreply. While the *Stacciata prima* is feistier and more humorous than Salviati's subsequent counterrebuttal, I concur with Weinberg that both installments of Salviati's debate with Pellegrino can be considered simultaneously (as they appeared in the *Infarinato secondo*) because the entire debate consists "of a group of variations on a central subject," rather than a "progressive set of stages in a developing polemic."[8]

From the start Salviati perceived that the debate about the merits of the *Furioso* centered around the issue of whether it was a different kind of poem from the epic defined by Aristotle and embodied in Homer's and Virgil's respective epics. Against Pellegrino's effort to establish its inferiority to these poems, Salviati's primary aim was to reassert that the *Furioso* was a modern *epos* equal to Homer's and Virgil's. He had to refute, therefore, every suggestion Pellegrino made that the romanzo Ariosto had chosen to compose was different from epic poetry. Thus one of his first interpolations in the *Stacciata prima* was to deny this generic difference as soon as he saw it implied in the dialogue. "Questa differenza da romanzo a eroico," he proclaimed, "è una vanità, e tanto è eroico il Danese e l'Aspramonte, e la Spagna, quanto Virgilio e Omero." The only distinction one can make, he went on to say, is between good and bad poetry.[9]

Interestingly enough, Pellegrino's reply to this opinion was one of the lengthiest he made in his subsequent *Replica*. It reveals how determined he was to distinguish Ariosto's practice from epic poetry. Restating that the principal parts of the *poema eroico* consist of a "favola d'una sola azione, il costume con decoro, la sentenza con lo splendore, e la favella magnifica, e non plebea," he maintains that the romanzo simply does not observe these requirements. Imperfections in these four respects are to be found not only in inferior *romanzi* like the *Danese*, but also in those written by the best authors, "non eccetuandone il Furioso" (p. 34). He then denies the Cruscans' claims that epic and romanzo deal with the same subject matter

> poiché l'uno intende per mezzo della perfetta imitatione di trattare i fatti illustri di una, o di più persone; ma che tutti insieme faccino una sola attione: & l'altro . . . imitando alle volte fatti indegni, & di huomini vilissimi, ha sempre per sua prima intentione una massa di cavalieri erranti & di donne, de' quali descrive le guerre e gli amori. (p. 35)

> [since one intends by perfect imitation to deal with the illustrious deeds of one or more characters, which together, however, make up one action, while the other, imitating at times unworthy deeds, and by the vilest kind of men, aims primarily to describe the wars and loves of a multitude of wandering knights and ladies.]

To support his distinctions Pellegrino not only cites Minturno's similar claims made twenty years earlier, but even recruits the support of Pigna and Giraldi, the first defenders of Ariosto to formulate and legitimize the differences of the romanzo from ancient epic.

Salviati will have none of it, and his counterreply in the *Infarinato secondo* is even lengthier. He argues that to differentiate the romanzo and the epic poem is to defy Aristotle's claims in the *Poetics*. Salviati, it must be understood, may be adamantly opposed to Pellegrino, but he is not an anti-Aristotelian. On the contrary, he bases his entire argument on Aristotelian principles. However, the way he interprets the *Poetics* yields, as we shall see, theoretical tenets quite contrary to the Aristotelian ones advanced by Pellegrino. In this instance, he proceeds to challenge the generic distinctions set forth by the opposition by pointing out that, according to Aristotle, it is the different subject ("soggetto"), the different means ("strumento"), and the different manner ("modo") that serve to distinguish different genres (he is referring to chapter 3 of the *Poetics*). Applying these three criteria to the romance and the epic, he maintains that both imitate the actions of illustrious persons, both use verse to do so, and both are narrative in their manner and mode. Both are therefore generically identical.[10]

Salviati then challenges Pellegrino's argument that in addition to imitating "fatti illustri" the romanzo, unlike epic, imitates "fatti indegni, e di huomini vilissimi." He does so by reminding his opponent that in Homer's epics, especially the *Odyssey*, one similarly finds baseborn individuals partaking in the action along with higher-ranking protagonists. As for basing a distinction on the unity versus the multiplicity of plot, he refutes it by pointing out that when Aristotle demands that the action of the epic poem be whole, complete, and of proper size, these are conditions imposed "non all'eroico ma al *perfetto* poema eroico" (p. 40; italics mine). If, he claims, these requisites are not fulfilled in some heroic poems, the latter do not lose their generic identity as a result. Aristotle may well praise Homer for the unity he achieves in his poems, but the epic poets castigated for not observing such unity do not cease to be epic poets because of it. He therefore proposes that, in similar fashion, Pellegrino should object to the *Furioso*, not on the grounds that it is an inferior, other kind of poetry, but because he finds it "un eroico diffetoso." If, as his opponent claims, it is imperfect in its plot, its characterization, and its diction, why, Salviati asks, "volete voi delle imperfezioni formare una nuova spezie? Perchè, se elle sono imperfezioni volete voi farci a credere di scusarle col nome di buona poesia di Romanzo? [on the basis of these imperfections, do you want to form a new poetic kind? Why, if these are imperfections, do you want to make us believe that they are excusable under the name of good romance poetry?]" (p. 43). Why excuse the *Furioso* on the grounds that it is no more than a romanzo?

Pellegrino did not get an opportunity to answer these rhetorical questions. It is possible, however, to better understand why these were urgent questions and why Salviati so adamantly opposed Pellegrino's generic distinction when one bears in mind that by the 1580s Aristotelian poetics were already gaining dominance in Italian culture. This was not yet the case in the 1550s and the 1560s, when Giraldi and his followers could less anxiously exempt the modern romanzo from being judged according to Aristotelian rules. By the 1580s, in the academic circles frequented by Pellegrino and Salviati, if a poetic work fell outside what was perceived as Aristotle's generic system (for example, any romanzo), then the very poetic legitimacy of that work was now open to question. Conversely, if a poetic work was seen to belong to one of Aristotle's generic categories (tragedy, comedy, epic, and, arguably, dithyramb), then its status as poetry would be more secure. That is why the most typical counterresponse to the critique of the *Furioso* in *Il Carrafa* is the argument, in one variant or another, that the poem conforms to Aristotle's generic system and rules.

For example, in his *Difese dell'Orlando Furioso* (1585), Orazio Ariosto manages to include the *Furioso* within Aristotle's generic categories by arguing at some length that these consist of more than tragedy, comedy, and epic. Positing that there are high, low, and also mixed kinds of narrative and dramatic poetry, he suggests that the *Furioso* is not a "high" epic like the *Iliad*, but a narrative poem that combines illustrious and plebeian persons, like the *Odyssey*.[11] Orazio's reinterpretation of chapter 3 of the *Poetics* results in a multiplication of the species of narrative poetry that, in turn, makes it possible for his granduncle's poem to belong in the Aristotelian system. Pellegrino, on the other hand, was so keen to prove that the *Furioso* did not belong to it that he was even willing to acknowledge Giraldi's argument that Ariosto's poem was a modern genre unknown to Aristotle and one that could not, therefore, be expected to conform to the requisites the Greek philosopher had set down.

Salviati was all too aware that such exemption from the dominant poetics would be tantamount to exclusion from the canon of respectable poetry. One must recall, too, that Salviati did not question the validity of Aristotle's poetics or their applicability to modern poetry. Having acknowledged the rationality of Aristotle's principles ("non ne lasciò ammaestramento nella poetica, che non fosse fondato sulla ragione"), he would have had to concede that any poetic practice that did not observe these principles might well be dismissed.[12] No wonder that he, too, had to leave no doubt that the *Furioso* conformed to Aristotelian rules and did not differ from the *Iliad* or the *Odyssey*.

In order to uphold his claim that the *Furioso* was a proper epic, Salviati had to demonstrate that it possessed unity of plot. From the start of his dispute with Pellegrino he asserted that the poem was organized around one main action, the war between Carlo Magno and Agramante. Pellegrino's spokesman, Attendolo, had maintained that the poem consisted of many unconnected actions, a fact acknowledged by Ariosto himself on the many occasions he announced to his reader that he had to shift from one plot line to another. After having been pressed by the Cruscans, Pellegrino offered further proof of the poem's lack of unity in his *Replica*. Pointing out that the single plot Aristotle demands has to be so integrated that none of its parts can be transposed without changing the whole design, he demonstrates that one can shift around or remove any number of parts of the *Furioso* without altering the poem in any significant way. That is because it does not consist of a single action. And if one should counter that various "favole" can be removed or rearranged because they are episodes appended to the poem's main argument, and that the same could be done with the episodes of the *Iliad* and the *Aeneid*, Pellegrino responds that the episodes in the ancient epics "nascono tutti secondo il verisimile, o secondo il necessario dell'argomento della favola e perciò non se ne può levar niuno senza . . . far notabil danno al poema; ma non così avviene di quelli del Furioso [all spring, according to verisimilitude, or necessity, from the argument of the plot, and hence not one of them can be removed without doing notable harm to the poem; but this does not occur with the episodes of the *Furioso*]" (p. 60). He goes on to provide even more examples of the shifts from one story line to another by which Ariosto confirms the multiplicity of his plot. Finally, he cites numerous prior critics, ranging from Minturno and Castelvetro to Pigna and Giraldi, who support his claim that Ariosto deliberately chose not to compose a unified epic but instead decided to treat a "soggetto variato di più azioni, qual conviensi a romanzo" (p. 63).

To this rebuttal Salviati replied that the possibility of transposing parts of its plot does not prove that the *Furioso* lacks unity. One could as easily move Odysseus's first voyage to where the second is, and vice versa, or have Aeneas land in Sicily before he lands in Carthage. Similarly, one could remove parts of the narrative from these epics without jeopardizing the unity of their plots. Moreover, Salviati denies Pellegrino's claim that numerous parts of the *Furioso*—for example, Orlando's madness, the loves of Angelica, Isabella, and Fiordiligi, the stories of Olimpia and of Ginevra— are extraneous. He argues that, on the contrary, their removal would alter the poem's overall design in precisely the way Aristotle suggests.

Nowhere in the *Poetics*, Salviati goes on to maintain, can one find the unity of action in the epic described. Aristotle makes passing observations about Homer's practice which subsequent interpreters take to be the norms of a unified single action. So will Salviati. Citing these passages (from chaps. 23 and 8 of the *Poetics*), he expounds at length on Aristotle's precepts in order to show how they are observed in the *Furioso*. According to his interpretation, the unity Aristotle posits for dramatic genres is different from the unity that obtains in the heroic poem. In drama, the beginning, middle, and end are each single and extend in a ribbon-like structure, whereas in epic, each of the parts, and especially the middle, may be filled out into an almond-shaped structure. Salviati actually provides an illustration of the almond-like structure that contains the breadth and variety of material called for in a properly designed epic plot (see p. 73). This "larghezza" is the "virtù propria di quella spezie," whereas the thinness of the "unità" desirable in tragedy is a flaw in the heroic poem.

To prove that the *Furioso* is constructed according to the precepts of plot unity he has derived from Aristotle, Salviati then provides the following synopsis of the poem's main argument, possibly the only such summary ever made that gathers so much of its action into one sentence:

Un Re cristiano con la sua oste stretto d'assedio nella sua terra da un Re, ed esercito barbaro, ne potendosi liberar con le sole forze de' suoi, per l'essere allora un suo principal guerriero per amor divenuto furioso; di poi per certi soccorsi venutigli, non pur liberatosi dall'assedio, ma dopo più e varie fazioni

divenuto superiore in campagna; e appresso rimessa con giuramento, per la
sua parte, tutta la somma della guerra in un suo campione (si come anche il Re
barbaro fece in un suo) dopo che esso Re barbaro, ingannato da false immag-
ini d'una maga, ebbe rotto quel duello e il giuramento; prima in terra, e poi 'n
mare sconfitto il detto Re barbaro, che se ne fuggiva nel regno suo, e per
mezzo del suo principal guerriero, in cui era cessato il furore, distruttagli la
città, e sedia reale, e appresso, per man del medesimo, in battaglia fra tre e tre,
privatolo della vita, restò non solo vittorioso, ma per parentela contratta tra i
suoi maggior baroni, e per l'acquisto fatto di cavalieri, e per la morte data da
un de' suoi in duello a un gran vassallo di quel Re barbaro, rimase in presente
gioia, e sicurezza nell'avvenire. (pp. 75–76)

[A Christian king and his army besieged in his own land by a barbarian king
and army, unable to liberate himself by relying on the strength of his men
alone, given that his chief warrior has become insane because of love; eventually, thanks to outside help that reaches him, he not only frees himself from
the siege, but after various subsequent battles he gains the upper hand in the
field; and later, on his sworn oath, he lets the outcome of the war be decided
by one of his champions (as does also the barbarian king) when this pagan
king stops the duel and breaks the oath, having been tricked by false images of
an enchantress; the Christian king defeats him, first on land, and then at sea,
and makes him flee to his own kingdom, and with the help of his chief warrior,
whose madness is over, he destroys his main city and royal seat, and after, by
the hand of this same warrior, in a duel of three against three, having taken
away his opponent's life, he not only remains victorious, but through family
contracts among his greatest lords, and through the acquisition of his knights,
and through the death inflicted by one of his own on a great vassal of the
pagan king, he achieves present joy, and future safety.]

After this summary (which makes Ariosto's plot seem more like the coordi-
nated and focused one that Tasso devised for the *Liberata*) Salviati maintains that the episodic parts of the poem do not jeopardize its unity since
they regroup together before the end.
  Pellegrino had argued that Angelica's escape in canto 1 jeopardized the
unity of Ariosto's plot from the start. Salviati counters by maintaining that
this opening does not threaten the unity of the *Furioso* any more than does
the voyage of Telemachus at the beginning of the *Odyssey*:

Ne nuoce all'unità del principio ciò che si dice prima d'Angelica, come il
viaggio di Telemaco all'unità non pregiudica dell'Ulissea, essendo l'uno e
l'altro episodio: e gli episodi non son parte dell'argomento, nel qual si consid-
era l'unità. (p. 76)

[Nor does what is said at first about Angelica harm the unity of the beginning,
just as Telemachus's voyage does not jeopardize the unity of the *Odyssey*,

given that one and the other are episodes: and episodes are not part of the
argument in which unity is taken into account.]

Similarly, to deny Pellegrino's claim that the plot's discontinuity is confirmed by Ariosto's recurring shifts from one story to another, Salviati argues that, although they are more frequent, these "saltamenti" (as he calls
the shifts) do not threaten the unity of the poem any more than do
Homer's shifts from Telemachus to Odysseus to the suitors in the *Odyssey*.
I will return shortly to Salviati's strategy of assimilating the so-called imperfections of the *Furioso* to recognizable features of the model epics of antiquity. But to finish with his argument about the *Furioso*'s unity, he concludes that Ariosto must be praised for having managed to provide more
amplitude and variety in his plot than any of his predecessors, yet without
forsaking the kind of unity Aristotle had called for.[13]

The argument about unity is taken up again later in response to Attendolo's accusation that Ariosto formed a "mostro di più capi e di diverse
membra non ordinate." Pellegrino elaborates this criticism in his *Replica*
by claiming that neither the middle nor the end of the *Furioso* is dependent
on what precedes it. These flaws, he concludes, simply reconfirm what he
must keep on repeating, namely, that the poem "ha molte imperfezioni,
come epico, ma è perfettissimo, come romanzo [has many imperfections as
an epic, but is absolutely perfect as a romance]" (p. 125). In his counterreply Salviati refers to the long demonstration of the poem's unity summa-
rized above. But he cannot leave unchallenged Pellegrino's closing remark—that the *Furioso* is a perfect romanzo, unacceptably flawed though it
is as an epic poem—and his rebuttal well represents his general tendency to
invoke ancient epic practice to refute his opponent.

Salviati argues that the imperfect beginning Pellegrino ascribes to the
Furioso is no different from the beginning of the *Odyssey*. After reviewing
the chronology of Odysseus's adventures, he proposes that, just as Pellegrino charged that the *Furioso* has no real beginning since it depends on
Boiardo's *Innamorato*, so one can see that the *Odyssey* is similarly dependent on the *Iliad* (p. 127). He also dismisses his opponent's suggestion
that Ariosto could have brought his poem to a proper close with the death
of Agramante by reminding Pellegrino that the *Iliad* does not end with the
death of Hector, or the *Odyssey* with the killing of the suitors. Salviati finally asserts what one has to conclude from the parallels he has drawn: that
the imperfections Pellegrino identifies as typical of the romanzo are features discernible in Homer's exemplary epics, thereby confirming that "tra
epico, e romanzo non ha divario, ma sono in tutto la stessa spezie [there is
no difference between epic and romance, but they are the same genre in
every way]" (p. 129).

Just as he interprets Aristotle so that the *Poetics* can be made to support
his argument, so Salviati exploits Homer's and Virgil's epic practice to

justify his claims. Particularly keen to challenge the limited and rigid notions of epic unity advanced by neo-Aristotelians like Pellegrino, he tries to demonstrate, as we have seen, that the ancient epics possess within their unified plots much the same sort of multiplicity castigated in the *Furioso*. Although Salviati refers most frequently to the *Odyssey* when making these analogies, he shows that the other canonical epics also share numerous parallels with Ariosto's poem. For instance, the many shifts in Ariosto's narrative, attacked as a source of discontinuity, can be found in the latter half of the *Aeneid* as well as in the *Odyssey* (see pp. 79–81). And when Salviati defends the stories or "novelle" in the *Furioso* against the charge that they are extraneous and unconnected, he reminds his opponent that the canonical epics contain similar digressions unrelated to the main action.

> E qual dependenza nell'Iliade, con la guerra troiana, o con l'ira . . . d'Achille avrà lo sbombettare, e l'addormentarsi, che fanno insieme Giunone e Giove? Quale col viaggio d'Ulisse nell'Ulissea, l'adulterio di Venere con lo dio Marte . . . ? . . . Quale con la venuta d'Enea in Italia, nell'Eneade di Virgilio, la favola d'Ercole, e di Cacco, raccontata da Evandro? (p. 142)

> [And in the *Iliad*, what connection do Jove's and Juno's heavy drinking and sleeping together have with the Trojan War or with Achilles' wrath? What has Venus's adultery with Mars to do with Odysseus's voyage in the *Odyssey*? In Virgil's *Aeneid*, what connection with Aeneas's coming to Italy has the story of Hercules and Cacus told by Evander?]

There is something quite refreshing about Salviati's humorous and irreverent assessment of the ancient classics. Earlier "assimilators" such as Fornari sought to elevate the *Furioso* by showing how it resembled the *Iliad* and the *Odyssey*. This meant that they had to occlude most of the modern poem's "unclassical" features.[14] Salviati, on the other hand, treats the ancient epics as equals. Rather than showing how the *Furioso* resembles them, he demonstrates how they resemble it. Even though assimilation is still the object of the rhetoric, the difference in argumentation is significant. The *Furioso* is no longer made to seem an ancient epic in modern dress; instead the ancient epics are revealed to be much more modern in certain respects than had been previously assumed. By demonstrating that they possess a unity that does not preclude the variety and multiplicity of Ariosto's poem, Salviati frees Homer's and Virgil's epics from the rigid standards of unity and coherence that some neo-Aristotelians had imposed on these poems; at the same time he challenges those standards.

Salviati applies his technique of assimilation to more than formal considerations. One finds him drawing analogies with the ancient epics once again when he defends Ariosto's depiction of his characters against Pellegrino's charges. Attendolo had first objected, it will be recalled, that the

Furioso included "persone sceleratissime, vili, e del tutto indegne." Epic protagonists, he maintained, had to be supremely virtuous. Already in the *Stacciata prima*, as spokesman for the Cruscans, Salviati counters that Homer's poems also included vile individuals. Besides, no "bel costume" can be learned from heroes like Achilles, Ajax, and Odysseus, he maintains, as he lists their moral flaws, beginning with Horace's characterization of Achilles as "Iracundus, inexorabilis, acer" (p. 179). Nor is Attendolo's demand that epic protagonists possess "bontà nel supremo grado" corroborated by the *Aeneid*. What kind of exemplary character, Salviati asks with characteristic irreverence,

> è quel d'Enea già maturo, e che aveva un figliuol già grande, che doveva imparare a . . . prendere esemplo da lui, nel tempo ch'egli aveva per le mani si grandi imprese . . . l'andarsi intabaccando, e perdendo negli amorazzi a guisa d'un giovinetto: e tradire con si scellerata fraude quella real femmina, che ignudo, e tapino, e diserto l'aveva raccolto nelle sue braccia, e apertagli l'anima, e 'l corpo? Udissi mai 'l più solenne tradimento di questo? (p. 179)

> [is that of Aeneas, already mature, and with a grown-up son to whom he should have served as a model when he had such great tasks to fulfill, . . . going around debauching himself with cheap loves like a youth: and with such wicked deceit betraying that royal lady who took him into her arms, naked, miserable, and abandoned as he was, and offered him her soul and body? Have you ever heard of a greater betrayal than this one?]

Virgil's hero is clearly not as virtuous as Pellegrino maintains epic heroes should be.[15] On the other hand, if Ariosto's Orlando is shown going insane, Salviati points out that he is not the main protagonist, and, besides, "gli fu levato o piuttosto sospeso il senno e l'arbitrio per divino giudicio [his mind and free will were removed or rather suspended by divine judgment]" (p. 180). One can see, as Salviati then goes on to rationalize Ruggiero's apparent misdemeanors, that he is keen to deny what Pellegrino will reassert in his *Replica*, namely, that one finds in the *Furioso* "malvagità de' costumi" in protagonists who should be virtuous. But when he realizes that Pellegrino will not relent, his final line of defense is to reassert that the vices ("peccati") criticized in the *Furioso* are as prevalent in the epics Pellegrino deems exemplary.

Ready as he is to employ Aristotelian principles to judge the *Furioso*, Salviati is willing to evaluate Ariosto's characterization according to the four requisites of *costume* Pellegrino derived from the *Poetics*. But, once again, he reinterprets Aristotle to suit his argument. Consider his justification of Ricciardetto's sexual escapade. Pellegrino, as I mentioned earlier, had found the latter's tricking and seduction of Fiordispina particularly objectionable. Not only did Ricciardetto's conduct breach decorum, it exemplified how immorally some of Ariosto's main characters behaved. Salviati excuses the young man's tricks precisely because he is a young man, and proposes that it would have been more inappropriate for someone his age not to have wanted to seduce the lovely Fiordispina! He then points out that Aristotle never demanded that the goodness of character of epic protagonists be as unadulterated as Pellegrino suggests. The precept of goodness (*khrestos*) should be construed with some discretion, applying only to the main protagonists of the plot,

> e non d'ogni genere di bontà, ma di quelle che son più proprie di cotal guisa di personaggi, come della sicurezza, o coraggio, e della prodezza . . . in compagnia delle quali non è disdetto in poema eroico, nè in tragedia, che si ritruovino per lo contrario de' costumi non commendabili, solo che non fossero scellerati o enormi. (p. 190)

> [and not every kind of goodness, but those kinds most appropriate for such protagonists, as confidence, courage, prowess. . . . In heroic poems and tragedies it is not inappropriate to find these characteristics accompanied by some that, in contrast, are not praiseworthy, as long as they are not wicked or terrible.]

It would appear from this passage that, in order to justify Ariosto's flawed protagonists, Salviati is ready to recommend that epic characters be as middlingly good as Aristotle's tragic protagonists (see *Poetics*, chap. 13), even though most of his contemporaries shared Pellegrino's belief that epic heroes should possess superior virtue.

When Salviati is not reinterpreting Aristotle to challenge his opponent, he is accusing him of misreading the *Furioso*. For instance, he dismisses (in one of his longer replies in the *Stacciata prima*) Pellegrino's critique of Rodomonte's characterization by demonstrating that the pagan knight is already inconsistent in Boiardo's *Orlando Innamorato* and that what is claimed to be contradictory about his behavior in the *Furioso* is Ariosto's observance of the "natural disegualità del costume di quel pagano" (p. 216). If, however, he cannot reinterpret Aristotle or Ariosto to disprove his opponent, he resorts to his other favorite strategy—citing parallel "imperfections" in the epics Pellegrino deems exemplary.[16]

Following Salviati's ingenious rebuttal of his opponent, one is more impressed by his rhetorical abilities than by his insights about the poem.[17] One becomes aware, too, that even though particular aspects of the *Furioso* are discussed, the more contested issues in the debate are the interpretation of Aristotle's *Poetics*, the authority of ancient epic models, and precisely what these models exemplify. These, at least, are the issues to which Salviati applies most of his rhetorical prowess. It is not that one questions his genuine admiration of the *Furioso*, or his commitment as an *Ariostista*.[18] Salviati, as we have seen, musters every possible argument to extend the definition of epic so that, on the one hand, it can include Ariosto's modern romanzo and, on the other, it still adheres to Aristotelian precepts. He leaves no doubt that the ostensible purpose of his argument is to prevent the *Furioso* from losing its identity as heroic poetry. Still, one becomes aware (and this is more discernible in the *Infarinato secondo* than in the *Stacciata prima*) that more is at stake in this debate than the generic status of Ariosto's poem. Salviati is not simply defying Pellegrino's attempt to exclude the *Furioso* from the canon of epic poetry. The reason he so "opens up" Aristotelian principles, and makes the ancient classics appear less monumental, is to preempt the marginalization of all modern Italian poetry that does not conform to the narrow strictures that far more conservative Aristotelians are seeking to impose. Although he does not state it explicitly, his claims for the *Furioso* extend to the prior and future achievements of Italian poetry that can similarly be shown to rank with the works of the ancients without being subservient to them. Ultimately his defense is a manifesto about what he takes Ariosto's poem to represent: the parity with ancient poetry that modern Italian poetry has attained.

If defending the *Furioso* became, for Salviati, an occasion to affirm the possibility of Italian poetry's rivaling that of Greece and Rome, for others, as I will show in the next chapter, it became an opportunity to advance various other views or theoretical positions about poetry. The dispute between Salviati and Pellegrino already reflects a phenomenon that other contemporary defenses of the *Furioso* will make even more evident: the poem was becoming a site for the debate of some of the culture's most pressing issues. In the 1580s *Orlando Furioso* often served as a conduit through which the virtues of poetic modernism were articulated and justified.

Chapter Seven

OTHER DEFENSES OF
ORLANDO FURIOSO IN THE 1580s

THE SENSE one is left with at the end of the *Infarinato secondo*—that *Orlando Furioso* has become a site of contestation over issues that are beyond the poem—is reinforced by the different and contradictory claims made in other defenses of the poem in the 1580s. Salviati's effort to preserve the epic identity of the *Furioso* notwithstanding, an ongoing defensive trend—which I will examine shortly—was to reaffirm the claim that Ariosto's romanzo constituted a modern kind of poetry different from ancient epic and exempt from Aristotelian and Horatian rules. But some of Ariosto's defenders took yet another tack: they argued that the reason his poem did not conform to classical epic norms was that it was a generic hybrid.

Such an argument is already advanced, albeit somewhat tentatively, in Orazio Ariosto's *Difese dell'Orlando Furioso* (1585). The *Difese*, as I mentioned earlier, was one of the initial responses to Pellegrino's *Il Carrafa*, and was published, along with Salviati's first response on behalf of the Cruscans, in the volume that also contained Tasso's *Apologia* in defense of the *Liberata*. Although most of the *Difese* consists of Orazio's specific rebuttals to various itemized assertions in *Il Carrafa*, the preliminary and more interesting part of his treatise consists of a reconstitution of Aristotle's generic system.

Given the authority accorded Aristotle's *Poetics* by Pellegrino and others, Orazio points out that one should bear in mind its unfinished state. Aristotle's principles, he maintains, are more open to modification than some of his interpreters allow. Thus, the generic distinctions set forth in the *Poetics*,

> combinate, o accoppiate in altri modi ancora, oltra a quelli che pone Aristotile, potranno constituire altre specie di poemi, che non saranno nè Epico, nè Tragedia, nè Comedia; le quali tuttavia confessarà Aristotile medesimo, che sian vere specie di poesia; poi che da i medesimi principij di lui si possono inferire; e così si potrà dire, ch'egli implicita, se non esplicitamente le habbia poste.[1]

> [combined and coupled in still other ways beyond those that Aristotle offers, can constitute other species of poems, which will be neither epic, nor tragedy,

nor comedy; nevertheless Aristotle himself will acknowledge that they are true
species of poetry since they can be inferred from his very own principles, and
thus it can be said that he has established them implicitly if not explicitly.]

Positing that there are high, low, and mixed kinds of poetry, Orazio goes
on to maintain that, like dramatic poetry, narrative poetry is divisible into
three species: "narrativa d'attion illustre, d'attion non illustre, e d'attion
illustre e non illustre insieme" (p. 204). The first type is exemplified by an
epic such as the *Iliad*, the second by Homer's lost *Margites* or Virgil's
Gnat, and the third type by the *Odyssey*. Although Orazio never states it
explicitly, the *Furioso* is presumably a narrative of the third type, since, like
the *Odyssey* (which it is shown to resemble in several other ways), it combines high and low actions. Such a mixture, Orazio intimates, need not
provoke the objections voiced by Pellegrino and other critics once his reconstitution of Aristotle's system of genres is taken into account. Nor will
the *Furioso* be attacked for lacking unity of action once it is recognized that
"diverse specie di poesia possano haver diverse proprietà; e tra quei, che
son nominati poeti Epici ve ne siano, che partano da questa regola della
stretta unità della favola [different species of poetry can have different prop-
erties, and that among those called epic poets there are some that depart
from the rule of strict unity of plot]" (p. 207).

As a relative of the poet, Orazio was undoubtedly motivated to defend
the *Furioso* against Pellegrino's charges. Nonetheless, one feels that it was
less the call to justify his granduncle's practice than the opportunity to
present his reconstitution of Aristotle's generic system that spurred him to
write his *Difese*. Torquato Tasso's eventual response to Orazio's *Difese*
confirms that the status of the *Furioso* was not the main issue in question.
For in his reply Tasso was not concerned with Orazio's defense of the
poem against Pellegrino's specific objections, but staunchly rejected the
validation of generic mixing that he correctly perceived to be the treatise's
primary agenda.[2]

A much less tentative effort to justify the *Furioso* as a generic hybrid
is to be found in Francesco Caburacci's *Breve discorso in difesa dell'Orlando Furioso*. Appended to a treatise on "imprese," published in 1580,
Caburacci's *Discorso* preceded the debate between the *Tassisti* and the
Ariostisti, and, possibly because it was not limited by the terms of that
debate, its justification of the poem is more original. It begins with a review
of the main objections currently brought against the *Furioso*. The list
includes one or two familiar complaints—that the poet speaks too much in
his own voice; that since he entitled the poem *Orlando* it should have
begun and ended with Orlando's exploits; that the action of the poem is
multiple, varied, and confused—but the list also highlights some objections that were seldom mentioned. For instance, this writer claims that

the poem is criticized for its "ridicolosi, & popolar concetti," especially those thoughts voiced by the poet in his own person. Objections are also made about Orlando's madness, a subject more fit for comedy than for heroic poetry. Also derided are the "molte, lunghe, & ridicolose narrationi" inserted in the poem, as well as the many popular proverbs and modes of expression, deemed too low for the epic.[3] The somewhat eccentric character of Caburacci's list becomes more apparent in the light of the more conventional litany of complaints reported in this period.[4] But why Caburacci's list of objections has its peculiar slant emerges only after he explains what kind of a poem he believes the *Furioso* to be. According to him, the basic error of the poem's critics is to have mistaken it for an epic, when what Ariosto chose to compose was a new kind of poetry aimed at producing variety in the feelings of its audience. Realizing that the traditional genres of tragedy, comedy, and epic did not, by themselves, create enough of this desired variety, he combined the materials of the three genres, treating them, however, in the epic mode.[5] Eventually, after he distinguishes this deliberate combination of genres from other kinds of poetic mixtures, Caburacci concludes that once Ariosto's intention is understood, "è agevole il difenderlo dalle obiettioni" (p. 91), and he proceeds to refute the various objections he had initially listed by showing that, however inappropriate the poem's mixtures of matter and style may be for epic, they are fully justifiable in the new poetic hybrid Ariosto composed.

One realizes, in retrospect, that virtually every seemingly objective claim in the *Breve discorso* is made to support Caburacci's thesis that *Orlando Furioso* consists of a successful mixture of the three genres. Thus, the list of objections against the *Furioso* that Caburacci initially draws is not a disinterested analysis of the contemporary criticism leveled against the poem. Rather, it is a rhetorical device by which the author can reinforce his subsequent argument, since the supposed imperfections of the poem cease to be so once Caburacci reveals that Ariosto intended to compose a generic hybrid. Similarly, when Caburacci records the broad appeal of the poem ("Io veggio l'opera sua manegiatta dai vecchi, letta dai giovени [sic], havuta cara dagli uomini, pregiato dalle Donne, tenuta cara da i dotti, cantata da gl'indotti") (p. 80), he does it not in order to vindicate the poem as such but rather to confirm how well the procedure of mixing together different genres succeeded in terms of affecting various kinds of readers. In other words, the success of the poem validates the poetic procedure Caburacci chooses to ascribe to Ariosto. The treatise may well be entitled a defense of the *Furioso*, but its argument makes apparent that the object of such a rhetorical exercise is no longer the justification of the poem but rather the justification of the critical or theoretical idea that the poem is made to represent.

This phenomenon can be discerned again in the major defense of Ariosto's modernism in the 1580s: Giuseppe Malatesta's *Della nuova poesia, o vero delle difese del Furioso* (1589). The efforts of the neo-Aristotelians, from Minturno to Pellegrino, to marginalize the romanzo did not deter "modernists" like Malatesta from championing the genre, and especially the *Furioso*, as a new form of poetry, more appropriate for the tastes of the present age than traditional epic. This argument had been first set forth by Giraldi in his exchange of letters with Pigna, and then in his *Discorso sopra il comporre dei romanzi* (1554). Giraldi, as we saw, took the position that the poetic norms of modern times were quite different from those of the ancients "che avevano altri costumi ed altri modi di poeteggiare." Ariosto's romanzo could not therefore be judged according to Aristotelian or Horatian principles, nor could it be measured against the different ancient epic practice to which these principles applied. In short, Giraldi justified the departures of the *romanzatori* from Aristotelian norms on historical grounds and sought, in the process, to establish a new poetics by which modern narrative poetry could be judged. In the 1580s such justification of the modern romanzo is most eloquently set forth in Malatesta's *Della nuova poesia*.[6] However, this dialogue does not simply present the *Furioso* as a new kind of poem that is different from ancient epic and therefore *exempt* from Aristotelian epic norms. It argues that Ariosto's romanzo deliberately defied these norms, that the *Furioso* is, in effect, a counterepic. Let us examine how this interpretation is reached.

Not long after he begins to respond to a list of specific objections against Ariosto's poem,[7] Sperone Speroni, Malatesta's spokesman in the dialogue, is confronted with the general claim that the *Furioso* is not a poem because it does not belong to any of the kinds of poetry, namely, tragic, lyric, comic, and heroic. According to Scipione Gonzaga, one of Ariosto's detractors in the dialogue, it does not qualify as a heroic poem because it lacks a single plot with one main protagonist to which all the action relates. When Speroni eventually responds to these objections, he starts by observing that Ariosto began his career by writing a poem about the single action of a single protagonist, following ancient epic models and rules. But he abandoned the project when he realized "che quella unità di favola in un poema in lingua nostra non havea molto gratia, e tenea più tosto del freddo, & dell'insipido [that this unity of plot in a poem in our language did not possess much grace but was rather cold and dull]."[8] On the other hand, the *Orlando Furioso* that he then chose to write followed neither Aristotelian precepts nor the example of the ancient epic poets but belonged to the new poetry called "romanzesca." The fact that it was a romanzo did not prevent it from being poetry. Moreover, Speroni maintains, far from ignoring the poetic art of the ancients, Ariosto chose to go against their precepts. Speroni does not elaborate on the motives for this defiance, but he does point out that it was prompted by Ariosto's realization that the Italian language was incapable of epic "grandezza" and majesty. The poet, he says, correctly recognized the inappropriateness of trying to achieve the "gravità" heroic verse required with a language primarily characterized by "facilità" and "dolcezza." He therefore abandoned the idea of imitating the ancient epics and espoused the new genre of the romanzo, much better suited to the Italian language and to his own times.[9]

Ariosto's critics in the dialogue refuse to consider his decision to write a romanzo so positively. Gonzaga maintains that Ariosto should not have transgressed the rules of poetic art for the sake of preserving the "proprietà della lingua." And the Abbate Lippomani, who represents the conservative neo-Aristotelian position, rejects the idea that a work of art can be produced by anyone who disregards the established rules of that art as well as its ancient examples. The laws of art, according to the abbot, are immutable and exist to preserve order, in the same way that civil laws do. If, he proposes, one granted poets the liberty to modify the laws of poetry as their whims dictated—as Ariosto apparently did—"sariano in breve più Arti, che huomini, & nascerebbe in essi confusion tale, che v'havremmo un altro Chaos [there would shortly be more arts than human beings, and out of these would grow such confusion that we would have another chaos]" (p. 76). Poets must be regulated by the laws of their art just as citizens are regulated by "le leggi civili." Ariosto, he concludes, deserves nothing but derision for having produced "un poema tutto ritroso alli dogmi dell'Arte Poetica [a poem altogether contrary to the dogmas of poetic art]" (p. 77). The abbot implies that Ariosto is not simply an artistic outlaw but a heretic as well, and Speroni will follow up on this association—but positively, as we shall see, by comparing the poet to a religious reformer.

At this juncture, however, Speroni takes advantage of these hostile remarks to develop his anticlassical position. He complains that the reverence shown toward the ancients is a prevalent error of his times. The authority that ancient authors such as Aristotle enjoy is unwarranted, since they are as fallible as all other human beings. If the abbot wants to cling "come ad anchora sacra, alla memoria degli antiqui [to the memory of the ancients, as to a sacred anchor]," Speroni asks him not to prevent others from exercising their divinely granted freedom of discourse, which allows them to disregard, if they so wish, the precepts and practice of "quei vecchi scrittori" (p. 81).

Speroni then challenges the notion that the laws of poetry are constant by pointing out that the art of poetry is subject to the mutability that governs all things in this world. He first illustrates how norms of poetry undergo historical change by recalling the modifications that occurred in ancient Greek comedy. The open mockery of actual individuals that characterized Old Comedy was not tolerated forever because, as he explains, "una certa modestia civile s'accorse della brutezza di questa usanza [a certain civil modesty became aware of the ugliness of this custom]," and consequently the convention of lampooning living citizens was replaced by the more impersonal satire of New Comedy (see pp. 86–87). By pointing out that similar vicissitudes mark the history of tragedy and epic, Speroni reveals that even ancient poetic norms were never uniform but underwent steady revision. Why, then, all this leads him to ask, should Ariosto be reproached for not composing poetry like Virgil and Homer, "se non fu ripreso Plauto o qualunque si fusse inventor della nuova Comedia, per non aver scritto alla guisa d'Eupollo, o di Cratino [if Plautus or whoever was the inventor of New Comedy was not reproached for not having written in the manner of Eupollus or of Cratinus]" (p. 102).

In the course of reviewing the history of epic, Speroni shows that the "pluralità delle attioni" criticized in Ariosto's poem can be found in numerous ancient epics, from the "little" *Iliad* to Statius's *Achilleid*. But, again, he cites these ancient instances not to validate, by association, Ariosto's multiplicity of plots, but to show that ancient practice is not constant and monolithic. On the contrary, he boasts that Ariosto's poem bears no resemblance to Statius's, nor to any other ancient poem, but embodies the changes that poetic art must continually undergo.[10] In short, he suggests that the modern poet must reject as obsolete ancient norms and practice, and that this is precisely what was admirable about Ariosto's decision to write *poesia romanzesca*. Should Malatesta's reader fail to appreciate the radical modernism of his spokesman, he makes Giorgio Gozzi, one of the participants in the dialogue, register shock at the idea that Ariosto should be admired for not having conformed to ancient norms. Gozzi admits that he has difficulty absorbing Speroni's claim that Ariosto would not be "così raro, & così miracoloso . . . se non si fusse scostato dall'antiquita, cioè da quella norma, & da quella Idea, che sempre ha dato nome di perfetto . . . ad ogni Poeta [so extraordinary and wonderful . . . if he had not moved away from antiquity, that is, from that principle, that ideal, which has always bestowed perfection . . . on every poet]" (p. 107).

To convince his interlocutors of the worth of Ariosto's innovation Speroni first maintains that poetry treats of pleasurable matters ("il dilettabile"), and that what people consider pleasurable changes over time with changes in tastes and customs. Later, in response to the abbot, he maintains that civil as well as artistic laws are modified because of changing "costumi" or "uso." His argument, reminiscent of Giraldi's over forty years earlier, is that "il costume di scrivere alla romanzesca" that became prevalent among the French, Spanish, and Italians was the "uso potente" that overcame "la forza degli antiqui precetti poetici." So when Ariosto rebelled against the so-called laws of art, he was, in effect, adhering "alla più ferma, e più approvata legge che sia, cioè questa dell'usanza [to the

steadiest and most approved law that exists, namely, that of custom]"
(pp. 130–31).

From the start, Speroni posits that pleasure is the proper end of poetry.
(Utility, in his view, is accidental and extrinsic.) This belief leads him to
propose that, because of its greater capacity to generate pleasure, *Orlando
Furioso* is not only different from ancient epic but superior to it. To sub-
stantiate this claim, he maintains that pleasure results from variety. Given
that the romanzo is a type of composition that allows for more variety than
epic, it is a more pleasurable and therefore a better kind of poem. In fact, it
is so clear that "varietà" is more readily produced by the many plots of the
romanzo than by the single plot of the epic that Speroni wonders why
Aristotle, aware as he was that pleasure was the end of poetry, advocated
unity of plot (p. 123).

At this point the main speaker launches into an attack on unity of plot,
which had become, as he well knew, one of the most cherished principles in
contemporary poetics. He discredits unity not only because variety is more
pleasurable for modern taste, but because variety has always been a source
of pleasure: "Se noi miramo bene alla natura dell'anima, chiaro è, ch'ella
tragge particolar dilettatione dalla varietà delle cose, & al contrario particolar noia, e stanchezza dalla uniformità, e identità loro [If we look closely at
the nature of the soul, it is clear that it derives special pleasure from the
variety of things, and on the contrary, special boredom and weariness from
their uniformity and sameness]" (p. 121). Aristotle and Horace, who must
have realized that "uniformità" produces nothing but weariness and boredom, should have required variety in plot structure. And, clearly, Virgil and
Homer would have produced more pleasurable poems had they enlarged
upon and multiplied their single plots. Through his spokesman, Malatesta
seeks to give multiplicity of plot the normative value that unity of plot had
recently come to enjoy.

It merits noting, however, that Speroni does not simply espouse the
principle of multiplicity to validate Ariosto's practice. To be sure, after he
has argued that multiplicity is superior, he does reassert "che quanto con la
varietà delle favole s'accosta alla dilettatione più il romanzo, che l'epico,
tanto maggior lode merita l'Ariosto d'haver scritto con esso, che non meri-
tan ne Virgilio, ne Homero, che scrissero con quell'altro [as much as the
romance with its variety of plots achieves more delight than epic, so much
more praise Ariosto deserves for having written that kind of poem than
either Virgil or Homer, who wrote the other kind]" (p. 128). But one
becomes aware, at this stage in the dialogue, that, rather than having to be
justified, Ariosto's successful practice simply serves to confirm Speroni's
(and, by extension, Malatesta's) modernist and even radical poetic principles. As a result, the *Furioso* becomes more and more secondary in the
latter half of the dialogue, part of which is taken up by Speroni's defense of

his recurring claim that the end of poetry is pure pleasure and not, as some of his interlocutors contend, moral utility or even utility combined with pleasure (see pp. 153–98). Whether the end of poetry was pleasure or profit, or a combination of both, was one of the central topics of discussion in late sixteenth century poetics. Nonetheless, the standard and more conservative view in Counter-Reformation Italy was that *docere* and not *delectare* had to be the primary aim of poetry, even if it was conceded that pleasure could serve to achieve didactic ends.[11] Speroni's uncompromisingly hedonistic theory is of a piece, therefore, with the defiant modernism he champions earlier. And as it served to support his call for multiple plots, Ariosto's successful practice serves to warrant Speroni's hedonistic claims. But the *Furioso* hardly enters in the discussion about the purpose of poetry. In fact, virtually the only time that Speroni brings up the poet in forty-five pages of discussion is to say that because Ariosto has, best of all, pursued "diletto" as an end, he thereby surpasses again all the ancient epic poets (p. 174).

This incidental reference to Ariosto's practice in the midst of a prolonged and intense argument about the function of poetry well illustrates my general point: the *Furioso* has ceased to be the object of debate but has become instead a *locus* to corroborate definitions of modern poetry and its function that are under contestation.[12] Malatesta may well maintain that *Della nuova poesia* is a defense of the *Furioso*, but, as the dialogue progresses, one realizes that Speroni's main goal is to defy the universal validity of ancient or traditional poetic principles and to affirm instead the validity of new ones while advancing, in the process, one of the most radical critiques of ancient authority in the period. *Orlando Furioso* is marshaled forth to serve this argument as an exemplary case, but virtually nothing specific about the poem is discussed.[13] The poem's tremendous success and universal appeal are described at some length (see pp. 137–39). But that, again, is because the undeniable success of Ariosto's modern composition can be made to validate the counterclassical poetics the work is made to embody.

Indeed, as the argument advances in *Della nuova poesia*, it is made progressively clear that Ariosto's poem is not simply unclassical (that had been Giraldi's argument): it is counterclassical. For example, after reasserting how boring and tiresome unity and single plots tend to be in narrative poetry, Speroni praises Ariosto for having had the good sense to shun Aristotelian principles. Eventually, he compares Ariosto's contribution to poetry to the contribution of the Reformers to religion. It seems, as he puts it at the close of his peroration, "che l'Ariosto fusse dell'Ordine de' Riformati: perché il Romanzo, col qual egli scrisse, non è altro in vero, che una riforma degli abusi dell'epico [that Ariosto was of the Order of the Reformed; for the romance, in which he wrote, is nothing else in truth but a reform of the abuses of the epic]" (p. 152). This equating of Ariosto's artistic reform to the Protestant one is striking and potentially quite explosive. While it is not discussed further by the interlocutors, the analogy Speroni draws between religious and artistic innovation makes one realize why the values promoted by the modernists (for example, multiplicity, or the defiance of outmoded and irrelevant dogma) might be threatening to those who supported the Catholic church's call for unity and conformity in the face of multiplying Protestant sects challenging its authority. Moreover, after Speroni hails Ariosto as a reformer, it seems less than accidental that the principal opponent of Ariosto in the dialogue is an abbot who associates the *Furioso*'s artistic transgressions with civil anarchy and who suggests that the poetic dogmas Ariosto violates are as sacred as religious ones.

When Speroni praises Ariosto for reforming the abuses of epic, presumably he means the monotony stemming from its unity, its gravity, and its concern with utility rather than pleasure. In any case, the multiplicity, the variety, the *allegrezza*, and the *diletto* that all these features produce in the *Furioso* lead Speroni to ascribe to Ariosto's romanzo a dialectical relationship to classical epic. This perception of the *Furioso* as a counterepic on the part of Malatesta's spokesman is quite extraordinary for its time. We have seen that the generic difference between the romanzo and the epic had been recognized by Italian critics (pace Salviati) ever since Giraldi proclaimed such a difference in his *Discorso* on chivalric romance. But Malatesta's claim that Ariosto's poetic composition was not simply un-epic but counterepic is unprecedented in the debate about the epic versus chivalric romance.

This perception, it should be made clear, does not stem from a superior reading of the poem, but is the product of a critical debate that postdates the poem. The anachronism of various observations in Malatesta's dialogue makes this particularly apparent. For example, on several occasions Speroni maintains, for the sake of his argument, that Ariosto deliberately shunned the "imperfettioni dell'Arte Aristotelica," obviously disregarding the historical likelihood that the poet was unfamiliar with the *Poetics*, and that he composed his poem forty years before Aristotle's theory began to exert any authority.[14] Malatesta is also keen, as we saw, to project an image of an Ariosto who deliberately opposed ancient epic norms. To this end, the story (originally told in Pigna's biography) that Ariosto abandoned an initial attempt at regular epic and opted instead to delight more readers with a romanzo is modified to make it seem that Ariosto's choice was to compose a counterepic. Such an argument is also anachronistic given that Ariosto composed his poem in the first years of the cinquecento and it was not until the 1550s that the issue of the romanzo's difference from epic, and, indeed, the question of what constituted epic poetry, began to be taken up in earnest.

One gradually realizes that Malatesta needs to create the historical fiction of an Ariosto defying Aristotelian precepts in order to authorize his late sixteenth century manifesto against imitating ancient poetry and its prescribed norms. But if this projection of Ariosto can, in fact, serve to validate his call for counterclassical poetics, it must mean that *Orlando Furioso* has achieved enduring value. Despite the ongoing hostile reactions to the poem that Malatesta's dialogue dramatizes, the very appropriation of Ariosto's authority suggests that it is not his poem that needs defending as much as the defiance of ancient dogma that the poem is being made to represent. There were, to be sure, some grounds for making the *Furioso* stand for a viable modern alternative to ancient epic practice. Yet, again, one has to understand that those grounds are not to be found in the poem as much as in the critical discourse of "moderns" such as Giraldi who promoted the idea that the narrative form of Ariosto's romanzo was the kind of poetry most amenable to contemporary taste. Of course, claims that the romanzo and not the old epic was the form that the times demanded could not have been as easily upheld without the manifest evidence of the *Furioso*'s appeal to high, low, learned, and unlearned readers alike. Nor could Malatesta have subsequently made the *Furioso* the exemplar of rebellious modernism without the poem's ongoing and universal appeal.

Giraldi's *Discorso* on composing romances (1554) had been the first treatise to exploit the broad appeal of the *Furioso* in order to warrant the right of Italian poets to depart from ancient and obsolete norms of poetic art. But, as we can see in retrospect, Giraldi's manifesto was ahead of its time. Not until twenty-five years later did Giraldi's strategy of invoking the poem to validate modern practices quite extrinsic to it become a common feature of what were ostensibly defenses of the *Furioso*. Contemporaries of Giraldi who championed Ariosto—for example, Fornari and Pigna—had been more concerned with legitimizing the poem as such rather than using it to justify something else. And to legitimize the poem, as we saw, Fornari, Pigna, and the midcentury Venetian editors brought out parallels between it and what were, at the time, the most respected examples of narrative poetry: Homer's and Virgil's epics. Their basic strategy consisted of making the new poem appear to be no different than canonical models of heroic poetry. By the 1580s, "defenders" of the poem, such as Caburacci and Malatesta, no longer sought to accommodate Ariosto's practice to prior, established norms of poetic composition. As Giraldi had done before them, they assumed that the poem was exemplary in its own right, and they used that exemplarity to warrant whatever departure from ancient tradition they were advocating. Whereas the midcentury "legitimizers" distorted the *Furioso* to make it look similar to ancient models of heroic poetry, these later defenders distorted the poem by making it embody various characteristics that clearly postdated it. They were projecting back onto Ariosto's poem contemporary problems or issues—for example, the right to mix genres, or, more generally, the need to defy ancient generic norms—because the success and the status of Ariosto's poem could serve to authorize their modernist claims.

The earlier kind of legitimation did not cease to be practiced. Salviati's cumulative defense of the *Furioso* amply demonstrates that strategies of assimilating Ariosto's poem to ancient epic models continued to be employed. However, Salviati's technique of assimilation differed from that of predecessors such as Fornari and Pigna. He established the parity of the modern poem and the ancient epics by bringing the latter down from their sacred heights, by showing that these exemplary poems possessed the same objectionable features that supposedly disqualified the *Furioso* from the ranks of the epic. It could be argued that, in Salviati's wanting to demonstrate that there were no grounds for excluding Ariosto's poem from the epic tradition, his defense of the poem was as much a manifesto for the right of modern vernacular works to be part of the poetic canon as was the more aggressively anticlassicist manifesto expressed in Malatesta's *Della nuova poesia*.

It is evident that the general tendency in the 1580s was to make defenses of Ariosto's poem serve as manifestos on behalf of modern vernacular poetry in which Ariosto's poem comes itself to function as an authoritative model for whatever form of modernism was being advocated. Giraldi's *Discorso* on composing romances (1554) was, as I have said, the pioneering manifesto of this kind. But Giraldi's assertion that the *Furioso* was already canonical had been an act of faith (or was it simply bravura?), based as it was on less than two decades of the poem's good fortune. By the time defenders like Caburacci and Malatesta were similarly making the *Furioso* serve as the touchstone for their modernism, the poem had enjoyed extraordinary popularity for fifty years, its manifest influence on subsequent narrative poetry could now well justify the exemplary role assigned to it, it had become a linguistic as well as a poetic model, its international reputation was steadily growing—it had, in short, secured the classic status that Giraldi had bravely conferred upon it. Perhaps the most telling sign that it had achieved this status is manifested by what was occurring to Ariosto's poem in the treatises examined in this and the previous chapter: it was increasingly functioning as a model or a "site" upon which various and often conflicting poetic ideologies could be projected.

Chapter Eight

HARINGTON'S ENGLISH REFRACTIONS
OF *ORLANDO FURIOSO*

ITALIAN CLAIMS that the *Furioso* was a poem equal to the ancient epics were gradually propagated outside of Italy in the latter half of the sixteenth century. As in Italy, other European readers began to recognize the poem as a modern classic largely because publishers presented it to them as such. For example, by 1553, Hieronimo de Urrea's Spanish verse translation of the *Furioso* (first published in 1549) was issued by Gabriel Giolito in Venice in exactly the same format (including Dolce's commentary in Spanish) as his successful editions of the original. The several editions of this Spanish version of the poem that were republished over the next two decades in Lyon, in Barcelona, and again in Venice played an important role in making Spanish readers perceive Ariosto as the laureate, and the *Furioso* as the epic, of his age. In contrast, in the second half of the century, French readers who did not know Italian had to depend on an anonymous and crude prose translation first published in 1543; as a result they did not take the *Furioso* to be different from native or imported works of popular chivalric fiction (for example, the Spanish *Amadís*). It is true that in Lyon, by the 1550s, Guillaume Roville had begun publishing the *Furioso* in Italian, in editions exactly similar in format and content to Giolito's Venetian editions. Among French readers knowing Italian these elegant annotated editions may have helped to corroborate claims such as Du Bellay's that Ariosto's achievement was comparable to Homer's and Virgil's. But the absence of a proper verse translation, "packaged" like Giolito's Spanish edition, definitely delayed the French recognition of the *Furioso* as a modern epic.[1]

In England it was Sir John Harington who was chiefly responsible for making his countrymen recognize the *Furioso* as a heroic poem equal to the ancient ones. In fact, Harington's translation, originally published in London in 1591, is the last significant proclamation of the poem as a classic in the sixteenth century. In the "Briefe Apologie" that precedes his translation he begins his defense of the *Furioso* by likening it to the *Aeneid*, a poem, he writes, "[h]allowed and approved by all men . . . whome above all other it seemeth my author [that is, Ariosto] doth follow as appears by his beginning and ending."[2] Citing the opening and closing lines of both the *Aeneid* and *Orlando Furioso*, he proceeds to draw other parallels between them: "*Virgil* extolleth *Aeneas* to please *Augustus*, of whose race he was thought to come. *Ariosto* prayseth *Rogero* to the honour of the house of *Este*. *Aeneas* hath his *Dido* that retaineth him; *Rogero* hath his *Alcina*; finally, least I should note every part, there is nothing of any speciall observation in *Vergill* but my author hath with great felicitie imitated it, so as whosoever will alow *Vergill* must *ipso facto* (as they say) admit *Ariosto*" (p. 10). Harington's efforts to inscribe the *Furioso* in the epic tradition did not stop with these prefatory remarks. As I will show in this closing chapter, his entire presentation of the poem—his apology, his translation, and the elaborate commentary that accompanied it—sought to make the English recognize it as a modern classic.

Not only does Harington maintain that one can find in Ariosto "whatsoever is praiseworthy in Vergill," he goes on to argue that, in terms of religious value, Ariosto actually surpasses Virgil, ignorant as the latter was of Christian doctrine and wisdom. After citing examples of Christian piety and "places full of Christian exhortation" in the *Furioso*, Harington proposes that "in this point my author is to be preferred before all the auncient Poetes in which are mentioned so many false Gods and of them so many fowle deeds, their contentions, their adulteries, their incest as were both obscenous in recitall and hurtful in example" (p. 11).

These last claims recall the preface to the 1553 Valvassori edition of the *Furioso*, in which Clemente Valvassori argued that Ariosto's Christian epic carried none of the liabilities inherent in the pagan, polytheistic universe represented by the ancient poets. Like Harington, Valvassori had argued that in the *Furioso* one did not find "la moltitudine de'Dei, né la lor discordia, non gli adulteri, né gli scelerati lor congiungimenti [the multitude of gods, nor their quarrels and adulteries, nor their wicked love affairs]" depicted in ancient epics, and that the Christian morality embodied in the Italian poem made it a more edifying work.[3] As Harington proceeds with his defense of Ariosto, his argument becomes even more reminiscent of the Italian legitimation of the poem articulated forty years earlier, especially when he brings up and then counters the criticisms that were or might be leveled against the poem. Such resemblance is hardly accidental, since one of the main sources of his argument was the "Apologia brieve" with which Simone Fornari began his *Spositione sopra l'Orlando Furioso* (1549–1550).[4]

At the start of this study it was pointed out that Fornari's "Apologia" listed the various objections that were being raised against the poem in the late 1540s, the main one being that it lacked unity of action. Other complaints, showing a similar neo-Aristotelian bias, were that Ariosto spoke too much in his own voice, that the disposition of his work showed a total

lack of art, and that the marvelous events or acts in his poem exceeded the
limit of all truth. Fornari's defense of Ariosto consisted of a systematic
rebuttal of these various objections. For example, after reporting that
"molti biasimano il Poeta del raccontar cose troppo maravigliose, & tali
che par che eccedino il termine della verità [many blame the poet for pre-
senting things which are so marvelous that they seem to exceed the limit of
truth]," he maintained that, according to Aristotle, it is verisimilar to depict events that fall outside the verisimilar. Moreover, epic requires marvelous events to achieve its wondrous effects. Less Aristotelian was his argument that, in his capacity as an inventor, the poet is entitled to narrate
fictitious events. Fornari also argued that Ariosto's marvels did not go beyond what Christians find credible. He defended the account of Astolfo
changing leaves into ships and stones into horses on the grounds that Ariosto shows Astolfo "aiutato della divina gratia, che egli adombra sotto 'l
nome di Giovanni percioché comunemente si crede dal popolo Christiano i
Santi adoperare cose alla natura impossibili [assisted by the grace of God
that he figures under the name of [Saint] John, because Christians commonly believe that saints can do things impossible to nature]."[5]

Harington, whose defense of Ariosto also included a refutation of a number of the objections countered by Fornari, clearly derived much of his
argument from the Italian. For example, after acknowledging that "Aristotle and the best censurers of Poesie . . . hold that nothing should be
fayned utterly incredible," Harington asserts that "Ariosto neither in his
inchantments exceedeth credit . . . neither in the miracles that *Astolfo* by
the power of *S. John* is fayned to do, since the Church holdeth that Pro-
phetes both alive and dead have done mightie great miracles" (p. 12). Yet,
while Harington was ready to appropriate Fornari's argument about the
Christian credibility of supernatural events in the *Furioso*, he was not interested in Fornari's more "Aristotelian" counterclaims—for example, that,
to achieve its wondrous effects, epic required more marvelous incidents
than a genre such as tragedy. This already suggests what will become more
evident later, namely, that Harington was not concerned (as Fornari already was by the midcentury in Italy) that Ariosto's marvels failed to meet
neo-Aristotelian criteria of verisimilitude. He simply wanted to preempt
the condemnation of these marvels as sheer lies.

From Fornari's "Apologia" Harington learned that objections were
made about Ariosto's narrative technique. Before he brought up the complaint about the excessive use of the marvelous, Fornari mentioned that
Ariosto was reproached for speaking too much in his own voice. There are
critics, he wrote, who accuse "il nostro poeta come colui, ch'habbia fatto il
contrario de quello, che tanto loda in Homero Aristotile cioé che egli
pochissime cose racconta come da se, ma fa che altri le dica [our poet as one
who has done the opposite of what Aristotle so praises in Homer, namely,

that he tells the very fewest things in his own person, but has others tell them]."[6] Harington similarly reports that Ariosto's recurring habit of speaking in his own voice met with criticism. Actually, he points out that two "reproofs" were made about Ariosto's narrative technique: "One, that he breaks off narrations verie abruptly. . . . Another fault is that he speaketh so much in his own person by digression" (p. 13). Fornari's remarks above probably made Harington aware of the second "reproof," but it was not from the "Apologia" that he learned about the hostility to Ariosto's sudden interruptions, since Fornari makes no mention of it. There were, however, several other ways that information could have come to Harington. If he had access to Minturno's *Arte poetica* (1563)—and scholars have surmised that he did—he would have found in this treatise a critique of the disruptive breaks that characterize the narrative structure of chivalric romance and could have inferred from it that Minturno's objections were particularly aimed at Ariosto's sudden interruptions.[7] It has been argued, moreover, that Harington knew and borrowed from Malatesta's *Della nuova poesia o vero delle difese del "Furioso"* (1589). If he did know Malatesta's dialogue, then he would have noted that at the beginning of it one of the speakers lists the main complaints then being made about Ariosto's poem. Second only to the complaint that the poem's multiplicity of actions was confusing was the charge that the author shifted from one narrative strand to another too unexpectedly.[8]

Even without these sources Harington could have inferred that the sudden narrative shifts in the poem were annoying readers simply from the marginal notes Italian editors began to provide at those instances in the narrative when such shifts occurred. These notes, which indicated where the interrupted story was taken up again further on in the poem, were one of the several aids for readers included in the 1584 Franceschi edition of the *Furioso*, which Harington used as his Italian text.[9] In fact, Harington himself imitated this feature. "Where divers stories in this worke seeme in many places abruptly broken off I have set," as he explained in the "Advertisement to the Reader," "directions in the margent where to find the continuance of every such storie." Presumably he provided these directions to offset the dissatisfaction produced by Ariosto's sudden suspensions of his stories.

Harington could also have learned about the second "reproof" against Ariosto's narration, the complaint that Ariosto "speaketh so much in his person by digression," from sources other than Fornari's *Spositione*. As we saw earlier, Ariosto's narratorial intrusions met with increasing hostility after 1550, and Harington may have been aware of this neo-Aristotelian criticism. It is more likely, however, that he learned about these objections from a source he relied on quite extensively in his notes: Alberto Lavezuola's "Osservationi" on Ariosto's borrowings, which were appended to the 1584 Franceschi edition of the *Furioso*.[10] Lavezuola brings up the opposition provoked by Ariosto's narratorial intrusions at the beginning of cantos in his note about the *proemio* of canto 2. "Hanno biasimato alcuni l'Ariosto," he writes, "nell'usare nel principio de' canti alcune moralità, stimando che ciò non habbia a far nulla con la testura della favola, et che l'interompere l'ordine dell'opera con simili digressioni sia cosa disdicevole & vitiosa [Some have blamed Ariosto for making moral pronouncements at the beginning of cantos, deeming that these have nothing to do with the structure of the plot, and that to interrupt the narrative sequence with such digressions is wrong and inappropriate]." Lavezuola then defends Ariosto's practice by citing ancient precedents (in Claudian) for these *proemi*. He counters the claim that the breaks in continuity they produce are inappropriate with the following argument:

> Dico che non è huomo, che quando ha letto il corso d'un canto intero, non senta haner [sic] mestiero di qualche pausa & riposo, a guisa di colui, che havendo tracorso grande spatio di via, ne cerchi col posarsi alquanto di ripigliar fiato, per poter poi un'altra volta più vigorosamente indirizzarsi al suo viaggio.

> [I say that there is no man who, having read through an entire canto, does not feel a need for some pause and rest, like a person who has traversed a great length of road looks for a place to rest awhile and catch his breath so that he can resume his voyage once again more vigorously.]

Harington, too, not only reports the opposition to Ariosto's intrusive addresses to the reader at the beginning of cantos, he also defends these *proemi*, and his argument is strikingly similar to Lavezuola's. When, at the start of cantos, Harington argues, Ariosto digresses to address his audience, it is

> both delightfull and verie profitable and an excellent breathing space for the reader, and even as if a man walked in a faire long alley to have a seat or resting place here and there is easie and commodious, but if at the same seat were planted some excellent tree that not onely with the shade should keepe us from the heat but with some pleasant and right wholsom fruit should allay our thirst and comfort our stomacke, we would thinke it for the time a little paradice, so are Ariostos morals and pretie digressions sprinkled through his long worke to the no lesse pleasure then profit of the reader. (p. 13)

Harington's translation confirms this prefatory endorsement of authorial commentary at the start of cantos. In fact, at the beginning of some cantos, the translator even amplified some of Ariosto's addresses to the reader by adding views of his own. But if he had no misgivings about the *proemi*, Harington was clearly disturbed by some of the other narratorial intrusions, enough, as we shall see, either to omit or to alter them. He also significantly modified Ariosto's sudden interruptions, revealing thereby that, despite his defense of them in his preface, he too found these premature breaks disconcerting. One must not forget that, as a translator, Harington had one distinct advantage over the Italian defenders of the poem whose arguments he appropriated. They could only domesticate (in order to more easily legitimize) the poem by extratextual or, at best, paratextual means. Translation, on the other hand, allowed Harington to rewrite parts of the text that he found troubling or objectionable, and he took advantage of this license. In the pages that follow I will examine some of the ways in which his translation tamed the Italian poem so that it could more readily function as the conventionally didactic work he claimed it to be. I intend to dwell on Harington's alterations of Ariosto's narrative technique, especially his efforts to moderate the sudden interruptions within cantos that he found in the original. Before doing so, however, I will consider what effects the objections against Ariosto's excessive use of the fantastic may have had on Harington's translation.

Harington's basic way of preempting objections about the marvelous or fantastic episodes in the poem was paratextual: he ascribed to these episodes allegorical meanings which the reader could find in the notes provided after each canto (or "book," as he called it). Despite the attention that has been given Harington's allegorization of the *Furioso*, not enough distinction has been made between his moralization of the narrative (to be found under the rubric "Morall" that always heads his notes) and his allegorization of it (to be found under the rubric "Allegorie").[11] The "moral" readings, he explained in the course of drawing one from canto 25, aimed "to make speciall note of all the good matters by which the honest reader might take profitt." For the most part, these consisted of conventional precepts derived from the actions of the characters in the canto, in much the same manner that Italian editors of the *Furioso* extrapolated these precepts in the summary *allegorie* that they placed at the head of cantos. Not infrequently Harington derived his moralization of a particular canto from the "sententiae" that Ariosto himself provided in the *proemio* to the canto.[12] Unlike his moralizations, however, Harington's allegorizations are reserved exclusively for the fantastic events in the poem. As he explains in his "Advertisement to the Reader," the "Allegorie" is of "some things that are meerely fabulous, yet have an allegoricall sence which every bodie at the first shew cannot perceive." The cantos, therefore, that receive the most allegorical annotation (some have none) are those in which fabulous or marvelous events are described.

For example, the magician Atlante, his winged horse, and his enchanted castle are ascribed the following meanings (derived largely from Fornari's *Spositione*) in the "allegorie" appended to the fourth book:

Atlant by many of his gestures and actions here specified may signifie Cupid or that fond fancie that we call love; and whereas he takes up such brave captaines and souldiers as well as women and weakelings, it seemes consonant to that pretie fantasticke verse of Ovid:

> Militat omnis amans & habet sua castra Cupido.
> All lovers warriours are, and Cupid hath his campe.

. . . .

Atlant takes and imprisons those he takes. Love is as close and inextricable a prison as his. The wayes to *Atlants* castell are described to be craggie, headlong and unpleasant. Such be the wayes of that passion. The castell is said to be placed in the middle of a rockie mountaine cloven in sunder, by which is meant that this folly we speake of possesseth us and dwels in us most of all about the middle of our age. . . . (pp. 56–57)

And, to support this last claim, he cites the opening lines of Dante's *Inferno*.

Not all the allegories are so elaborate. Here, as another example, is the interpretation of the episode in canto 22 when Astolfo destroys Atlante's enchanted palace by means of the book he was given by the fairy Logistilla and the magical horn:

> *Astolfo*, that with the helpe of his booke dissolves the inchaunted pallace and with his horne drave away those that assaulted him and put him in great daunger, signifieth allegorically (as I have in part touched before) how wisdome with the helpe of eloquence discovereth the craftiest and tameth the wildest. (p. 249)

As this and the earlier example sufficiently illustrate, *allegoresis* permits Harington to rationalize and domesticate the fantastic so that what is "meerely fabulous" at the literal level becomes credible at the allegorical level. This procedure obviously serves to justify the poem's fabulous impossibilities, but the objections it aims to counter are not complaints that Ariosto's marvels defy neo-Aristotelian notions of verisimilitude (see note 18). Instead, Harington's allegorizations reflect a more basic concern that, if taken as such, the fabulous elements in Ariosto's poem will confirm the accusation that poetry is a nurse of lies. To warrant the poet's license to describe literal impossibilities, Harington shows that these are invented and put in the poem to signify important moral truths. His allegorizations also serve to show that Ariosto's marvels are not there merely to excite or amuse readers but to edify them.

Because *allegoresis* enabled Harington to justify the "meerely fabulous" episodes of the poem, he did not have to tamper much with the fantastic events he found there. He did, however, modify Ariosto's presentation of these events, especially when the Italian poet treated these events too play-fully. One can well understand the translator's interventions. Given that Harington warranted the fantastic episodes by the allegorical meanings he imposed on them, he had to make sure that the presentation of these episodes did not undermine or render problematic their allegorization.

Not surprisingly, therefore, he regularly suppresses Ariosto's habit of calling attention to the fictionality of his more fanciful tales. Consider, for example, the first description of the Hippogryph as it flies through the sky carrying an armed rider and is observed by Bradamante, an innkeeper, and his attendants (at the beginning of canto 4). Bradamante has been busy keeping a close watch on the crafty Brunello when a great commotion distracts them:

> Ecco all'orecchie un gran rumor lor viene.
> Disse la donna:—O gloriosa Madre,
> O Re del ciel, che cosa sarà questa?—
> E dove era il rumor si trovò presta.
>
> E vede l'oste e tutta la famiglia,
> e chi a finestre e chi fuor ne la via,
> tener levati al ciel gli occhi e le ciglia,
> come l'eclisse o la cometa sia.
> Vede la donna un'alta maraviglia,
> che di leggier creduta non saria:
> vede passar un gran destriero alato,
> che porta in aria un cavalliero armato.
>
> Grandi eran l'ale e di color diverso,
> e vi sedea nel mezzo un cavalliero,
> di ferro armato luminoso e terso;
> e ver ponente avea dritto il sentiero.
> Calossi, e fu tra le montagne immerso:
> e, come dicea l'oste (e dicea il vero),
> quel era un negromante, e facea spesso
> quel varco, or più da lungi, or più da presso.

(4.3–5)

The context of the "low mimesis" of inn life makes the appearance of a winged horse flying through the sky seem even more fantastic than it would be were it to occur in the remote setting of the previous canto. In addition, the innkeeper's claim that the magician's flights occur regularly—and the narrator's intervening confirmation ("e dicea il vero")—rather than reassuring us about the veracity of the event, makes us even more aware of its improbability. When Harington comes to the episode, he not only compresses it, he omits the original fifth octave altogether:

Now while these two did to confer begin,
She to his fingers having still an eye,
The host and other servants of the Inne
Came on the sodaine with a wofull crie,
And some did gaze without and some within
(As when men see a Comet in the skie):
The cause of this their wondring and their crying
Was that they saw an armed horseman flying,

And straight by th'host and others they were told
How one that had in Magike art great skill
Not far from thence had made a stately hold
Of shining steele and plast it on a hill
To which he bringeth Ladies young and old
And men and maids according to his will,
And when within that castl they have bene
They never after have bene heard or seene.

                                                    (4.3–4)

Ariosto's description of the Hippogryph is left out, as are the remarks by
the innkeeper and the narratorial interjection. In short, by reducing the
fantastic event to a couple of lines ("The cause of this their wondring . . .
Was that they saw an armed horseman flying") Harington removes all
traces of Ariosto's playful and ironic manner of making the surreal appearance of the Hippogryph and its rider seem an almost quotidian event. He
alters the original in this way whenever a passage similarly collocates fantastic occurrences with daily reality in a facetious manner.[13]

Harington would not, of course, object if Ariosto actually meant to
make his marvels seem less unreal. On several occasions when Ariosto facetiously makes his more fantastic creations appear to be part of this world,
Harington translates the text quite literally but removes the ironic or
tongue-in-cheek tone of the original. Harington's efforts to make other
marvelous events or figures in the poem gain more credibility reinforces
the impression that when he translates Ariosto's truth claims, he makes
them quite unironic. Sometimes he tries to lend credibility to fantastic
events by arguing in the notes that such events are not "meerely fabulous"
(and therefore will not require allegorical interpretation), but were held as
true either in the past or in popular opinion.[14]

At other times he will invoke Turpin, mistakenly believed to be the original chronicler of Carolingian *gesta*, to authenticate the historicity of some
extraordinary event. Ariosto, to be sure, also uses the *topos* of invoking
Turpino to warrant the more fantastic occurrences in his poem, but (as
Boiardo had already done earlier) he does so in jest, and almost always as a
ploy that makes the occurrences being authenticated appear all the more
fictive. Harington, on the other hand, translates these references to Turpin

quite earnestly, wrongly assuming, as Fornari did as well, that they were invoked as genuine truth claims.[15]

The earnest renditions of Ariosto's appeals to Turpin as well as his other mock authentications are part of Harington's overall effort to rationalize and make less patently fictive the fantastic events in the *Furioso*. It has been shown that overtly fabulous episodes like Ruggiero's adventures on Alcina's island and Astolfo's voyage to the moon are modified by Harington and accompanied by marginal explanations in order to make them less strange and otherworldly. Such changes reflect the translator's desire to lessen the distance between the world of the Elizabethan reader and the fictive universe of the *Furioso*.[16] It is no wonder, then, that Harington suppressed Ariosto's flaunting of the fictiveness of his poem: such self-consciousness could only serve to detach the reader and so work against the translator's efforts to make the poem's fictions more assimilable.

Consider, as an example of Harington's interference, the description of Ruggiero's fierce combat with the Orca when he rescues Angelica from the jaws of the monster at the end of canto 10. The original episode imitates Ovid's account of Perseus's rescue of Andromeda in the *Metamorphoses* (4.663–764). Ariosto even recalls that when Ovid described Perseus's struggle with the monster he pointed to a logistic difficulty besetting the hero: namely, his fear that his winged feet will not allow him to stay airborne, so drenched have they become from the monster's spray (see *Metamorphoses* 4.730). In his account of the awesome encounter between Ruggiero on the Hippogryph and the sea monster, Ariosto develops the problem of waterlogged wings to more comic proportions:

> Sì forte ella nel mar batte la coda,
> che fa vicino al ciel l'acqua inalzare;
> tal che non sa se l'ale in aria snoda,
> o pur se 'l suo destrier nuota nel mare.
> Gli è spesso che disia trovarsi a proda;
> che se lo sprazzo in tal modo ha a durare,
> teme sì l'ale inaffi all'ippogrifo,
> che brami invano avere o zucca o schifo.

(10.106)

[So powerfully did the orc thrash the water with its tail that the seas surged up to the skies, and Ruggiero could not tell whether his mount was beating the air with its wings or swimming in the waves. Many times he wished himself safely on dry land, fearing that if the Hippogryph continued having to endure the flying spray, his wings would be so sodden that he would vainly wish for something floatable, be it only a cockle-shell.]

By shifting from the hyperbolic description of the monster splashing heaven to Ruggiero's very pressing concern about a drenching his winged steed cannot withstand, the narrator succeeds in detaching us sufficiently from the epic struggle to make us smile. Harington omitted the entire stanza in his version of the struggle (see his translation at 10.90–92). He did so because he realized that bringing up such a rational consideration on Ruggiero's part would not only serve to detach his readers, but also make them too aware of how utterly fantastic the entire episode was. By repeated modifications of this sort he diminished the distancing effects that Ariosto intended to produce, effects that jeopardized the transference Harington wanted readers to make between the events in the poem, however marvelous, and their own lives.[17]

There are indications that the neo-Aristotelian critics in Italy who objected to the marvels in Ariosto's poem also dismissed the rationalization that these incredible fantasies served as vehicles of allegorical meaning. For example, in his "Discorso contro l'Ariosto," Filippo Sassetti maintained that impossible creatures like the Hippogryph or incredible exploits like Astolfo's capturing of the South Wind in a wineskin could not be justified on the grounds that they have allegorical meaning: "scusare non si può con il campo larghissimo della Allegoria."[18] The new Aristotelians were dubious about the viability of *allegoresis* as a method of interpreting poetry in any case, but it is possible that Sassetti and others were even more disposed to deny the allegorical intention of Ariosto's fantasies as a result of his self-conscious and facetious presentation of them. Whether or not Harington was aware of these critics' doubts, he perceived how Ariosto's playful treatment of the marvelous could undermine his claims about the allegorical intentions of the poem. He took the one preventive measure he could exercise as a translator: he removed from Ariosto's account of the fantastic its original humor and irony.

The narrative discontinuity of the poem also disturbed him considerably, despite his prefatory defense of Ariosto's interruptions. As I mentioned earlier, the first telling sign of Harington's preoccupation is that, in imitation of the 1584 Franceschi edition, his text carried marginal notations indicating, at those places within cantos where a plot line is suspended, where later in the poem the reader can find the same plot line continued. These paratextual aids had already begun to appear in midcentury Venetian editions (starting with the Valgrisi edition of 1556), presumably in response to the dissatisfaction provoked by Ariosto's premature breaks. Readers, one assumes, who found the interruptions frustrating or yearned for more continuity than Ariosto had intended could, with the help of these indices, skip the intervening narrative and go straight to the sequel. Harington was well aware that, while these marginal directions served to alleviate the poem's discontinuity, they could also encourage too much skipping. In his "Advertisement to the Reader" he writes that "where divers stories in this worke seeme in many places abruptly broken off I have set directions in the margent where to find the continuance of every such storie, though I would not wish any to read them in that order at the first reading." His respect for the poem's integrity notwithstanding, Harington took other measures to reduce the dissatisfaction produced by its discontinuities. These interventions were not paratextual, however, but are to be found in the actual translation of Ariosto's text.

Sudden interruptions regularly occur in the *Furioso* at the end of cantos as well as within them when one plot line is abandoned for another. We observed, two chapters ago, that one of Ariosto's favorite ploys is to defy the expectation of closure at the end of a canto by terminating it in the midst or at the start of a dramatic action. He often does this to prompt his unrequited reader to go on to the next canto, where, after a preliminary authorial comment, the narrative previously cut off is resumed. Harington is not so unfaithful as to reduce the suspenseful effects at canto ends altogether. But when such closures occur too abruptly, he attenuates this suddenness and the dissatisfaction it may produce.

Consider, as an example, the memorable end of canto 10. Having just rescued the naked Angelica from the Orca, Ruggiero is carrying her off on the Hippogryph when, suddenly overwhelmed by sexual desire, he alights in a meadow; while he frantically tries to remove his armor in order to ravish the girl, the canto is brought to a sudden halt. The last three octaves of the canto, in the original and in the translation, read as follows:

> Non più tenne la via, come propose
> prima, di circundar tutta la Spagna;
> ma nel propinquo lito il destrier pose,
> dove entra in mar più la minor Bretagna.
> Sul lito un bosco era di querce ombrose,
> dove ognor parche Filomena piagna;
> ch'in mezzo avea un pratel con una fonte,
> e quinci e quindi un solitario monte.
>
> Quivi il bramoso cavalier ritenne
> l'audace corso, e nel pratel discese;
> e fe' raccorre al suo destrier le penne,
> ma non a tal che più le avea distese.
> Del destrier sceso, a pena si ritenne
> di salir altri; ma tennel l'arnese:
> l'arnese il tenne, che bisognò trarre,
> e contra il suo disir messe le sbarre.
>
> Frettoloso, or da questo or da quel canto
> confusamente l'arme si levava.
> Non gli parve altra volta mai star tanto;

che s'un laccio sciogliea, dui n'annodava.
Ma troppo e lungo ormai, Signor, il canto,
e forse ch'anco l'ascoltar vi grava:
si ch'io differirò l'istoria mia
in altro tempo che più grata sia.

(10.113–15)

He leaves his Spanish journey first assignd
And unto litle Brittain doth repaire,
But by the way be sure he did not misse
To give her many a sweet and friendly kisse,

And having found a solitarie place,
A pleasant grove well waterd with a spring
Where never herd nor herdsman did deface,
Where *Philomela* used still to sing,
Here he allights, minding to stay a space,
And hither he the Ladie faire did bring,
But sure it seemd he made his full account
Er long upon a better beast to mount.

His armour made him yet a while to byde,
Which forced stay a more desire did breed,
But now in him it was most truly tryde,
Oftimes the greater hast the worse the speed.
He knits with hast two knots while one untyde,
But soft, tis best no furder to proceede.
I now cut off abruptly here my rime
And keepe my tale unto another time.

(10.95–97)

Harington's version slows down the tempo of the original narration by altering the rapidly accelerating account of Ruggiero's efforts to alight, dismount, and unbuckle in order to ravish the girl. The action of Ariosto's octave 114 is not only compressed into the second half of Harington's stanza 96. Instead of dwelling on Ruggiero's frustrated unbuckling, which, in the original, carries over to the last octave and serves to build up suspense, Harington prolongs the stop in the meadow and brings the octave to a more pronounced close as he describes Ruggiero's mounting sexual desire. The pause, in the English version, between 96 and 97 reduces the tension and involvement Ariosto seeks to produce by providing no such pause. In the last octave Harington tries to defer the break rather than letting it occur right in the middle. And after the interruption, instead of translating the narrator's ironic comment about the excessive length of the canto, Harington explicitly declares, "I now will cut off abruptly here my rime," in the hope, it would seem, that such a forewarning will somehow placate the reader. This heavy-handed, almost apologetic declaration reflects the translator's misgivings about Ariosto's intent to leave the reader as unrequited as Ruggiero.

Harington's modifications of narrative breaks within cantos are generally more pronounced than his alterations of canto ends. It will be recalled that in the course of each canto the narrator constantly has to abandon one strand of the narrative and resume the progress of another in order to advance more or less simultaneously the separate strands of the *Furioso*'s multiple plot. But, as Harington himself acknowledged, when Ariosto makes these shifts he tends to interrupt his narrative abruptly, and always, one might add, when he is sure the reader is captivated by the action taking place. His defense of these transitions notwithstanding, Harington clearly felt that they did not have to be as abrupt and aggravating as Ariosto made them. Take, as a first example, the sudden break that occurs near the beginning of canto 11 after Angelica, thanks to the magic ring, has escaped Ruggiero's sexual assault. The abandoned Ruggiero is eventually distracted by the noise of a duel between a giant and a knight. As he watches the giant overcome the knight, he recognizes that the victim is none other than Bradamante (she turns out to be a fabricated double of his beloved), whereupon he rushes to assist her. The giant seizes Bradamante, slings her over his shoulder, and runs away, furiously pursued by Ruggiero.

> e se l'arreca in spalla, e via la porta,
> come lupo talor piccolo agnello,
> o l'aquila portar ne l'ugna torta
> suole o colombo o simile altro augello.
> Vede Ruggier quanto il suo aiuto importa,
> e vien correndo a più poter; ma quello
> con tanta fretta i lunghi passi mena,
> che con gli occhi Ruggier lo segue a pena.
>
> (11.20)

In the next octave, just as the chase reaches a crescendo, the narrator interrupts it abruptly and shifts to Orlando's adventures, left in abeyance for more than a canto.

> Così correndo l'uno, e seguitando
> l'altro, per un sentiero ombroso e fosco,
> che sempre si venia più dilatando,
> in un gran prato uscir fuor di quel bosco.
> Non più di questo; ch'io ritorno a Orlando,
>
> . . . .
>
> (11.21)

Harington's translation is as follows:

> So have I seene a wolfe to beare away
> A lambe from shepherds fold; so have I seene
> An Egle on a silly Dove to pray
> And oare aloft the skie and earth betweene.
> *Rogero* hies him after as he may
> Untill he came unto a goodly greene,
> But th'other ev'rie step so much out stept him
> That in his view *Rogero* scantly kept him;
>
> But now a while of him I speake no more,
> And to *Orlando* I returne againe
>
> .   .   .   .

(11.18–19)

Harington not only abbreviates the action; he also slows down its accelerating tempo. He does this chiefly by containing the giant's hasty departure and Ruggiero's pursuit within the bounds of separate octaves rather than letting the action spill over without pauses from one octave to the next, as in the original. Harington also avoids (and this is a characteristic change) making the transition in midoctave—Ariosto's usual strategy—but rather lets the pause between octaves 18 and 19 serve to diminish the abruptness of the break. One also notes that the translator omits the entire first half of octave 21. Instead, he interrupts the pursuit at the moment when the giant virtually disappears from view—a moment that makes the break more acceptable to the reader than if it were to occur in the middle of the next phase of the chase, which is when Ariosto chose to interrupt it. Overall, one can see that to cushion the suddenness of the interruption, Harington rearranges the text so that both the form and the content of the narrative make the break appear less untimely and therefore less dissatisfying. And, as usual, he also provides a marginal indication for the reader who may want to continue with Ruggiero's chase rather than shift to Orlando's adventures as the original text demands.

Ariosto was occasionally obliged to suspend a segment of his narrative because its sequel depended on developments still to be unraveled in other strands of the plot. However, he did not have to suspend his narrative at the untimely moments he chose if he did not deliberately seek to frustrate his readers. That this was indeed his aim becomes apparent in instances when the narrative shifts do not turn out to be necessary (even for the sake of variety) but seem to take place simply to deprive the reader of continuity. The best examples of these seemingly gratuitous interruptions are to be found in cantos 16 to 18, where the narrator oscillates between the military conflict in and around Paris and the Middle Eastern adventures of Grifone and other knights. In the course of these cantos the reader comes to feel that there is no reason for the recurring suspension of the epic struggle between the Saracens and the Christians. This momentous action does not have to await developments in other strands of the plot in order to be continued. It is simply and steadily interrupted by the separate goings-on in Damascus. Ariosto's shifting back and forth between these two narratives allows him, as a result, to make some of his most perverse interruptions.

Consider the first segment of canto 17, which, after describing Rodomonte's single-handed devastation of Paris and its inhabitants, focuses on Charlemagne's efforts to rally together his knights and overcome this Saracen invader. After haranguing his retainers to display their former courage, he leads the charge against Rodomonte, but at the very moment at which he and his knights close in to strike the pagan warrior, the action is abruptly cut off as the narrator shifts back to Grifone's arrival at Damascus:

> Al fin de le parole urta il destriero,
> conl'asta bassa, al Saracino adosso.
> Mossesi a un tratto il paladino Ugiero,
> a un tempo Namo e Ulivier si è mosso,
> Avino, Avolio, Otone e Berlingiero,
> ch'un senza l'altro mai veder non posso:
> e ferir tutti sopra a Rodomonte
> e nel petto e nei fianchi e ne la fronte.
>
> Ma lasciamo, per Dio, Signore, ormai
> di parlar d'ira e di cantar di morte;
> e sia per questa volta detto assai
> del Saracin non men crudel che forte:
> che tempo è ritornar dov'io lasciai
> Grifon, ...
>
> (17.16–17)

Before Harington comes to this shift, he omits most of the preceding octaves that described Rodomonte's onslaught inside Paris and thereby diminishes the sense of urgency that prompts the old emperor's call for a counterattack. In the original, Charlemagne's oration rouses forth a number of knights (individually named) who join their leader in the charge, suspended just as they are about to strike Rodomonte. Harington tries to make the break less abrupt by having it occur after the clash has occurred, which he does by having Charlemagne charge and strike the Saracen alone right after his speech, ending the octave, and then having the other knights (who are not named) join in the assault:

> . . . .
> No death can make a princely heart to quaile,
> And with that word with couched spear in rest
> He runnes and smites the Pagan on the brest,

> And straight the other of the chosen crew
> On ev'rie side the Pagan do beset;

Then, before abandoning the confrontation, he feels that he has to relieve the suspense of Ariosto's break by revealing the outcome of the momentous encounter:

> But how he scapt and what did then ensew
> Another time ile tell, but not as yet;
>
> (17.10–11)

Needless to say, in the original interruption the reader's frustration is not alleviated by this disclosure of Rodomonte's escape.

Nearly a canto later, the narrator does return to Rodomonte to describe his forced exit from Paris. He then devotes twenty octaves to the massive battle raging around the city, eventually focusing on the outstanding feats of the young Saracen prince Dardinello (18.47ff.). One of Ariosto's memorable interruptions occurs just as Dardinello's victorious *aristeia* reaches its crescendo at 18.57–59. Dardinello has just slain Lurcanio, and his brother Ariodante, trying to seek revenge, is described cutting his way through the Moorish ranks in vain pursuit of Dardinello:

> Urta, apre, caccia, atterra, taglia e fende
> qualunque lo 'mpedisce o gli contrasta.
> E Dardinel che quel disire intende,
> a volerlo saziar già non sovrasta:
> ma la gran moltitudine contende
> con questo ancora, e i suoi disegni guasta.
> Se' Mori uccide l'un, l'altro non manco
> gli Scotti uccide e il campo inglese e 'l franco.

The two fail to meet, but Dardinello encounters the more formidable Rinaldo, and just as their fateful duel is about to begin, Ariosto defers the tragic pathos of Dardinello's untimely death and shatters our involvement with the young prince by gratuitously suspending the action to resume Grifone's adventures in Damascus:

> Fortuna sempremai la via lor tolse,
> che per tutto quel dì non s'accozzaro.
> A più famosa man serbar l'un volse;
> che l'uomo il suo destin fugge di raro.
> Ecco Rinaldo a questa strada volse,
> perch'alla vita d'un non sia riparo:
> ecco Rinaldo vien: Fortuna il guida
> per dargli onor che Dardinello uccida.

> Ma sia per questa volta detto assai
> dei gloriosi fatti di Ponente.
> Tempo è ch'io torni ove Grifon lasciai,
> che tutto d'ira e di disdegno ardente
> facea, con più timor ch'avesse mai,
> tumultuar la sbigottita gente.
>
> . . . .

(18.58–59)

Now consider Harington's translation:

> But *Ariodant* (that deare his brother loved)
> And sees him in such paine and daunger lye
> Was therewithall in wrath so greatly moved
> He meaneth to avenge his hurt or dye;
> But though that he attempted oft and proved,
> Yet could he not to *Dardanell* come nye.
> For still of other men the throng and number
> Did him in this attempt molest and cumber.
>
> No doubt the heav'ns had *Dardanell* ordained
> To perish by a more victorious hand;
> *Renaldos* blade must with his blood be stained
> And was, as after you shall understand.
> By him this praise and glorie must be gained,
> The fame whereof must fill both sea and land;
> But let these westerne warres a while remaine,
> And of *Griffino* talke we now againe.

It followes
in this booke
68st.

(18.23–24)

Already the different stanza numbers reveal how many octaves Harington has omitted. His drastic cutting includes most of Dardinello's *aristeia* (oct. 47–55 in the Italian) so that much of the involvement with Dardinello and the dramatic buildup experienced in the original are not to be found in Harington's version. By not giving the reader the chance to become as fully engrossed in Dardinello's exploits, the translator can interrupt them without producing as much of a sense of deprivation as he found in the original text. Moreover, Harington reduces the suspense and tension he found at the break by previewing much more explicitly than did Ariosto Rinaldo's forthcoming killing of Dardinello. Other modifications—making the shift coincide with the end of the stanza rather than having it occur in the course of the next octave; the marginal indication of where to find the sequel—are changes, we have seen, that he regularly makes when he translates Ariosto's narrative breaks. Overall Harington so diminishes the abruptness and frustration produced by the original break at 18.59 that his

English reader remains virtually undisengaged from the narrative, despite the shift from one plot line to another. This final example illustrates more vividly than the others that it was not discontinuity as such that disturbed Harington but rather the disengagement from the narrative that Ariosto's sudden shifts produced. And, as we shall soon see, in his efforts to remove Ariosto's distancing effects the translator tampered with more than the poem's interruptions.

Whereas Ariosto's interruptions within cantos unsettled him enough to cause him to rewrite them, Harington did not similarly modify the *proemi* at the beginnings of cantos, even though he knew that these narratorial addresses were deemed disruptive and inept by some Italian critics. The *proemi*, it will be recalled, were often the narrator's moral reflections on actions of the previous canto or on an episode about to be told. Harington obviously found such reflections worth preserving since they reinforced his own interpretations (in the "moral" section of his notes) of each canto's ethical pertinence. In fact, as we observed earlier, a number of his moralizations of individual cantos begin by reiterating or developing *sententiae* originally voiced in the *proemi* of these cantos.[19] Such elaboration of the *proemi* in the "Morals" that he appended to the cantos confirms how valuable he found them and that he meant what he said in the preface when he praised Ariosto's narratorial comments at the beginnings of cantos for the "rests" and the wisdom they provided. That they broke up the continuity of the narrative from one canto to another does not seem to have bothered him.

He was less appreciative, however, of the narratorial intrusions and asides that he found within the cantos. Of course, Harington was aware that shifts from one plot line to another had to be announced by the narrator. And even though he omitted or modified the remarks that Ariosto specifically addressed to his patron Ippolito d'Este, he rendered quite faithfully the announcements that regularly accompanied the transitions in the narrative:

> Now was *Rogero* mounted up so hie
> He seemd to be a mote or little pricke,
>
> . . . .
> But let him on his way, God speed him well,
> For of *Renaldo* somwhat I must tell.

(4.38)

> But here a while I cease of her to treat
> Or *Sacrapant* or of the knight of Spayne.
> First I must tell of many a hardie feat
> Before I can returne to them agayne.

(12.51)

He was also careful to include certain comments at the moments of transition: for example, when the narrator explains that the need or the pleasure of *varietà* motivates his frequent plot shifts (see, for example, 8.29).

The narratorial comments that bothered him and that he systematically altered were Ariosto's flippant or tongue-in-cheek asides. On several occasions Ariosto playfully exposes the artifice of his fiction as he shifts from one character's adventures to another. A notable instance is to be found at the start of canto 15 when the narrator suspends his account of the siege of Paris to resume the story of Astolfo. The shift comes right after he begins to list the various Christian knights and leaders that have rallied to Charlemagne's side to oppose the besieging Saracens:

> gente infinita poi di minor conto,
> de' Franchi, de' Tedeschi e de' Lombardi;
> presente il suo signor, ciascuno pronto
> a farsi riputar fra i più gagliardi.
> Di questo altrove io vo' rendervi conto;
> ch'ad un gran duca è forza ch'io riguardi;
> il qual mi grida, e di lontano accenna,
> e priega ch'io nol lasci ne la penna.
>
> (15.9)

The narrator's witty notion of being beckoned by a neglected character yearning to be reinscribed in the text serves to advertise the fictional status of Ariosto's characters as well as the ultimate control of the author over his poetic creation. Harington clearly found such wit problematic, since he removed the image of Astolfo clamoring for attention when he came to this transition and, instead, simply reminds the reader of the English knight's former metamorphosis into a tree (the shift, as usual, is made not in the middle but at the beginning of the octave):

> But here I cease untill another time
> To tell of these assaults the hard successe,
> Of damage like to both sides: now my rime
> Unto the English Duke I must addresse,
> *Astolfo* sonne of *Oton* whom somtime
> *Alcyna* switchcraft held in great distresse,
> Who like another *Cyrce* men transformed
> To trees, to beasts, and foules of shapes deformed.
>
> (15.6)

Even when Harington translates one of these witty transitions more faithfully, he leaves out the details that highlight, if only momentarily, the fictionality of Ariosto's construct. Consider the shift, in canto 41, from the decisive battle about to take place at Lipadusa to Ruggiero, who had been last reported swimming for his life after being thrown overboard in a storm:

> Nel biancheggiar de la nuova alba armati,
> e in un momento fur tutti a cavallo.
> Pochi sermon si son tra lor usati:
> non vi fu indugio, non vi fu intervallo,
> che i ferri de le lancie hanno abbassati.
> Ma mi parria, Signor, far troppo fallo,
> se, per voler di costor dir, lasciassi
> tanto Ruggier nel mar, che v'affogassi.
>
> Il giovinetto con piedi e con lancia
> percotendo venia l'orribil onde.
>
> . . . .
>
>   (41.46–47)

Despite Harington's usual omission of Ippolito d'Este as the addressee, his rendering is not completely unfaithful:

> Thus parted they and rested all that night,
> But readie they were all by breake of day,
> All armd and readie for the future fight.
> Small speech was usd, no lingring nor no stay.
> They couch their speares and run with all their might,
> But while I tell you of this bloodie fray
> I doubt I do unto *Rogero* wrong
> To leave him swimming in the sea so long.
>
> The gallant youth had labourd manie an howre
> To swim and save him selfe from being drownd.
>
>   (41.46–47)

Yet by leaving out Ariosto's final witty "che v'affogassi" and going on to explain that Ruggiero had been struggling "manie an howre" Harington tries to sustain the illusion of Ruggiero's dramatic plight as he returns to it. Ariosto, in contrast, flippantly suggests that if he does not return to his chief protagonist, Ruggiero will drown—and that simply can not happen, because he needs him to conclude his poem. As a result, Ariosto advertises, if only momentarily, that his poem and its characters are a fictive construct, quite separate from actuality and quite securely in his control. Harington's changes suffice to make the narrative transition occur more smoothly, or at least without this abrupt laying bare of the artifice.

Harington alters Ariosto's narratorial intrusions for the same reasons that he modifies the Italian poet's playful treatment of the fantastic: to remove all the signals the narrator provides of the poem's fictional autonomy. Actually, this is true of all of Harington's refractions of the Italian text examined in this chapter. One can see that Ariosto's abrupt interruptions also disturbed Harington because they, too, serve to expose the poem as a fictional construct manipulated at the author's will. The narrative shifts and interruptions would not have bothered Harington had they been less sudden and did not so often disengage the reader from the narrative. Eventually, as Harington must have recognized, most readers become habituated enough that they no longer feel frustrated by the sudden breaks of continuity but meet them with more amused detachment, having learned to anticipate the likelihood of being left unsatisfied. Harington, I contend, did not want his readers to acquire such detachment or, as a result, to become aware that the fictive illusion that had so absorbed them was mere illusion. Ultimately it was the distancing effects of Ariosto's sudden shifts that he sought to remove, just as he changed the narratorial interventions to preempt the amused detachment they originally produced.

At one point in his commentary Harington explains that the point of it was "to make speciall note of all the good matters [in the poem] by which the honest reader might take profit" (p. 286)—a didactic aim fulfilled primarily by the moralizations that headed his notes to each canto. From canto 8, for example, he proposed that readers could derive the following maxims:

> In the hard adventures of *Angelica* we may note how perilous a thing beautie is if it be not especially garded with the grace of God and with vertue of the mynde, being continually assayld with enemies spirituall and temporall. In *Orlandos* dreame we may see how unquiet thoughtes are bred in the myndes of those that are geven over to the passion of love or ambicion or whatsoever else may be understood by *Angelica*. Lastly in that *Orlando* abandons his prince and country in their greatest extremitie we may observe the uncomely and carelesse actes that dishonest or unordinat love do provoke even the noblest onto if once they get harbour in their myndes and be not overruled with reason and grace. (p. 99)

So, after commenting on Ariosto's own moral observations at the beginning of canto 15, Harington finds these lessons to be gained from the rest of the canto:

> In *Charles* is to be noted the providence of a wise and valiant prince; In *Astolfo* that by the power of his horne ridds the country of theeves and malefactors we may learne to apply the talents are given us to good uses; In *Griffin* that after all his devotions at Jerusalem comes again to *Origilla* we may note the frailtie of flesh and withall that outward holynesse without inward zeal availeth nothing. (p. 174)

In extrapolating such conventional precepts from the actions of the principal characters in each canto Harington was following a tradition that began in the 1540s when Dolce and other Italian commentators began to head

Ariosto's cantos with summary *allegorie*. Clearly, one purpose of these sober readings was to affirm that serious morality underlay the deceptively comic surface of the text. Examining Harington's moralizations, a modern reader is struck not simply by their disregard of the comic surface but by their indifference to the surface of the text altogether. As examples of a proper reading of the poem, they reveal that the translator wanted his readers to move through the *litera* to the more general moral truths they supposedly signified. It was not that the interpretations were to be unconnected to the literal contents of the narrative. One can see that Harington moralizes actions and issues that do occur in Ariosto's cantos. Yet, in order to reduce these actions to assimilable—that is to say, conventional—precepts, their superficial idiosyncrasies had to be most rapidly laid aside.

Harington's exegesis served to reveal the poem's function as an ethical instrument, and his moralizations indicated what, ideally, the reader was to do independently: apply the lessons of the fiction to his or her own comportment and "to the amendment of the same" (p. 17). Harington was, nonetheless, an intelligent enough reader of the *Furioso* to perceive that in many instances Ariosto sought to distinguish his fiction from actuality by flaunting in various ways the fictionality, the artifice, and the surface of his verbal creation. Do not virtually all the passages of the original poem examined in this chapter serve, in their own ways, to advertise the autonomy of Ariosto's fiction, its separateness from actuality? Harington had to alter these passages in the manner that he did because he realized that they impeded and occasionally even jeopardized the moral transfer his readers were to make from the fiction to their lives.

From its beginning in the 1540s, the process of legitimizing the *Furioso* entailed taming its idiosyncrasies. The midcentury Italian commentators who initiated that process had to do this, as we have seen, by devising paratexts that reduced the poem's "strange," equivocal, or otherwise problematic aspects and that thereby made the work more assimilable. Harington followed their example by providing, along with his translation, a commentary which also served, overall, to domesticate the poem and stabilize (usually by reducing) its equivocal meanings. But Harington also exploited the opportunity he had as a translator to redress some of the poem's formal idiosyncrasies. Like prior sixteenth-century readers, he was disturbed by Ariosto's jarring interruptions. So, as part of his normalization of the poem, he made these breaks less jarring. Certain aspects of the *Furioso* that had dismayed or offended earlier Italian readers clearly did not disturb Harington. For instance, he did not share the Italian Aristotelians' view that the poem's lack of plot unity violated fundamental norms of poetic art. Nor, defensive though he was about the poem's fantastic episodes, did he try to excise or abbreviate them. His main concern was that the poem operate as the exemplary and formative text he assumed a proper heroic poem had to be. The poet's art, as Sir Philip Sidney had written a decade before Harington's translation appeared, was "not wholly imaginative, as we are wont to say by them that build castles in the air: but so far substantially it worketh, not only to make a Cyrus . . . but to bestow a Cyrus upon the world to make many Cyruses, if they will learn aright why and how that maker made him."[20] Harington similarly believed that the examples formed by the heroic poet, once decoded by the reader, exerted an immediate educative influence upon that reader. And, having proclaimed that the *Furioso* was as morally edifying as the *Aeneid*, he had to make sure that nothing in the Italian fiction jeopardized its supposed educative function. The main idiosyncracy he had to redress was Ariosto's tendency to flaunt the separateness of his fiction from life. That is why he suppressed, as we saw, the various means Ariosto employed (including the abrupt interruptions) to foreground the artifice, the fictionality, the autonomy of his verbal creation.

If, as a result, the poem lost much of its playful self-consciousness—one of its most cherished features among modern readers—Harington's revision definitely served to increase the poem's status among late Tudor readers. For, like most of his refractions, this one helped to reinforce the idea that the *Furioso* was a modern classic. It was, in fact, largely owing to Harington's translation and commentary that Ariosto's poem won that reputation among the English.

CONCLUSION

IN THE last section of his *Osservationi nella volgar lingua* (1550), where Lodovico Dolce reviews the various forms of Italian poetry, he presents the history of the development of *ottave rime* (or *stanze*, as he also calls them) in the following manner:

> Il Boccaccio . . . ne fu inventore, e primo in esse materia di arme descrisse. Dapoi nella seguente età alcuni bassi ingegni, parendo loro questo modo di rimar facile, in cantar diverse menzogne e favole di Orlando e de Paladini le adoperorarono, di maniera, che per lungo tempo in queste non si raccolse cose degne di esser lette. Dopo vario tempo un Francesco Cieco da Ferrara vi scrisse pure in soggetto di Paladini assai comportevolmente. Ma costui fu poscia lasciato a dietro dal Boiardo si di stilo, come d'inventione. Indi il Policiano [sic] altamente cantando primo adornò così fatta maniera di versi di dottrina, di vaghezza, e di leggiadria; & aperse la strada, per laquale caminando l'Ariosto pervenne a tanta altezza, che non solo si puo dir, che egli davero le Stanze illustrasse, ma che le habbia ridotta a quella perfettione, alla quale tra Latini Virgilio, e tra Greci Homero, ridussero il verso Hessametro; che da ambedoi alhora degnamente prese, & conservò il nome di Heroico.[1]

> [Boccaccio invented them, and was the first to describe epic matter in them. Then in the following era some inferior talents, to whom this manner of rhyming seemed easy, used them to compose various falsehoods and stories about Orlando and the Paladins, so that for a long time these rhymes offered nothing worth reading. After some time one Francesco Cieco of Ferrara wrote about the Paladins in this rhyme much more acceptably. But he was left behind by Boiardo, as much in terms of style as of invention. Then, singing loftily, Poliziano first adorned this kind of verse with doctrine, grace, and loveliness. He also opened up the way by which Ariosto, when he took it, reached such heights, that not only can one say that Ariosto made octaves illustrious, but also that he raised them to that perfection to which Virgil, among the Latins, and Homer, among the Greeks, had raised the hexameter, from both of whom it then took and kept the worthy name of heroic verse.]

This evolutionary account of ottava rima from Boccaccio's *Teseide* to Ariosto's poem affirms an idea that became dear to many Italians in the middle decades of the cinquecento: in the *Furioso* the verse form of Italian narrative finally attained heights that made it equal to the heroic hexameters of Homer and Virgil.

Indeed, when one looks back at the editorial publicity that the *Furioso* was given, beginning in the 1540s, the recurring theme in that promotion was that the poem equaled, and in certain ways even surpassed, the achievement of the ancient epic poets. The publisher Gabriel Giolito was one of the first to proclaim (at the beginning of his 1542 edition) that Ariosto "la bassezza de' romanzi ha con l'ali del suo raro e felice ingegno a tanta altezza recata, che per aventura a più sublime segno il gran Virgilio non recò l'arme di Enea." So Niccolo Eugenico similarly announced in his dedication for a 1551 edition (published by Bartolomeo dell'Imperatore) that Ariosto had elevated Italian poetry to a level that matched Virgil "per altezza di stile eroico." Clemente Valvassori maintained in his 1553 dedication that Ariosto even surpassed the ancients: "In questa nostra lingua Volgare, ha col suo Orlando Furioso rilevata l'Eroica composizione a tanta altezza, a quanta giammai s'alzasse per Virgilio, ed Omero nella loro favella." Not only, he went on to say, was the poem a better epic than the ancient ones, but embodying as it did Christian rather than pagan doctrine, it was that much more edifying. More usually, however, editors and commentators proclaimed that the *Furioso* equaled the ancient epics in ethical or pedagogical value. The following parallel that Toscanella makes in the dedication of his *Bellezze del Furioso* (1574) is typical:

> Non fu mente di Omero di scrivere le sue opere per ciancia, o capriccio; ma per insegnare nell'Iliade le forze del corpo; & nell'Odissea le virtù dell'animo: & per mostrare anco i vicii, i dolori, l'allegrezze, i timori, & i desiderii de gli huomini sotto diverse finte persone, accio che specchiandosi nelle opere loro . . . imparassero ad imitare i buoni; & ad havere in odio i malvagi. Tale mente, & animo hebbe Virgilo Prencipe de i Poeti Latini; e tale mente parimente il nostro dottissimo M. Lodovico Ariosto in questo suo Furioso; come io a canto per canto vo mostrando.[2]

> [It was not Homer's intention to write his works idly or whimsically; but to teach the strengths of the body in the *Iliad*; and the virtues of the soul in the *Odyssey*; and also to represent in various fictional characters the vices, pains, joys, fears, and desires of mankind, so that, mirroring themselves in their works, readers would learn to imitate the virtuous, and hate the wicked. Virgil, the Prince of Poets, had the same intent; and so, equally, did our most learned Lodovico Ariosto in his *Furioso*, as I proceed to show canto by canto.]

Again, when Harington argued, in his defense of the *Furioso*, that it was as instructive and praiseworthy as the one poem "[h]allowed and approved by all men," namely, the *Aeneid*, he was affirming, once more, the Italian work's primary value for its sixteenth-century readers: it could be matched with the most admired poems of antiquity.

While various inherent features of Ariosto's poem can serve to explain why it was deemed a modern classic, there were extrinsic factors more directly responsible for the rapidity with which the poem was elevated to that status. The most important of these was the need that existed, by the time the final version of the *Furioso* appeared, for a modern vernacular equivalent of the ancient epics. As I pointed out in the first chapter, that need was intensified by the fact that no trecento or quattrocento poem, Dante's *Commedia* included, could be favorably matched with the ancient epics. The poetic achievements of Petrarch, Boccaccio, and Dante enabled Renaissance Italians to boast that their language was the first European vernacular to reach heights comparable to Greek and Latin. But they were aware that to make that boast undeniable they needed to be able to point to a native heroic poem that measured up to the ancient epics. The 1532 *Furioso* fulfilled such a need.

Not only was the *Furioso* rapidly acclaimed as the heretofore missing classic of Italian narrative poetry, but the poem was even perceived to be the result of a deliberate effort on Ariosto's part to match the heroic poems of antiquity. Claims of this sort were made, as we saw earlier, in Pigna's biography of Ariosto in *I romanzi* (1554), excerpts of which were reprinted in the numerous Valgrisi editions of the poem. Ariosto, according to Pigna, was fully aware that no one had managed to achieve in Italian narrative poetry what the ancients had done, and, given this "room at the top," he set out to occupy it:

> Veggendo egli quanto fosse il numero de' poeti Latini; e quello che più pesa, quanto alcuni di loro in alto saliti fossero, & dall'altro lato considerando che nella nostra lingua un luogo vi era non ancora occupato, & in che egli atto si sentiva a poter entrare; voltatosi alla Toscana poesia, prese per suo oggetto il comporre Romanzevolmente, Havendo tal componimento per simile all' Eroico, e all'Epico, nel quale egli conosceva di potere haver buona lena, & nel qual tuttavia non vedeva alcuno che con dignità, & magnificamente poeteggiato avesse.[3]

> [Seeing how numerous were the Latin poets, and what is more important, to what heights some of them had risen, and considering, on the other hand, that in our tongue there was a place that had not yet been taken, and one which he felt he could suitably occupy, having turned to Tuscan poetry, he set out to write a romance. He deemed that such a composition was similar to heroic and epic poetry, and one in which he had the necessary strength, and yet he saw no poet who had written such heroic poetry with dignity and magnificence.]

Even though he knew the poet's sons, it is doubtful that Pigna had privileged knowledge of Ariosto's original intent. But, given his belief that the *Furioso* met the need for a modern epic, it is more likely that he made up an account of its origins that corroborated his belief.

More than a decade later, in a preface to a 1568 edition of the poem, Lodovico Dolce presented a similar account of the genesis of the *Furioso*. Ariosto, Dolce claimed, wrote to achieve immortality. Aware that it could not be won by writing poetry in Latin, "essendo non solo malagevole, ma impossibile agguagliar gli antichi, . . . deliberò con molta prudenza di scriver nella Volgar lingua [given that it was not only difficult but impossible to equal the ancients, he prudently decided to write in the vulgar tongue]." But, Dolce went on, considering which kind of poetry to write, Ariosto

> vide quella del Lirico occupata del Petrarca: alquale il Sannazaro e'l Bembo . . . si erano per comun giudicio più, che altri, avicinati, & ottenevano le prime lode: deliberò d'indrizzar la sua Penna al Poema Heroico . . . e vedendo il nome d'Orlando e de gli altri Paladini della corte di Carlo Magno esser non pur celebri presso al Volgo, ma anco presso gli huomini letterati . . . hebbe l'occhio a questa materia.[4]

> [saw that lyric poetry was taken by Petrarch: and, according to general opinion, more than any others, Sannazaro and Bembo had come nearest to him, and were granted foremost praise. He decided therefore to apply his writing to heroic poetry, and seeing that the name of Orlando and the other knights of Charlemagne's court were renowned not only among the common people, but also among learned men . . . he turned his attention to this subject matter.]

Dolce's claims, of course, are all made after the fact. It was Ariosto's sophisticated treatment of the Carolingian matter of romance (infusing it as he did with the learned *koiné* of his time) that first pleased learned readers as well as the more "vulgar" audience who had traditionally enjoyed the adventures of Carlomagno's paladins. Their deeds were not so universally appealing a subject until Ariosto made them so. The retrospective and anachronistic nature of Dolce's account becomes even more evident when one recalls that Ariosto began composing his poem at least two decades before the accomplishments of modern lyric poets like Sannazaro and Bembo were deemed illustrious enough to deter a writer from choosing that genre to attain immortality. Dolce's account seems hardly conceivable before Bembo's *Prose della volgar lingua* (1525) established the canonicity of Petrarch's lyrics and made it apparent (by omission) that there was still room to write a narrative poem of equal stature. Dolce deemed that the *Furioso* was indeed that poem; therefore, like Pigna, he also fabricated a history of its genesis that corroborated his evaluation of the result. However, the point of Dolce's fiction, and also of Pigna's earlier account, was to make readers believe that parity with the classics was not simply being conferred on the *Furioso* but was the author's original intention: Ariosto had aspired to achieve that parity from the start.

How keen Italian literati were to confer the status of a classic on the *Furioso* is revealed by more than the various assertions to that effect made in the prefaces of the midcentury editions of the poem. At the same time that Venetian editions puff Ariosto as the Virgil of the age, there begin to appear anthologies and *florilegia* that contain, along with selections from the already canonized trecento poets, choice lines and *sententiae* from Ariosto's poem. The first of these poetic *florilegia* to include Ariosto seems to have been Fabricio Luna's *Vocabulario di cinque mila vocabuli Toschi . . . del Furioso, Boccaccio, Petrarca e Dante*, published in Naples as early as as 1536.[5] But it is another decade before one begins to find Ariosto regularly cited along with the trecento "masters" for his *sententiae*, or his exemplary use of Italian. Volumes with titles like *Versi morali et sententiosi di Dante, del Petrarca, di messer L. Ariosto. Per utilità comune raccolti . . .* (1544) offer perhaps the most obvious evidence of the exemplary function so rapidly being granted the *Furioso*. A popular topical dictionary of the period, Francesco Alunno's *Fabbrica del mondo*, also reflects the growing prominence of the *Furioso* as an exemplary text. As the title page of this dictionary announced in the original 1548 edition, it contained "tutte le voci di Dante, del Petrarca, del Boccaccio, e d'altri buoni autori . . . con le quali si ponno scrivendo isprimere tutti i concetti dell'huomo di qualunque cosa creata." Ariosto was already cited occasionally as one of the other "buoni autori" in this original edition. But by 1562, after the drive to raise the *Furioso* to the status of a classic is accomplished, the amplified edition of Alunno's dictionary cites Ariosto almost as often as Petrarch, Boccaccio, and Dante.

Already in the 1550s Girolamo Ruscelli was ready to make Ariosto a more exemplary model of Tuscan poetic usage than Petrarch himself! In his letter to Alfonso d'Este prefacing the 1556 Valgrisi edition of the *Furioso* (of which, it will be recalled, he was himself the editor), Ruscelli announced that in another work of his, still in progress, he demonstrates the capacity of the Italian language to achieve every form of stylistic or expressive excellence by citing examples from poetry. In doing so, "ho proposto," he writes, "e nominato sempre il Petrarca, e il Furioso; e questo poi tanto più, quanto è più importante in se stesso il poema eroico, che il lirico [I have always brought up or named as examples Petrarch and the *Furioso*; and the latter all the more so, as the heroic poem is, in itself, more important than the lyric]." Interestingly enough, this elevation of Ariosto's poem as a supreme model of Italian usage did not go unchallenged. That Ruscelli was being irresponsible in ranking Ariosto higher than Petrarch as a model of proper linguistic—that is to say, Tuscan—usage was pointed out and lamented by the astute Florentine critic and scholar Vincenzio Borghini. But while discrediting the Venetian editor's ploys, Borghini himself acknowledged that Ruscelli could get away with granting Ariosto such unfounded linguistic authority because of the enormous and virtually unimpeachable reputation that the *Furioso* had already achieved.[6]

The rapidity of its canonization can be attributed to the need, which the *Furioso* evidently met, for a vernacular narrative poem that measured up to ancient heroic poetry. One might have thought that the efforts of hostile neo-Aristotelians to refute the claims that it was a "poema eroico" would have made the literate public relinquish the idea that the poem belonged to the epic tradition. But this did not happen. As I suggested at the end of the first chapter, the increasing vociferousness of the neo-Aristotelians in the 1560s and 1570s was itself an indication that Italian readers had accepted the status conferred upon the poem in its numerous Venetian editions. These hostile critics had to demonstrate how unclassical the *Furioso* was in order to dispel the view that it was, as Sassetti lamented in his attack on the poem, a "quasi Iliade novella."

The neo-Aristotelian critique did have some effect. It spurred champions of Ariosto such as G. B. Giraldi to argue that the *Furioso* was a modern romanzo, different from ancient epic, but heroic poetry nonetheless. Those who espoused this argument hardly abandoned the idea that the poem was a modern classic. On the contrary, much of their rhetoric sought to advance the idea that the *Furioso* was at once modern (that is, unlike ancient poetry) and a classic of its kind. Just as Petrarch, whose lyric output was quite unclassical, was preeminent in comparison with prior Tuscan poets, so Ariosto, Giraldi had written, "rimase appresso gli altri che a così fatte compositioni s'erano dati, ch'egli solo tra tutti . . . si è scoperto degno di essere imitato [stands among those that have devoted themselves to composing romances; he is the only one who has shown himself worthy of imitation]." By so ascribing to Ariosto exemplary "autorità" in modern narrative poetry Giraldi had, in effect, elevated his poem to the rank of a classic as early as 1554.

Giraldi and his followers argued that if the *Furioso* violated ancient epic conventions, it was because, as a modern romanzo, it observed different norms, but its modernity could not be used to deprive it of the canonical status it had won. Still, by the 1580s neo-Aristotelian orthodoxy had become dominant enough that the demotion of the poem to the rank of a vulgar and illegitimate romanzo seemed a possibility, especially since the neoclassicists could now boast of Tasso's *Gerusalemme Liberata*, a modern Italian poem that was, in their opinion, a genuine equivalent of ancient epic. As a champion of vernacular poetry, Salviati feared—and Pellegrino's *Il Carrafa* confirmed that fear—that if the neoclassicists had their way, any modern poem, not simply the *Furioso*, risked being marginalized if it was perceived as an illegitimate kind of poem, that is, undefined by Aristotle. To preempt such an outcome Salviati countered Pellegrino's efforts to disqualify the *Furioso* as heroic poetry by marshaling every possible argument to prove that it was an epic, as defined by Aristotle and as embodied in Homer's and Virgil's practice. In the *Infarinato secondo* his assimilation of Ariosto's poem to the canonical epics of antiquity was original, as we saw, in that it showed that most of the so-called imperfections of the *Furioso* were also recognizable features of the *Iliad*, the *Odyssey*, and the *Aeneid*. If Salviati was proclaiming once again that the Italian poem was a modern equivalent of the ancient epics, that parity was no longer being asserted to elevate the Italian poem as much as to bring down the ancient classics from their sacred heights. Still, despite his irreverent treatment of the ancients, Salviati's main intent was to affirm the continuity between ancient and modern poetry, and to affirm Ariosto's place in the tradition he was consolidating. His larger objective was not simply to retain the *Furioso* within the poetic canon that was being established, but to ensure that this canon would generally remain open to works that did not observe the narrow strictures that far more conservative Aristotelians wanted to impose. Ariosto's poem could not be allowed to be dispossessed of its newly gained reputation as a classic because what was at stake was the status of all modern vernacular poetry not subservient to so-called ancient poetic rules and practice.

Instrumental as Salviati's eloquent defense was in reinforcing the canonical status of the *Furioso*, it was simply reinforcing it. As I proposed earlier, the fact that in both *Il Carrafa* and the *Infarinato secondo* (and the other defenses of the poem in the 1580s) the *Furioso* could become a site of contestation about issues ultimately extrinsic to it (for example, the question of what proper heroic poetry is) was in itself a sign that the canonical status bravely conferred on it by the previous generation had been achieved.

Even Ariosto's neo-Aristotelian opponents recognized by the 1580s that the idea of the *Furioso* as the modern equal of the great ancient epics had become so entrenched that their counterclaims might not succeed in dislodging it. At the end of Pellegrino's *Il Carrafa*, Attendolo maintains that, his preference for Tasso as an epic poet notwithstanding, it is unlikely that his argument will diminish the lasting popularity that Ariosto had secured for himself. "La loda e fama dell'Ariosto," he explains,

> è così invecchiata, et ha preso così salde radici nella mente della maggior parte degli uomini [this is claimed, one should recall, a little more than fifty years after the publication of the 1532 *Furioso*], che par loro un sacrilegio di scemargliene pur un poco. E continuandosi questa buona opinion di lui d'età in età, non è fuor di ragione il credere che egli viva e che abbia ad aversi in pregio fin che si ragioni la volgar lingua.[7]

[Ariosto's praise and fame are so established and have taken such firm root in the minds of most men that they think it a sacrilege to diminish his fame even a little. And with this good opinion of him continuing from generation to generation, it is not unreasonable to believe that he shall live and be held in esteem as long as the vulgar tongue is spoken.]

Attendolo's prediction turned out to be correct. What Pellegrino's spokesman was not ready to acknowledge—was it because he was trying to make that case for Tasso's epic?—was the reason that the *Furioso* so quickly "rooted itself" as a classic: it best embodied the capacity of modern Italian poetry to equal that of Greece and Rome at a time when Italians most needed that capacity of their vernacular to be affirmed.

NOTES

Introduction

1. Klaus Hempfer's recent bibliography of sixteenth-century sources that discuss Ariosto and his poem lists 116 works, most of them published in the second half of the century. See his *Diskrepante Lektüren: Die Orlando-Furioso-Rezeption im Cinquecento* (Stuttgart: Steiner, 1987), pp. 301–9.

2. Giuseppina Fumagalli, *La fortuna dell'"Orlando Furioso" in Italia nel sec. XVI* (Ferrara: Zuffi, 1912). I also found useful Giuseppe Fatini, *Bibliografia della critica ariostea (1510–1956)* (Florence: Le Monnier, 1958), especially the entries for the period from 1532 to 1600. Overall surveys of Ariosto criticism, for example, Walter Binni, *Storia della critica ariostesca* (Lucca: Lucentia, 1951), and Raffaello Ramat, *La critica ariostesca dal sec. XVI ad oggi* (Florence: Nuova Italia, 1954), have proved less useful precisely because their more extensive coverage forces their authors to deal with cinquecento criticism too selectively and superficially.

3. Bernard Weinberg, *A History of Literary Criticism in the Italian Renaissance* (Chicago: University of Chicago Press, 1961), pp. 954–1073.

4. For the purposes of this study I make no distinction between a classic and a text that acquires canonical status, but they may not always be identical. Since standards of canonicity change, and thus some texts cease to be canonical, classics might be defined as texts that are always deemed canonical.

To those readers who find anachronistic my use of *canonization* to describe the elevation of Ariosto or of his poem to the rank of a classic, I should point out that by the end of the sixteenth century one can already find the adjective *canonizzato* or *canonizato* used by Italian writers in this more secular sense. For example, in the following passage from G. B. Guarini's *Verrato contra M. Jason Denores* (1588) the author maintains that Sperone Speroni only attacked famous poets, that is, poets already "canonized" as comparable to Virgil: "Egli [Speroni] non è censore se non dell'opere più lodate, poichè sdegna di sindicare alcuna cosa che già da tutti celebrata non sia. Per modo che tanto vien a dire Poeta esercitato dal sottilissimo ingegno suo, quanto Poeta canonizato per eccellente e degno di paragonarsi a Virgilio" (*Delle opere del cavalier Battista Guarini* . . . [Verona: G. A. Tumermani, 1737–1738], 2:215).

5. On the adoption of the *Furioso* in the syllabi of Venetian vernacular schools see Paul F. Grendler, "Chivalric Romances in the Italian Renaissance," *Studies in Medieval and Renaissance History* 10 (1988): 87. Again, in his *Schooling in Renaissance Italy: Literacy and Learning* (Baltimore: Johns Hopkins University Press, 1989), p. 298, Grendler points out that the *Furioso* was adopted in the curricula of vernacular schools in the late cinquecento and was "the only vernacular classic to win such approval." According to him, however, there is no evidence of how the poem was taught.

6. On the canon as an aristocracy of texts see the illuminating opening remarks by John Guillory in "The Ideology of Canon-Formation: T. S. Eliot and Cleanth Brooks," *Critical Inquiry* 10 (1983), esp. pp. 173–74.

CHAPTER ONE
THE SUCCESS OF *ORLANDO FURIOSO* IN THE SIXTEENTH CENTURY

1. On the average size of editions of nondevotional literature in the sixteenth century see R. Hirsch, *Printing, Selling, and Reading, 1450–1550* (Wiesbaden: Harrassowitz, 1967), p. 125. For estimates of the print runs of the 1516 and 1532 editions of the *Furioso* see Conor Fahy, "Some Observations on the 1532 Edition of Lodovico Ariosto's *Orlando Furioso*," *Studies in Bibliography* 40 (1987): 75.

2. These various Venetian editions are described in Giuseppe Agnelli and Giuseppe Ravegnani, *Annali delle edizioni Ariostee* (Bologna: Zanichelli, 1933), vol. 1.

3. Aside from the *Annali* cited in note 2, for my count of editions (not distinguished from issues) of the *Furioso* I have consulted the *Censimento* of *cinquecentine* now being published by the Istituto Centrale per il Catalogo Unico: *Le edizioni italiane del XVI secolo: Censimento nazionale: Volume "A"* (Rome, 1985). My count of Petrarch editions is based on those listed in the Catalogue of the Petrarch Collection at Cornell University.

4. Giolito's claims prefacing his edition of the Spanish translation are cited in Fatini, *Bibliografia della critica ariostea (1510–1956)*, p. 27 [no. 107]. Dolce's claim was made in his preface to *L'Amadigi di Gaula del S. Bernardo Tasso* (Venice: G. Giolito, 1560).

5. *Operum Bartholomaei Riccii Lugiensis* . . . (Batavia: J. Manfré, 1747–1748), pp. 434–35. Ricci goes on to say that "nulla enim adhuc Gens, nulla Europa Natio est . . . qui librum hunc summa non excolant reverentia."

6. On the "epigoni del *Furioso*" see Fumagalli, *La fortuna dell' "Orlando Furioso,"* pp. 258–310; Ulrich Leo, *Angelica ed i "Migliori Plettri": Appunti sullo stile della Controriforma* (Krefeld: Scherpe-Verlag, 1953); and, most recently, Marina Beer, *Romanzi di cavalleria: Il "Furioso" e il romanzo italiano del primo Cinquecento* (Rome: Bulzoni, 1987), pp. 141–206 and app. 2, esp. pp. 342–69.

7. *Delle lettere di M. Bernardo Tasso* (Padua: Comino, 1733), 2:425. Unless otherwise indicated, all translations are my own.

8. Trissino's envious slur about "l'Ariosto col 'Furioso' suo che piace al vulgo" is to be found in bk. 24 of his *Italia liberata dai Goti* (1547), a poem that, despite its imitation of Homeric epic norms, was a resounding failure. The reading public simply preferred *romanzi* to imitations of the ancient epics. As G. B. Giraldi wrote to Bernardo Tasso in 1556, the imitations of Homer and Virgil revived "ne' nostri tempi, nella nostra lingua sono poco meno che odiose; e se ne puote avere l'esempio dall'Italia del Trissino. Il quale siccome era dottissimo, così fosse stato giudicioso in eleggere cosa degna della fatica di venti anni! avrebbe veduto che così scrivere, come egli ha fatto, era uno scrivere a' morti: e non avrebbe biasimata la composizione dell'Ariosto come cosa degna del favore del vulgo, e non dei dotti, e dei giudiciosi [in our times, in our tongue, are little less than odious; and one can take the example of Trissino's *Italia*. Extremely learned as he was, had Trissino been as judicious in choosing a work deserving twenty years of effort, he would

have seen that writing in the way he did was writing for the dead; and he would not have condemned Ariosto's composition as one worthy of common folks' acclaim but not that of learned and discriminating readers]" (*Delle lettere di M. Bernardo Tasso* 2:198).

9. *Lezzioni di M. Benedetto Varchi* . . . (Florence: F. Giunti, 1590), p. 585. Varchi delivered the "lezione" in which this statement is made in 1553. While he had words of praise for the *Furioso*, Varchi preferred Luigi Alamanni's more unified *Giron Cortese* (1548).

10. In her recent study of the romanzo in the sixteenth century Marina Beer points out that the universal readership of Ariosto's poem was exceptional since the genre traditionally appealed not to everybody but rather to two opposite sectors of society, "il pubblico della corte" and "il pubblico della piazza." The *Furioso*, as she points out, "riesce miracolosamente a unificare proprio il pubblico differenziato dall'universo tipografico, innestando sul corpo di un genere largamente popolare tutte le conquiste dell'alta cultura della letteratura volgare della svolta del secolo" (*Romanzi di cavalleria*, p. 210).

11. I will not give signature marks (page numbers are rare) when I cite from prefatory or appended texts or notes in sixteenth-century editions of the *Furioso*, but I will describe these passages specifically enough so that they can be readily located. In my citations of sixteenth-century sources in Italian I have chosen to modernize the accentuation, as well as to make it more consistent, but I have not modernized spelling or punctuation.

12. Fumagalli, *La fortuna dell'"Orlando Furioso,"* pp. 181–83; see also pp. 405–37 for her comments on the editions of the *Furioso* in the various Italian dialects. For useful statistical surveys of the editions of the poem from 1516 to 1615 according to format and typeface see Enrica Pace, "Aspetti tipografico-editoriali di un 'best seller' del secolo XVI: l'*Orlando furioso*," *Schifanoia* 3 (1987): 103–14.

13. On the *Furioso* in the inventories of Florentine merchants see Christian Bec, *Les livres des florentins (1413–1608)* (Florence: Olschki, 1984), esp. pp. 61–62; see also Beer, *Romanzi di cavalleria*, pp. 244–45. Except for claims that they were fond of memorizing it and setting it to music (see note 15 below), we have virtually no record of how Ariosto's unlearned audience responded to the poem. On the adoption of the *Furioso* in the syllabi of Venetian vernacular schools see Grendler, "Chivalric Romances," p. 87, and *Schooling in Renaissance Italy*, pp. 298–99.

14. *Trattato di M. Francesco Caburacci da Immola. Dove si dimostra il vero, & novo modo di fare le imprese. Con un breve discorso in difesa dell'Orlando Furioso di M. Lodovico Ariosto* (Bologna: G. Rossi, 1580), p. 80.

15. *Della nuova poesia o vero delle difese del Furioso, dialogo del Signor Gioseppe Malatesta* (Verona: S. delle Donne, 1589), pp. 137–38. A little later in the dialogue we are told of the "infima plebe così studiosa di questo poema, che molti fra loro vi sono, i quai, non sapendo legger . . ., voglion pur tutto il giorno distratiare i versi del Furioso, & impararne qualche stanza a mente, per poter la poi biscantare su la ribeca, o su'l gravicembalo [lowest class of people so keen about this poem that there are many among them who, though not knowing how to read, wish all day long to botch verses of the *Furioso* and to memorize a few stanzas from it, in order to then sing them badly, accompanied by a ribeck or a harpsichord]" (p. 147).

16. Pietro Bembo, *Prose della volgar lingua* (II.xx), in *Trattatisti del Cinquecento*, ed. Mario Pozzi (Milan and Naples: Ricciardi, 1978), 1:161. Carlo Dionisotti observes that this judgment of Dante's poem "che nei termini della poetica rinascimentale non era controvertibile . . . ebbe un peso decisivo . . . sulla fortuna di Dante nel Cinquecento." See his entry on Bembo in the *Enciclopedia Dantesca* (Rome: Istituto della Enciclopedia Italiana, 1970), 1:568.

17. On the reputation of Dante's *Commedia* in sixteenth-century Italy see Michele Barbi, *Della fortuna di Dante nel secolo XVI* (Pisa: Nistri, 1890), esp. pp. 1–76. Lodovico Dolce, who was the most important editor of the *Furioso* in the mid–sixteenth century, also edited Dante's *Commedia* (Venice: G. Giolito, 1555). In the dedicatory letter of this edition he gave the following assessment, which reflects how much more valued Dante's poem was for its content than for its style: "E benché nella prima fronte si dimostri privo di quella vaghezza che contengono molti altri poemi, è poi tanto più ricco di dottrina e di maestà; simile a quelle dipinture che sono più nobili per artificio di disegno che per politezza di colori [And even though at first sight it seems to lack that grace which many other poems possess, it then turns out to be so much richer in learning and in majesty; like those paintings which are nobler because of artful design than the finish of their colors]." As the following chapter will make evident, neither Dolce nor other contemporary editors of the *Furioso* ever express such qualifications in their praise of Ariosto's poem. According to Bernard Weinberg, arguments about whether the *Commedia* was or was not to be considered an epic poem do not fully emerge until the appearance of the "Discorso di messer Anselmo Castravilla, nel quale si mostra l'imperfettione della comedia di Dante . . .," which began circulating in manuscript in 1572. For the "quarrel over Dante" that this manuscript provoked see Weinberg, *Literary Criticism*, pp. 831–911.

18. Beer, *Romanzi di cavalleria*, p. 142.

19. For a detailed account of the reception of Aristotle's *Poetics* in this period see Weinberg, *Literary Criticism*, esp. pp. 349–423. On the conflation of the *Poetics* with Horace's *Ars poetica*, see pp. 111–55. For another, briefer, account of the assimilation of Aristotle's *Poetics* see Enzo Turolla, "Aristotele e le 'Poetiche' del Cinquecento," in *Dizionario critico della letteratura italiana*, ed. Vittore Branca (Turin: UTET, 1974), pp. 133–39. See also Baxter Hathaway, *Marvels and Commonplaces: Renaissance Literary Criticism* (New York: Random House, 1968), pp. 9–19.

20. *La spositione di M. Simon Fornari da Rheggio sopra l'Orlando Furioso di M. Lodovico Ariosto* (Florence: L. Torrentino, 1549), p. 32. Not very much is known about Simone Fornari, the first important commentator on the *Furioso*. Originating from Reggio Calabria, he spent time at the University of Padua, and the Studio in Pisa, and was active in literary circles in Florence around 1550. In the "Life" of Ariosto that he included in the *Spositione*, Fornari mentions that he also resided in Ferrara, where he met Ariosto's brother, Gabriele, and Virginio, the poet's son.

21. "Accusano etiandio il nostro poeta come colui, ch'habbia fatto il contrario di quello, che tanto loda in Homero Aristotile, cioè che egli pochissime cose racconta come da se, ma fa che altri lo dica [They also accuse our poet of having done the opposite of what Aristotle so praises in Homer, namely, that he narrates very few things in his own voice, but has other individuals speak]" (ibid., p. 38).

22. Ibid., p. 39.

23. Ibid., pp. 40–41.

24. *Delle lettere di M. Bernardo Tasso* 2:424, 425. "S'Aristotele nascesse a questa età," he writes, "e vedesse il vaghissimo Poema dell'Ariosto, conoscendo la forza dell'uso, e vedendo che tanto diletta, come l'esperienza ci dimostra, mutasse opinione, e consentisse che si potesse far Poema Eroico di più azioni [If Aristotle had been born in this age, and had seen Ariosto's most beautiful poem, knowing the power of custom, and seeing that the poem delights so much, as experience shows, he would have changed his opinion, and would have agreed that one could write a heroic poem of many actions]."

25. Torquato Tasso, *Discorsi dell'arte poetica*, in *Prose*, ed. E. Mazzali (Milan and Naples: Ricciardi, 1959), p. 372. Later, in the second Discourse, Tasso acknowledges "che 'l diletto sia il fine della poesia," and he concedes "quel che l'esperienza ci dimostra: cioè che maggior diletto rechi a' nostri uomini il *Furioso* che l'*Italia liberata* [by Trissino], o pur l'*Iliade* o l'*Odissea* [what experience shows: that is, that the *Furioso* gives people of our time greater delight than the *Italia liberata*, or even the *Iliad* or the *Odyssey*]" (ibid., pp. 385–86).

26. On this Latin lecture, which he dates about 1580, see Weinberg, *Literary Criticism*, pp. 978–79.

27. On the declining fortune of *Orlando Innamorato* in the sixteenth century see Carlo Dionisotti, "Fortuna e sfortuna del Boiardo nel Cinquecento," in *Il Boiardo e la critica contemporanea*, ed. G. Anceschi (Florence: Olschki, 1970), pp. 220–41. Boiardo's poem became unfashionable largely because its language and style lacked the "pulitezza" that poetic diction was deemed to have acquired in the fifty years since the work had first appeared. By the 1540s the original version of the *Innamorato* was replaced by the *rifacimenti* of Berni and Domenichi. In fact, Boiardo's original poem was never republished from 1544 to 1830–1831.

28. Klaus Hempfer argues that the role ascribed to Aristotle's newly reclaimed *Poetics* in generating hostile and then defensive criticism of the poem has been exaggerated. He maintains that even if the *Poetics* had not been reclaimed and absorbed, the *Furioso* would have been criticized for its violation of Horatian poetic norms. (See his *Diskrepante Lektüren*, pp. 60–61.) To be sure, there were factors other than the ascendance of Aristotle's authority that provoked both opposition to and defense of the poem, but I would stress much more than does Hempfer that these were cultural factors external to the text. I suspect that he wants to diminish the importance of growing neo-Aristotelian opposition to Ariosto's poem because this clearly discernible cultural development that occurs almost two decades after the publication of the 1532 *Furioso* challenges his thesis, namely, that the contradictory responses to the *Furioso* in the sixteenth century are the product of the poem as a paradoxical and "problematischer" text, rather than of the extrinsic agendas of its readers.

CHAPTER TWO
THE LEGITIMATION OF *ORLANDO FURIOSO*

1. The one early defense of the poem that was not provoked by neo-Aristotelian criticism was the very first, Lodovico Dolce's "Apologia . . . contra ai detrattori

dell'Ariosto," appended to the 1535 edition of the *Furioso* published by Mapheo Pasini. Dolce does suggest that, even in the 1530s, "detrattori" complained about the irregular disposition of the plot. One of the objections was that Ariosto should have titled the work *Ruggiero* and not *Orlando Furioso*. The other main complaints, however, were aimed at Ariosto's language and style.

2. Giovambattista Giraldi Cinthio (1504–1573) was, in the 1540s and 1550s, a leading scholar and literary theorist at the university and the court at Ferrara. He was also one of the first writers of vernacular tragedies in the sixteenth century, and the author of a collection of *novelle* entitled the *Hecatommithi*. He was attached to the Este court, where he served as secretary to Ercole II.

Giovanni Battista Nicolucci detto Pigna (1529–1575) was also a scholar at Ferrara (where he held a chair at the Studio), and a disciple of Giraldi, until they accused each other of plagiarism (see below). Pigna was even more successful than Giraldi at the Este court, serving, from 1552, as secretary for Alfonso II, then as his minister, and also as his historiographer.

For Pigna's letter to Giraldi see G. B. Giraldi Cinzio, *Scritti critici*, ed. Camillo Guerrieri Crocetti (Milan: Marzorati, 1973), pp. 246–47. Giraldi made public this 1548 letter from Pigna in a pamphlet published in 1554 to disprove Pigna's subsequent allegations that he had plagiarized Pigna's *I romanzi* in his *Discorso intorno al comporre dei romanzi*, both of which were also published in 1554. Pigna claimed that the early date ascribed to his letter and to Giraldi's reply was spurious. For further comments on this exchange, see Weinberg, *Literary Criticism*, pp. 957–63, and, more recently, Giancarlo Mazzacurati, *Il Rinascimento dei moderni* (Bologna: Il Mulino, 1985), pp. 306–9.

3. In Pigna's words, the additional complaints are as follows: " . . . oltre di ciò che fuori del decoro molte cose vi sono, come in due luoghi l'aversi fatto esso pazzo per amore, e massime nella fronte del libro; come l'introdurre tanti lunghi lamenti nelle giovani donne innamorate, e come fare tanto piangere tanti cavallieri per amore, e che non si conviene fare quelle digressioni così spesso fatte da lui, e che è poco dicevole, trattando cose pastorali e poscia reali, mescolare le persone basse ed umili con l'alte e con le gravi; che parimente disdice proporci una cosa di cattivo esempio, volendo far impazzire un uomo savio [. . . in addition to this, that many things transgress decorum, as, when in two places, he [the poet] presents himself mad because of love, and above all, at the beginning of the book; as by inserting so many long laments on the part of young women in love, and making so many knights weep so much because of love; and that it is not appropriate for him to make those digressions so often; nor is it proper when he deals with pastoral and then with royal matters, to mix low, humble persons with high-ranking serious ones; that it is equally unbecoming to set forth wicked examples, as choosing to make a wise man go insane]."

4. Giraldi, *Scritti critici*, p. 249. Giraldi's entire letter to Pigna is to be found on pp. 247–53.

5. Ibid., p. 70.

6. Ibid., pp. 67–68.

7. Near the beginning of his treatise Giraldi claims that both Boiardo and Ariosto "sono come due duci in così fatti componimenti; le vestigia dei quali debbono seguir con ogni studio coloro che di materie finte vorranno ben scrivere in tal poesia

[are like two leaders in such compositions; those who wish to write romances well must follow in their footsteps]" (p. 49). By the end of the *Discorso*, however, Boiardo no longer shares with Ariosto this preeminent status.

8. Giraldi, *Scritti critici*, p. 143.

9. See *I romanzi di M. Giovan Battista Pigna* (Venice: V. Valgrisi, 1554), p. 14.

10. At one point (p. 65) Pigna states that Aristotle "quivi ne Romanzi è stato la nostra guida: benche egli mai ne parlasse [has been our guide here in *I romanzi*, even though he never spoke of romances]."

11. Ibid., pp. 78, 80.

12. Ibid., pp. 87–88. The precedent miraculous transformations in the *Odyssey* and the *Aeneid* are cited on p. 85.

13. Fornari's *allegoresis* brings to mind another contemporary contribution that served, in its own particular way, to enhance the poem's moral value: the *Discorso sopra tutti i primi canti d'Orlando Furioso. Fatti per la Signora Laura Terracina* (Venice: G. Giolito, 1549). Terracina's work consisted of forty-two cantos of seven octaves each that elaborated upon the *sententiae* she found in the opening octave or *proemio* of each of Ariosto's cantos. Terracina, moreover, artfully devised each of her octaves to end with a line from Ariosto's original octave. Her first octave ended with the first line, the second octave with the second line, and so forth, until her seventh octave ended with the closing couplet of Ariosto's first octave. Her expansion and elaboration rendered the sententiousness of Ariosto's *proemi* less pithy and less ambiguous, and obviously allowed her to moralize at greater length.

Terracina's work was published at least a dozen times in the course of the century. According to Paul Grendler, some teachers in the vernacular schools assigned their pupils her *Discorso* to supplement (or possibly to replace) their reading of the *Furioso*. (See his *Schooling in Renaissance Italy*, p. 298.)

14. See Fornari, *Spositione . . . sopra l'Orlando Furioso*, pp. 40–43.

15. Ibid., p. 43.

16. Ibid., p. 39.

17. The Venetian edition of the *Furioso* published by Bindoni and Pasini in the same year, with its learned annotations by Fausto da Longiano, also initiated the editorial trend toward promoting the poem as a modern classic. But the Bindoni edition was immediately eclipsed by Giolito's. On Fausto da Longiano's commentary see Chapter 3.

18. The various prefatory or appended "paratexts" from which I cite are often not paginated, and the signature marks are not always the same in various editions. Therefore, rather than referring to the pages by signature marks, I will situate the text specifically enough, or provide enough information about it, to enable the reader to locate the citations in the respective editions.

19. Leonardo Bruni, *De studiis et litteris liber*, in *Il pensiero pedagogico dell'Umanesimo*, ed. Eugenio Garin (Florence: Sansoni, 1958), p. 160. The original reads as follows: "Quid Homero deest, quominus in omni sapientia sapientissimus existimari possit? Eius poesim totam esse doctrinam vivendi quidam ostendunt, in belli tempora pacisque divisam; et in bello quidem quae provisis ducis, qui aut astus aut fortitudo militum, quod insidiarum genus cavandum vel faciendum, quae monitio quod consilium ab eo est pratermissum."

20. "Quod autem ad bene, beateque vivendum pertinet quis non videat omnia quibus vita humana recte instituatur." Cristoforo Landino, "Praefatio," in Publius Virgilius Maro, *Opera* . . . (Venice: L. A. Giunta, 1533). Landino goes on to say, "Maronis poema omne humanae vitae genus exprimit, ut nullus hominum ordo, nullus aetas, nullus sexus sit, nulla denique conditio, quae ab eo sua officia non integre addiscat."

21. I cite from George Sandys' 1632 translation of Regio's preface. The original, first published in 1493, reads: "Nihil est enim quod ad rei militaris peritiam gloriamque pertineat: cuius illustria exempla in Ovidii Metamorphosi non habeantur. . . . Iam civiliter vivendi rationes unde facilius sumamus autorem invenies neminem."

22. Lodovico Dolce edited more than 180 texts for Gabriel Giolito during his collaboration with his publishing house from 1542 to 1568. While he produced important editions (in some cases, of more than one work) of Boccaccio, Ariosto, Dante, Sannazaro, Berni, Castiglione, Bembo, and Bernardo Tasso, it was his edition of *Orlando Furioso* that was the best known and the most frequently republished. For more on Dolce's prolific editorial and literary activities see Claudia di Filippo Bareggi, *Il mestiere di scrivere: Lavoro intellettuale e mercato librario a Venezia nel Cinquecento* (Rome: Bulzoni, 1988), pp. 58–60, 99, 285–86, 323–27, and the numerous other references to Dolce cited in the index.

23. On the woodcuts that adorn the Valvassori edition see E. Falaschi, "Valvassori's 1553 Illustrations of *Orlando Furioso*: The Development of Multi-Narrative Technique in Venice and Its Links to Cartography," *La bibliofilia* 77 (1975): 227–51.

24. For Ruscelli's defamatory attack on Dolce see his *Tre discorsi . . . a M. Lodovico Dolce* (Venice: P. Pietrasanta, 1553). On Ruscelli's activities as an editor for Valgrisi and other Venetian publishers, see di Filippo Bareggi, *Il mestiere di scrivere*, pp. 78–80, 283–84, 290–91, and, for an account of his quarrel and rivalry with Dolce, 296–301.

25. In the first Valgrisi edition of 1556, Pigna's "Life" of Ariosto corresponds to the biography he had included in bk. 2 of *I romanzi*. But in the 1558 edition and, again, in the 1560 edition, the "Life" was amplified, possibly by Ruscelli. In the 1560 edition, the new passage in which the diversity of styles in Ariosto's works is compared to Virgil's reads as follows: "Et così quello a punto che si dice de' tre stili di Virgilio, si dirà ancora sopra l'Ariosto, essendo l'humiltà, la mediocrità, e l'altezza nelle Commedie, nelle Satire & nel Furioso di esso, non meno che ne' Bucolici, & ne' Georgici, & nell'Eneide di Virgilio. Anzi questa varietà è maggiore e più pregiata nell'Ariosto, per essere tutti questi ordini Poetici, la ove i Georgici non sono sotto alcuna sorte di Poesia."

26. The full title of Toscanella's compendium was *Bellezze del Furioso di M. Lodovico Ariosto, scelte da Oratio Toscanella: con gli argomenti et allegorie de i canti: con l'allegorie de i nomi proprii principali dell'opera: et co i luochi communi dell'autore, per ordine di alfabeto; del medesimo* (Venice: P. dei Franceschi, 1574). Toscanella would have been very familiar with the earlier editorial promotion of the *Furioso*, since, a decade after Ruscelli and Dolce, he too worked as an editor and literary consultant for several Venetian publishers. On Toscanella's editorial activities in Venice see, again, di Filippo Bareggi, *Il mestiere di scrivere*, pp. 86–87, 360–61.

27. See Carlo Dionisotti's valuable comments on the ascendance of more ortho-dox classicism in the 1560s, in comparison to the previous two decades, in "La letteratura italiana nell'età del concilio di Trento," in *Geografia e storia della lettera-tura italiana* (Turin: Einaudi, 1967), pp. 246ff.

28. *L'arte poetica del Sig. Antonio Minturno* (Venice: G. A. Valvassori, 1564), p. 28.

29. Filippo Sassetti, "Il discorso contro l'Ariosto . . .," ed. Giuseppe Castaldi, *Rendiconti della R. Accademia dei Lincei* 22 (1913):496. The refutation of the other parallels with classical epics that Pigna and others had drawn is to be found on pp. 493–96.

CHAPTER THREE
COMMENTARIES ON IMITATIONS IN *ORLANDO FURIOSO*

1. There were, to be precise, two Bindoni editions in 1542, one in octavo and one in quarto. For a full description of the two editions see Agnelli and Ravegnani, *Annali delle edizioni Ariostee* 1:56–60. Quotations are from the quarto edition. I give no page references, because the original commentary appended to the poem is not paginated. Instead of referring to the pages by signature marks, I provide enough information about the particular lines or octaves of the poem to enable the reader to locate Fausto da Longiano's remarks.

2. Quotations from the original commentary are taken from the Venice Giolito edition of 1542. Because the commentary is unpaginated, I provide references to particular lines or octaves. In this chapter I will not translate the shorter comments that simply identify Ariosto's models, nor the poetic passages juxtaposed.

3. In her brief discussion of cinquecento commentaries on Ariosto's similes, Kristen Murtaugh (*Ariosto and the Classical Simile* [Cambridge, Mass.: Harvard University Press, 1980], pp. 29–30) mistakenly assumes that this observation of Dolce's was originally made by Ieronimo Ruscelli in his 1556 commentary on Ari-osto's imitations. This is an understandable mistake, because Ruscelli appropriated Dolce's earlier commentary and passed it off as his own.

4. The one exception is Dolce's reference to Ariadne's lament to Theseus in *Heroides* 10 as a model for Olimpia's similar lament when she is abandoned by Bireno in canto 10.

5. See Agnelli and Ravegnani, *Annali delle edizioni Ariostee* 1:68–69.

6. In the third of his *Tre discorsi*, a critique of Dolce's recent translation of Ovid's *Metamorphoses*, Ruscelli begins by referring to the commentary on Ariosto's imitations and the publisher's letter to the readers that were appended to the numer-ous contemporary Giolito editions of *Orlando Furioso* and calls into question Dolce's authorship of the commentary: "Nel fine di quanti Furiosi ha stampati l'honorato M. Gabriel Giolito . . . voi sapete honoratissimo M. Lodovico mio, che avanti a quelle espositioni & luoghi da quel Poeta in diversi antichi autori imitati, le quali, *essendo di chi sa Iddio*, vanno sotto il nome vostro, si legge una epistola di esso M. Gabriello a i lettori [At the end of so many Furiosos that the esteemed Gabriel Giolito has published . . . you know my most honored Lodovico that one can find a letter of the same Gabriel to the readers that precedes those commentaries on and citations of Ariosto's imitations of various ancient poets composed by God knows who, but that go under your name]" (*Tre discorsi di Gerolamo Ruscelli a M. Lodo-*

vico Dolce . . . [Venice: P. Pietrasanta, 1553], p. 83; italics mine). This comment suggests that Ruscelli felt he could appropriate Dolce's "Brieve dimostratione" because he believed Dolce's commentary was itself appropriated from elsewhere, presumably Fausto da Longiano's earlier "Annotazioni."

7. In *Il mestiere di scrivere* (p. 85) Claudia di Filippo Bareggi suggests that the "collage" of commentaries in the revised Valvassori edition of 1566 (see my comments in Chapter 2 on the prior Valvassori edition of the *Furioso*, which first appeared in 1553) was put together by Tomasso Porcacchi, another active Venetian editor of modern literature and history. Porcacchi's own "Dichiarazione d'historie et di favole" was one of the new paratexts in this 1566 *Furioso* and followed Dolce's updated commentary at the end of each canto.

8. I cite from *Orlando Furioso di M. Lodovico Ariosto; delle annotazioni de' più celebri autori che sopra esso hanno scritto* . . . (Venice: S. Orlandini, 1730). Dolce's revised commentary is easier to find in this famous synoptic edition than in the editions published by Valvassori in the 1560s.

9. Erasmo di Valvasone (1523–1593) lived most of his life in Friuli. Aside from his translation of the *Thebaid*, he also wrote *I primi quattro canti del Lancilotto* (1580), the *Lagrime di Santa Maria Maddalena* (1586), and the *Angeleida* (1590), a minor epic known for its influence on Milton's *Paradise Lost*. He knew and was in touch with Venetian literati (he was elected to the Accademia degli Uranici, a literary academy established in Venice in 1587), but little seems to be known about his relations with Lodovico Dolce. For further biographical and literary information see F. Foffano, "Erasmo di Valvasone," in *Ricerche letterarie* (Livorno, 1897), pp. 87–131.

10. Consider, for example, the twin similes at 11.20 describing the giant carrying off what seems to be Bradamante:

> e se l'arecca in spalla, e via la porta,
> come lupo talor piccolo agnello,
> o l'aquila portar ne l'ugna torta
> suole o colombo o simile altro augello.

Dolce refers only to *Aeneid* 9.561–66 as a model. Emilio Bigi notes in his recent edition of the poem that Ariosto may also have been imitating Pulci's simile of the wolf in *Morgante* (21.38), or Boiardo's in *Orlando Innamorato* (1.23.12), or Cieco's in *Mambriano* (6.440); these possibilities, however, are quite overlooked.

11. There is one significant exception to Dolce's usual assumption that Ariosto imitates one and only one model: the observation he adds to his original note on the episode of Olimpia abandoned by Bireno in canto 10. Originally he had claimed that Ariosto's account was modeled solely on Ovid's *Heroides* 10, Ariadne's lament after being abandoned by Theseus. In the revised commentary, he notes at 10.28–29 that Catullus 64 should also be consulted as a model: "Leggasi ancora il lamento, che fa la medesima Arianna presso Catullo nell'Argonautica; a' versi del quale molti di questi dell'Ariosto son simili." Dolce probably refers to Poem 64 in this way because some of the earliest manuscripts of Catullus's poem entitled it "Argonautia" on the basis of the opening line.

Catullus's account of Ariadne is indeed the other subtext in Ariosto's episode, but Dolce still wants the reader to think that some parts of Ariosto's text imitate

Ovid, other parts Catullus, not both models at once. Dolce also fails to point out that in *Heroides* 10 Ovid imitated Catullus 64—a chief reason why Ariosto wanted to evoke both ancient texts.

12. By midcentury, Italian critics had begun to appreciate the broad formal resemblances, in contrast to the structural norms of classical epic, between Ovid's *Metamorphoses* and the modern Italian romanzo, especially Ariosto's. When Giraldi defended the romanzo in his *Discorso intorno al comporre dei romanzi* (1554), he cited Ovid's departure from classical epic norms (e.g., multiplicity of stories, repeated narrative digressions, the sheer variety of matter) as an ancient precedent for the contemporary romanzo's similar challenge of these norms. For Dolce's awareness of the affinities between the nonepic structure of the *Furioso* and the *Metamorphoses*, see my comments in Chapter 4.

13. See, for example, his extensive analysis of the verbal parallels between the account of Brandimarte's funeral at 43.165ff. and the account of Pallas's funeral in *Aeneid* 11.

14. For instance, Lavezuola comments about the description at 7.54 of Ruggiero's effeminate attire while in the company of Alcina as follows: "Questo passo se bene alcuni hanno detto esser fatto a sembianza di quello di Virgilio nel quarto dell'Eneide, parmi molto somigliante a quel d'Ovidio nell'epistola di Deianira, la quale rinfaccia al marito, che per gradire al vile amore di Onfale porti il monile al collo [Even though some maintain that this passage sought to resemble Virgil's in the fourth book of the *Aeneid*, it seems to me very similar to that of Ovid in the epistle of Deianara, who reproaches her husband for wearing a necklace in order to enjoy the base love of Onfale]." He then cites *Heroides* 9.55–60. Among other references to the *Heroides*, see his comments at 7.24, 8.47, 16.68, 19.33, 33.61, and 44.62.

15. Consider, for instance, his "osservazioni" about the story of Olindro and Drusilla included in the Marganorre episode (37.56ff.). Olindro, the beloved companion of Drusilla, is killed in an ambush set up by Tanacro, one of Marganorre's two sons, who covets Drusilla for himself. Disguising her hatred, Drusilla pretends, after an unsuccessful suicide attempt, that she is ready to become Tanacro's spouse. At the ceremonies preceding their marriage she manages to make him drink a goblet of poisoned wine, which she also consumes. Expiring, she curses the dying Tanacro and expresses her satisfaction at having avenged her beloved Olindro. When he reaches this tale in canto 37, Lavezuola notes: "Questa novella di'Olindro, & di Drusilla fu tolta dall'Erotico di Plutarco. Se ne servì il Castiglione, traducendola quasi di parola in parola di Plut. nel suo Cortegiano. Fù descritto con grandi ornamenti di parole da Apuleio nell'8 dell'asino d'oro, che con avanzarlo altamente, imitò l'Ar [This novella of Olindro and Drusilla was taken from Plutarch's "Eroticus." Castiglione uses it in his *Cortegiano* translating it almost word for word from Plutarch. It was recounted with much verbal ornament by Apuleius in the eighth book of the *Golden Ass*, which Ariosto imitated while surpassing it greatly]." He then draws some specific parallels between Ariosto's and Apuleius's modifications of the story as told by Plutarch. Although modern commentators do not share his view that Apuleius is the most significant model for this tale, they confirm Lavezuola's perceptive indications that it was a retelling of Plutarch's story, partly drawn as well from Castiglione's recent retelling of Plutarch. The only source

Lavezuola overlooks is the Latin version of Plutarch's story in Francesco Barbaro's *De re uxoria* (2.1), which had apparently served as Castiglione's source. Nonetheless, he identifies enough of the prior versions to allow the reader to figure out the elaborate genealogy Ariosto sought to invoke. Incidentally, although the other stories and *novelle* recounted within the poem rarely have such a complex ancestry, Lavezuola is fond of identifying their sources or prior analogues, and this in itself is a novel feature of his commentary.

16. This partiality may stem from the fact that Poliziano was himself so often imitative. Ariosto's borrowings from Poliziano therefore allowed Lavezuola to reveal further receding genealogies of texts. For example, at 14.61 and 16.68 he cites both Poliziano and his classical Latin precedents as Ariosto's models.

17. At 1.18, before he cites the verse borrowed from an anonymous *Tristano*, Lavezuola observes: "Nota come l'Ariosto non s'è sdegnato di servirsi in questo suo poema delle cose anco de i pessimi auttori, che gli sono venuti a proposito [Observe how Ariosto did not disdain from also using in his poem matters from the worst authors that suited his purpose]." After citing the verse, he adds, "onde si vede che gli andava giudiciosamente raccogliendo l'oro dello sterco, come rispose Vergilio a chi lo riprese della frequente lettione d'Ennio [from which one sees that he judiciously extracted the gold from the excrement, as Virgil replied to those who criticized him for his frequent use of Ennius]."

18. When Lavezuola discusses the account of Caligorante's horrible dwelling at 14.49, he cites several ancient models, beginning with the cave of Caccus in *Aeneid* 7, but he totally ignores the most prominent model: Boiardo's description of the Rocca Crudele, *Orlando Innamorato* 1.8.25. The linguistic prejudice that prevailed among cinquecento readers against Boiardo's poem, and the fact that by the latter half of the century Italians read Berni's and Domenichi's *rifacimenti* of the *Orlando Innamorato* rather than the original, can also serve to explain Lavezuola's disregard of Ariosto's verbal borrowings from the *Innamorato*.

19. According to Agnelli and Ravegnani's *Annali delle edizioni Ariostee*, after 1566 Dolce's "Brieve dimostratione" was reprinted in the following thirteen Venetian editions: Comin da Trino di Monferato, 1567; Gieronimo Scotto, 1567; Domenico et G. B. Guerra, 1568, 1570, 1577; Domenico Farri, 1580, 1594; Giovanni Alberti, 1589, 1597, 1598; G. Domenico Imberti, 1590, 1612; Paulo Ugolino, 1602.

20. For further details on the debate that followed the publication of Pellegrino's *Carrafa* see Chapter 6.

CHAPTER FOUR
AFFILIATIONS WITH OVID'S *METAMORPHOSES*

1. G. B. Giraldi Cinzio, *Discorso intorno al comporre dei romanzi* (1554), in *Scritti critici*, ed. Camillo Guerrieri Crocetti (Milan: Marzorati, 1973), p. 70.

2. Ibid., p. 79.

3. For an informative account of these translations of Ovid and their cultural context see Bodo Guthmüller, "Literarische Übersetzung im Bezugsfeld Original-Leser (Am Beispiel italienischer Übersetzung der Metamorphosen Ovids im 16.

Jahrhundert)," *Bulletin d'humanisme et renaissance* 36 (1974): 233–51. See also his *Ovidio Metamorphoseos vulgare. Formen und Funktionen der volkssprachlichen Wiedergabe klassischer Dichtung in der italienischen Renaissance* (Boppard am Rhein: Boldt, 1981), pp. 252–61.

4. For a useful prepublication history of the *Trasformationi* see Salvatore Bongi, *Annali di Gabriel Giolito de'Ferrari* (Rome: Ministero della Pubblica Istruzione, 1890–1895), 1:396–97.

5. Interesting polemical comments about the genesis of Dolce's *Trasformationi* are to be found at the beginning of Girolamo Ruscelli's discourse on this translation in his *Tre discorsi*, esp. pp. 83–89. Ruscelli claims that it was Dolce, not Giolito, who actually composed the "Avvisi" to the readers appended to the various editions of the *Furioso*, and while criticizing Dolce for referring to rival translators as "Pedanti o Simie" Ruscelli maintains that Dolce's slur was aimed specifically against Anguillara (see p. 88).

6. It should be pointed out that in the late 1530s Dolce began a translation of the *Metamorphoses* in unrhymed *versi sciolti*, but only book 1 of this translation was published in 1538. Clearly, when Dolce returned to Ovid's poem later in his career, he had modernized his views about rhyme and recognized that ottava rima was a more appropriate verse form for the translation he finally completed.

7. The end of canto 5 of the *Trasformationi* (of which the last octave is also reproduced in plate 1) offers a good example of the Ariostean manner in which Dolce closes his cantos in order to arouse his reader's curiosity and prompt him to read on. We learn, before this canto ends, that Cadmus's companions, having gone in search of water, are devoured by a horrible serpent inhabiting the hidden spring they have found. (Ovid describes this fatal expedition more economically in *Metamorphoses* 3.28–49). Cadmus, in the meantime, growing increasingly worried about the delay of his men, decides to go find them. As he sets off, fully armed, to encounter instead the monstrous serpent, Dolce closes his canto:

> Ne l'una mano una lung'hasta tiene,
> Ch'un grosso ferro havea lucido e netto:
> Ne l'altra un Dardo; e più non li conviene,
> Peró, che troppo havea sicuro petto.
> Mentre serba la via, ch'al Fonte viene,
> Ne l'altro Canto ad ascoltar v'aspetto;
> Nel quale io vi verró forse contando
> Prove, che tal mai non ne fece Orlando.

Needless to say, Ovid's original narrative makes no such interruption before Cadmus's victorious battle with the serpent (cf. *Metamorphoses* 3.50–94). Dolce, on the other hand, not only chooses this moment to imitate Ariosto's tantalizing technique of closing a canto at the start of a dramatic episode—his last line actually boasts that Cadmus's exploits, about to be told in the next canto, will outshine those of Ariosto's titular hero! While such an anachronistic reference to one of Ariosto's protagonists is rare in the translation, it suffices to indicate how intent Dolce was to have his readers associate his narrative with Ariosto's.

8. Giraldi's *Discorso* on romances was also published by Giolito. Even though Giraldi claimed that it was completed in 1549, it is likely that he knew of Dolce's

translation in ottava rima before he finished his treatise, and that it intensified his awareness of the affinities between the *Metamorphoses* and the *Furioso.*

9. For a detailed account of Dolce's "rifacimento" of Virgil in ottava rima see Luciana Borsetto, "Riscrivere l'*historia*, riscrivere lo stile; il poema di Virgilio, nelle 'riduzioni' cinquecentesche di Lodovico Dolce," in *Scritture di scritture,* ed. Giancarlo Mazzacurati and Michel Plaisance (Rome: Bulzoni, 1987), pp. 405–38.

10. Anguillara's translation of the first book of the *Aeneid* was published in Padua in 1564, and that of the second book in Rome in 1566. On the lack of appeal of the *Aeneid* in ottava see Guthmüller, *Ovidio Metamorphoseos vulgare,* p. 253.

11. For a careful study of Anguillara's infidelities as a translator see Maria Moog-Grünewald, *Metamorphosen der "Metamorphosen." Rezeptionsarten d. Ovid Verwandlungsgeschichten in Italien u. Frankreich im 16. u. 17. Jh.* (Heidelberg: Winter, 1979), pp. 27–112. We both concur about Anguillara's frequent imitation of the *Furioso,* but her study treats the allusions to the *Furioso* as just one instance, albeit a major one, of Anguillara's tendency to contaminate his translation with allusions to various contemporary works of Italian literature fashionable at the time.

12. See, for example, *Metamorfosi 7,* oct. 266–69, and *OF* 43.35; or *Metamorfosi 7,* oct. 291ff., and *OF* 43.38ff. Moog-Grünewald shows (in *Metamorphosen der "Metamorphosen,"* pp. 87–98) that Anguillara's version of Cephalus and Procris, like Ariosto's story of the Mantuan host in *OF* 43, was also influenced by Niccolo da Corregio's tragicomedy, *Cephalo,* originally produced in Ferrara in 1487.

13. I discuss medieval representations of Perseus on Pegasus, as well as Ariosto's imitation of Ovid, in "Rescuing Ovid from the Allegorizers," *Comparative Literature* 30 (1978): 97–197. For more on Perseus riding Pegasus see Rensselaer Lee, "Ariosto's *Roger and Angelica* in Sixteenth Century Art: Some Facts and Hypotheses," *Studies in Late Medieval and Renaissance Painting in Honor of Millard Meiss,* ed. Irving Lavin and John Plummer (New York: New York University Press, 1977), esp. pp. 305–10.

14. How consciously Anguillara emulated Ariosto in his "translation" of Perseus's rescue of Andromeda can be seen by juxtaposing Anguillara's and Ariosto's descriptions of their heros' reactions to and exchanges with the respective damsels chained to the rock.

> *Le Metamorfosi d'Ovidio . . . di G. A. dell'Anguillara* (Venice: G. Griffio, 1561),
> 4, oct. 417–21:
>
> Perseo fa che l'augel nel lito scende,
> E più dappresso le s'accosta, e vede,
>
> . . . .
>
> Senza sapere chi sia, di lei s'accende
> Et ha del suo languir maggior mercede,
> E 'n lei le luci accese avendo fisse,
> Pien d'amore, e pietà così le disse.
>
> Donna del ferro indegna, che nel braccio
> Fuor d'ogni humanità t'annoda, e cinge,
> Ma degna ben dell'amoroso laccio,

Che i più fedeli amanti abbraccia e stringe;
Contami, chi t'ha posto in questo impaccio,
E quale Antropofago ti constringe,
A farti lagrimar su'l duro scoglio,
Che 'l lito e 'l mar fai pianger di cordoglio.

Contami il nome, il sangue, e 'l regio seno,
Che t'han dato per patria i sommi Dei;
Ch'io veggio ben nel bel viso sereno
La regia stirpe, onde discesa sei;
Che se quel, che in me può, non mi vien meno,
Ti sciorrò da quei nodi iniqui, e rei.
China ella il viso, e sì commove tanto,
Che invece di risposta accresce il pianto.

E se i legami con l'havesser tolto
Le man, vedendo ignudo il corpo tutto,
Celato avrebbe il lagrimoso volto,
L'ignudo fianco, la vergogna e 'l lutto:
Pur sì la prega il Greco, che con molto
Pianto e con poche note il rende istrutto
De l'arroganza della madre, e poi
Palese fè la patria e i maggior suoi.

Ecco, mentre che parla, un romor sorge,
E in baleno il mar tutto turbare.
Perseo alza gli occhi, e mentre in alto scorge,
Pargli un monte veder, che solchi il mare.
. . . .

Ariosto, *Orlando Furioso*, ed. Emilio Bigi (Milan: Rusconi, 1982), 10.96–99:

Creduto avria che fosse statua finta
o d'alabastro o d'altri marmi illustri
Ruggiero, e su lo scoglio così avinta
per artificio di scultori industri;
se non vedea la lacrima distinta
tra fresche rose e candidi ligustri
far rugiadose le crudette pome
e l'aura sventolar l'aurate chiome.

E come ne' begli occhi gli occhi affisse
de la sua Bradamante gli sovenne.
Pietade e amore a un tempo lo traffisse,
e di piangere a pena si ritenne;
e dolcemente alla donzella disse,
poi che del suo destrier frenò le penne:
—O donna, degna sol de la catena
con chi i suoi servi Amor legati mena,

e ben di questo e d'ogni male indegna,
chi è quel crudel che con voler perverso
d'importuno livor stringendo segna
di queste belle man l'avorio terso?—
Forza è ch'a quel parlare divegna
quale è di grana un bianco avorio asperso,
di sè vedendo quelle parte ignude,
ch'ancor che belle sian, vergogna chiude.

E coperto con man s'avrebbe il volto,
se non eran legate al duro sasso;
ma del pianto, ch'almen non l'era tolto,
lo sparse, e si sforzò di tener basso.
E dopo alcun' signozzi il parlar sciolto,
incominciò con fioco suono e lasso:
ma non seguì; che dentro il fe' restare
il gran rumor che si sentì nel mare.

15. As Orologgi points out in his "Annotationi del nono libro," Anguillara's translation of Byblis's lament, after she dreams of incestuous love with Caunus (*Metamorfosi* 9, esp. oct. 254–56), rivals Ariosto's description of Bradamante's lament after she dreams of Ruggiero (*OF* 33, esp. 62–63): "[Anguillara] si è affaticato di fare, come ha fatto in molti luoghi di queste sue traformationi una virtuosa concorrenza all'Ariosto, nel lamento, che fa Bradamante mentre godeva più soavemente il suo Ruggiero dormendo in sogno che non facea veggiando." Again, his translation of Iphis's pathetic complaint about her impossible homosexual love (*Metamorfosi* 10, esp. oct. 353–58) imitates and seeks to rival Fiordispina's impassioned lament upon her discovery of Bradamante's female identity (*OF* 25. 34–37). One must recall that both Bradamante's and Fiordispina's monologues in the *Furioso* were themselves imitations on Ariosto's part of the very passages in the *Metamorphoses* that Anguillara "translates."

16. *L'arte poetica del Sig. Antonio Minturno* (Venice: G. A. Valvassori, 1564), pp. 34–35.

17. *Poetica di Iason Denores . . .* (Padua: P. Meietto, 1588), p. 58.

18. Lodovico Castelvetro, *Poetica d'Aristotele vulgarizzata e sposta*, ed. Werther Romani (Bari: Laterza, 1978–1979), 1:239–40.

19. Giovanni de' Bardi, "In difesa dell'Ariosto," in *Della Imp. Villa Adriana e di altre sontuosissime gia adiacenti alla città di Tivoli* (Florence: Magheri, 1825), p. 67. I am grateful to Dennis Looney for this reference. See his Ph.D. dissertation, "Ovidian Influence on the Narrative of the *Orlando Furioso*" (University of North Carolina, 1987), pp. 31–33.

20. Weinberg, *Literary Criticism*, p. 989.

21. See, for example, Joseph Solodow's illuminating contrast of the *Metamorphoses* and the *Aeneid* in *The World of Ovid's Metamorphoses* (Chapel Hill: University of North Carolina Press, 1988), pp. 110–56.

22. W. R. Johnson, "The Problem of the Counter-Classical Sensibility and Its Critics," *California Studies in Classical Antiquity* 3 (1970): 125.

CHAPTER FIVE
CRITICAL RESPONSES TO NARRATIVE DISCONTINUITY IN *ORLANDO FURIOSO*

1. Malatesta, *Della nuova poesia*, pp. 17–18.
2. Here and henceforth I cite from Ludovico Ariosto, *Orlando Furioso*, ed. Emilio Bigi (Milan: Rusconi, 1982). The translation is by Guido Waldman (Oxford: Oxford University Press, 1974). All subsequent translations are from this edition.
3. Among other examples, see *OF* 8.29, 13.80–81.
4. Giraldi Cinzio, *Scritti critici*, p. 68.
5. I provide and discuss examples of such interruptions in my analysis of Harington's English translation and attenuation of them in Chapter 8.
6. In an earlier article that sought to explain the motives underlying these frustrating interruptions I proposed that Ariosto thus deprived his readers of continuity and fulfillment in order to duplicate the frustration of desire and of expectation constantly experienced by the characters in his poem. That the poet seeks and achieves this duplication becomes particularly obvious when both character and reader are made to suffer their frustration more or less simultaneously. At the end of canto 10, for example, Ruggiero, having just rescued the naked Angelica from being devoured by the Orca, carries her off on the Hippogryph. Suddenly, overwhelmed by sexual desire, he alights in a meadow. While he frantically and clumsily tries to remove his armor in order to ravish the girl, the canto is abruptly brought to a halt that is as frustrating as Ruggiero's effort to shed his gear. Considered in the context of what then follows in canto 11—the naked Angelica will manage to disappear before Ruggiero can get undressed—this interruption duplicates the sexual frustration Ruggiero is about to suffer. As readers, we are subjected repeatedly to such unpleasant deprivations and, even though these frustrations do not regularly occur at the same moment that they afflict his characters, it becomes clear that Ariosto wanted us to share this inevitable existential condition. In other words, he not only wanted the various adventures of his protagonists to illustrate the wayward discontinuity of human existence, he also managed to exploit the formal necessity of interrupting his many plots to make his readers experience that discontinuity directly. See my *"Cantus Interruptus* in the *Orlando Furioso," Modern Language Notes* 95 (1980): 66–80.
7. *I romanzi di M. Giovan Battista Pigna* (Venice: V. Valgrisi, 1554), p. 44.
8. *Scritti critici*, p. 68.
9. See *Delle lettere di M. Bernardo Tasso* (Padua: Comino, 1733), 2:323–27 and 370–72, for Bernardo's letters to Sperone Speroni; pp. 343–46 for his letter to Vincenzo Laureo; pp. 362–65 for his letter to Girolamo Molino. All these letters were written between 1557 and 1558.
10. *Opere di M. Sperone Speroni degli Alvarotti* . . . (Venice: D. Occhi, 1740), 5:521. After criticizing Ariosto's *proemi*, Speroni goes on to challenge the rationalization such authorial addresses were given by the defenders of the romanzo. Both Giraldi and Pigna had sought to justify the *proemi* as conventions that originated when the romances were oral poems and their singers turned to their listeners, especially during pauses between cantos. In the *Discorso intorno al comporre dei*

romanzi (p. 48) Giraldi proposed that these oral conventions went back to the heroic songs performed by the rhapsodes of ancient Greece. Canto divisions, he pointed out, were originally determined by the constraints of oral performance, namely, the length of recitation that an audience found tolerable before a pause was needed. Speroni flatly counters these claims in his critique of the modern romanzo. According to him, the addresses to the audience at the beginning of cantos do not predate Boiardo's *Orlando Innamorato*. The divisions into cantos, as one can see in Dante's *Commedia* and Petrarch's *Trionfi*, allow for welcome pauses and make the narration more intelligible. But, he writes, "che la divisione in canti sia fatta, perché si cantassero, o si debbano cantare, è una pazzia [that the division into cantos occurred because they were sung aloud or had to be sung is a mad claim]" (p. 521). The dozens upon dozens of editions of the *Furioso* already printed by 1560 made Speroni all too aware of the fiction of Ariosto's pretense of addressing his *canti* to a group of courtly auditors. It is not surprising, therefore, that he thought it "pazzia" to justify the romanzo's narrative technique on the grounds that it was still performed orally.

Speroni's polemic suggests that the hostility of the neoclassical literati toward the modern romanzo stemmed, in part, from the fact that, although it was printed, this kind of poetry retained too many conventions and traces of the earlier oral tradition of *cantastorie* from which it descended. Besides their other objectionable qualities, the *proemi* and other authorial addresses to the audience may have already been considered formal anachronisms inappropriate in poetry intended for readers in the new age of print.

11. *Delle lettere di M. Bernardo Tasso* 2:363.

12. *L'arte poetica del Sig. Antonio Minturno* (Venice: G. A. Valvassori, 1563), p. 35.

13. Filippo Sassetti, "Discorso contro l'Ariosto," MS BNF Magl. 9, 125, fols. 189–204, was first published by Giuseppe Castaldi in *Rendiconti della Reale Accademia dei Lincei* 22 (1913): 473–524. I cite from this published version, pp. 502–3. The critique of Ariosto's interventions follows immediately after.

14. *Aristotle's Poetics*, trans. James Hutton (New York: Norton, 1982), p. 73.

15. Torquato Tasso, "A i lettori," in *Rinaldo*, ed. G. Bonfigli (Bari: Laterza, 1936), p. 5.

16. Lodovico Castelvetro, *"Poetica" d'Aristotele vulgarizzata e sposta*, ed. Werther Romani (Bari: Laterza, 1978–1979), 2:164–65.

17. *Annotationi di M. Alessandro Piccolomini, nel libro della Poetica d'Aristotele . . .* (Venice: G. Guarisco, 1575), pp. 385–86.

18. *Orlando Furioso, Translated into English Heroical Verse by Sir John Harington (1591)*, ed. Robert McNulty (Oxford: Clarendon, 1972), p. 13. See Chapter 8 for my discussion of Harington's modifications of Ariosto's interruptions.

Alberto Lavezuola provides further evidence of late cinquecento criticism of the *proemi* when he defends them in his *Osservationi . . . sopra il Furioso* appended to the 1584 Franceschi edition of the *Furioso*. In his comments on canto 2 Lavezuola begins by observing that "hanno biasimato alcuni l'Ariosto nell'usare nel principio de' canti alcune moralità, stimando che ciò non habbia a far nulla con la testura della favola, et che l'interrompere l'ordine dell'opera con simili digressioni sia cosa disdicevole & vitiosa [some have blamed Ariosto for making moral pronouncements at the beginning of cantos, deeming that these have nothing to do with the structure of the plot, and that to interrupt the narrative sequence with such digressions is wrong and inappropriate]." He then justifies the *proemi* on the grounds that they have ancient precedent, and that they give the reader a needed respite after every canto. He denies that these pauses obstruct the flow of the narrative, since readers who find them a hindrance can simply disregard them and go on with the story. This notion that readers can merely skip the *proemi* and read on was obviously entertained by the various editors of the poem who provided marginal indices telling readers where suspended narratives were resumed so that they could go to the sequels directly without having to be bothered by Ariosto's interruptions.

CHAPTER SIX
LIONARDO SALVIATI'S DEFENSE OF *ORLANDO FURIOSO*

1. One of the first modern accounts of the quarrel between Tasso's and Ariosto's champions is to be found in Angelo Solerti, *Vita di Torquato Tasso* (Turin: Loescher, 1895), 1:414ff.; for a more detailed account of the quarrel see Weinberg, *Literary Criticism*, pp. 991–1073. I am indebted to Weinberg's study. See also Peter M. Brown, "The Historical Significance of the Polemics over Tasso's *Gerusalemme Liberata*," *Studi secenteschi* 11 (1970): 3–23, and his *Lionardo Salviati: A Critical Biography* (Oxford: Clarendon, 1974), pp. 205–27.

I pay virtually no attention to Tasso's own contribution to the quarrel (namely, his *Apologia in difesa della sua Gierusalemme liberata*), nor to the responses it provoked, because they concern the *Liberata* more than the *Furioso*. For Tasso's role in the debate see, aside from Solerti and Weinberg, the penetrating study of Tasso's *Apologia* in Margaret Ferguson, *Trials of Desire: Renaissance Defenses of Poetry* (New Haven: Yale University Press, 1983).

2. Camillo Pellegrino, *Il Carrafa, o vero della epica poesia, dialogo di Camillo Pellegrino all'Illustrissimo Signor Marco Antonio Carrafa*, in *Trattati di poetica e retorica del Cinquecento*, ed. Bernard Weinberg (Bari: Laterza, 1972), 3:317. Hereafter page numbers to this edition will follow immediately after the citations.

Pellegrino is known primarily for *Il Carrafa* and his role in the debate that ensued. Born in Capua around 1527 (he also died there in 1603), he was not only an early champion of Tasso's poetry but also one of his important Southern admirers. On Pellegrino and Tasso's other Southern champions in Naples see Amedeo Quondam, *La parola nel labirinto: Società e scrittura del Manierismo a Napoli* (Rome: Laterza, 1975), pp. 25–61.

3. Weinberg, *Literary Criticism*, p. 994.

4. For some useful discussion of the cinquecento interpretations of Aristotle's four requisites for *ethos* (*Poetics* 1454a16–33) and their translation into more Horatian notions of character portrayal, see Marvin Herrick, *The Fusion of Horatian and Aristotelian Literary Criticism, 1531–1555* (Urbana: University of Illinois Press, 1946), pp. 48–57; and Antonio Garcia Berrio, *La formación de la teoría literaria moderna* (Madrid: CUSPA, 1977), pp. 129–35, 158–62. Bernard Weinberg also discusses this topic in numerous sections of his *Literary Criticism* (see the index under "Character, requisites for").

5. Attendolo cites further examples of inconsistency in Rodomonte's characteri-

zation: "Nel ponte poi del sepolcro d'Isabella, gitatto da cavallo da Bradamante, vien finto che fuori del suo costume perda l'usato ardire; e d'infido che egli era (avendo detto di lui: 'e nel mancar di fede / Tutta a lui la bugiarda Africa cede'), fa che divenga osservantissimo della promessa da lui fatta a Bradamante di liberare i prigioni mandati in Africa, dove il costume richiedeva che non osservasse la fede ne si donasse per vinto [Then on the bridge by Isabella's tomb, unhorsed by Bradamante, he is presented out of character having lost his usual daring. From the faithless individual that he was (having said of him: 'in breaking faith, / the whole of deceitful Africa yielded to him'), the author makes him become totally respectful of his promise to Bradamante to free the prisoners sent to Africa, whereas his character required that he not be faithful and that he not admit defeat]" (p. 327).

6. On Pellegrino's elevation of "locuzione artificiosa" as a source of invention, and its importance in his evaluation of Tasso, see Amedeo Quondam, *La parola nel labirinto*, pp. 32–43.

7. See Weinberg, *Literary Criticism*, pp. 997–1073.

8. Ibid., p. 1039. Italian readers have been inclined to emphasize the jocular aspects (pointing, for example, to the droll imagery of milling and sifting flour adopted by the Cruscans) of Salviati's attack against Pellegrino and tend, therefore, to take the debate less seriously than American or Anglo-Saxon readers (e.g., Weinberg, Brown). Because I also consider that the issues at stake in the debate are no laughing matter, some may fault me for not dwelling enough on Salviati's pugnacious wit despite my subsequent discussion of his irreverent and humorous treatment of Homer and Virgil.

9. *Lo 'Nfarinato secondo ovvero dello 'Nfarinato Accademico della Crusca, risposta al libro intitolato Replica di Camillo Pellegrino ec. Nella qual risposta sono incorporate tutte le scritture, passate tra detto Pellegrino, e detti Accademici intorno all'Ariosto, e al Tasso, in forma e ordine di dialogo* . . . (Florence: A. Padovani, 1588), p. 34. Hereafter page references to this edition will immediately follow the citations. This text was virtually reprinted, with its spelling modernized, as *Il Carrafa ovvero dell'epica poesia dialogo di Camillo Pellegrino coll'aggiunta delle chiose della Crusca, della Replica di Pellegrino, e della Risposta dell'Infarinato secondo*, in *Opere di Torquato Tasso colle controversie sulla Gerusalemme*, ed. Giorgio Rosini (Pisa: Capurro, 1827), vol. 18.

Lionardo Salviati (1540–1587) played an important role in Florence's literary life in the latter decades of the cinquecento and was one of the founders and principal supporters of the Accademia della Crusca. For more on his role as a man of letters see Brown, *Lionardo Salviati*.

10. In his *Discorsi dell'arte poetica* (composed in the early 1560s, but not published until 1587) Tasso had denied any generic difference between epic and romance on similar Aristotelian grounds. "Da la convenienza dunque delle azioni imitate e degli istrumenti e del modo d'imitare, si conclude essere la medesima spezie di poesia quella ch'epica vien detta e quella che romanzo si chiama" (*Prose*, ed. Ettore Mazzali [Milan and Naples: Ricciardi, 1959], p. 377). Tasso's motives for asserting the generic sameness of epic and romance differed, however, from Salviati's. First, the argument supported Tasso's claims that *Orlando Innamorato* and *Orlando Furioso* were not another kind of poetry but defective examples of heroic poetry. Second, his argument served to occlude the actual generic mix of

romance and epic that characterized his *Liberata*. For further discussion of this second motive see my "Self-Justifying Norms in the Genre Theories of Italian Renaissance Poets," *Philological Quarterly* 67 (1988), esp. pp. 205–14.

11. See my comments on Orazio Ariosto's *Difese* in the next chapter.

12. Salviati makes it clear that he does not accept Aristotle's guidelines in the *Poetics* because of the Greek philosopher's "autorità," but because these recommendations are based on rational principles. In one of his early objections in the *Stacciata prima* he stated: "Le regole dell'arte sono veramente nella poesia, come le massime nelle scienze: ma non per ciò, che dice l'Attendolo, cioè per l'avere avuti più chiari scrittori, ma per l'essere fondate su la ragione: senza la quale non basterebbe nè l'esempio d'Omero, nè l'autorità d'Aristotile, il quale non ne lasciò ammaestramento nella poetica, che non fosse fondato su la detta ragione [The rules of art in poetry are really like rules in the sciences: but not on the grounds claimed by Attendolo, namely, because the most famous writers held them, but for their being founded on reason: without which Homer's example would not suffice, nor the authority of Aristotle, who did not leave us one precept in his *Poetics* that was not based on reason]" (p. 144).

13. "La favola del Furioso," he concludes, "è di perfetta unità, ma in essa, senza punto scemarle quella perfezione, ha saputo il poeta ritrovar modo d'allargarla, e di renderla ampia, e magnifica, e varia, e dilettevole per conseguente, più che altro poeta sapesse mai, accozzando due virtù insieme, che quasi son contrastanti [The plot of the *Furioso* has perfect unity, yet without diminishing this perfection at all, the poet knew how to find a way of enlarging the plot, and make it ample, magnificent, and various, and delightful as a result. More than any other poet ever knew how to, he thus combined two nearly opposite qualities]" (p. 77).

14. It should be said that in one or two instances the parallels Fornari draws between Ariosto's and Homer's poems in his 1549 "Apologia" anticipate Salviati's technique of showing precedents for Ariosto's so-called flaws in Homer's epics. Thus Fornari argues that when Ariosto is accused of inserting apparently extraneous tales into the narrative, he is simply following Homer, who also introduced incidental episodes into his epic. And these episodes, Fornari writes, "tal volta si veggono esser tali, che niuna convenienza haranno con quella unica actione, come nella Iliade il ragionamento di Glauco con Diomede sopra i fatti di Bellerophonte, & nell'Odissea i discorsi del porcaio ad Ulisse co quali essempi potrassi francamente, il nostro poeta difendere [are occasionally such that they have no connection to the main single action—for instance, Glaucus's discussion with Diomedes about the deeds of Bellerophon in the *Iliad*, and, in the *Odyssey*, the swineherd's speeches to Odysseus. With such examples, our poet can openly defend himself]" (*Spositione*, p. 37). But unlike Salviati, whose emphasis on the many "unclassical" features of Homer's poems is intended to bring them down to the level of modern vernacular poetry, and to defy the notions of their classical exemplarity advanced by the more conservative neo-Aristotelians, Fornari remains much more respectful of Homer's authority, and does not question the superior and normative status that Homer's epics have in relation to Ariosto's poem.

15. Two years before Pellegrino's *Carrafa* appeared, Salviati had already countered the criticism of *costume* in the *Furioso* by a similar criticism of the *Aeneid*. In a letter to Giovanni de' Bardi, dated 28 September 1582, Salviati demonstrated how

Virgil "havesse peccato nel costume" in his presentation of Aeneas at Carthage. Using much the same language that he employed in his subsequent debate with Pellegrino, he asks, "E poi che bella cosa è quella, un huomo di quella qualità, e che haveva un figliuol già si grande, e che haveva si gran fini, e si grandi imprese alle mani, andarsi a perder nelli amorazzi, come se fosse stato un giovinetto di prima barba? E se mi sarà risposto, che l'Ariosto fece Orlando furioso, replicherò che Orlando non è la principal persona dell'azion del Furioso, ma Carlo, et Agramante ai quali non fa mai il poeta far cosa sconvenevole [And what, then, is admirable about a man of this quality, who already had so grown a son, and who had such great purposes and undertakings at hand, who goes and gets lost in love entanglements as if he were a youngster? And if someone were to reply that Ariosto made Orlando go insane, I would answer that Orlando is not the principal character in the action, but Charles and Agramante, and they are not ever made to do anything inappropriate]." For the full text of the letter see Peter M. Brown, "In Defence of Ariosto: Giovanni de' Bardi and Lionardo Salviati," *Studi secenteschi* 12 (1971): 6–10. As Brown shows, other parts of the defense of the *Furioso* in this letter are later reiterated in the anonymous *Stacciata prima* (1585), and can therefore serve to confirm Salviati's authorship of the Cruscans' first response to Pellegrino's dialogue.

16. Even Pellegrino himself had to admit that Homer and Virgil occasionally disregarded epic rules. For example, when he had faulted Ariosto for failing to make Orlando "similar" to the wise and chaste paladin of previous chronicles, he had acknowledged that Virgil was also blamed by some for a similar transgression: when he depicts Dido killing herself because of her unrequited love for Aeneas, when history claimed she had died for the sake of her husband Sichaeus. Since his opponent has already brought it up, Salviati cannot counter the charge about Orlando by citing Dido in *Aeneid* 4, but he does reply that if Ariosto had modified history as much as Virgil did in this instance, opponents would not have ceased to clamor about it (p. 210).

Again, at the end of the discussion of *costume* in Pellegrino's dialogue, Carrafa had pointed out that in the *Poetics* (chap. 15) Aristotle had cited various infractions of decorum in ancient Greek drama and even in Homer. He correctly recalls that Aristotle refers to a play (the lost *Scylla* of Timotheos) in which Odysseus is depicted crying, an inappropriate state for such a fearless hero. In his response, Salviati, who is so keen to "desacralize" the revered poems of antiquity, cannot resist reminding Pellegrino that Homer's Odysseus, who is so often a cheat and a fraud, and Achilles, who cries "come un bamboccio intorno alla mamma" over the loss of Briseis, could also be added to Aristotle's list (p. 148).

17. The sense that Salviati is not infrequently arguing just for the sake of arguing is confirmed in a letter he wrote to his opponent in 1586 assuring Pellegrino that in his other writings on poetry, where he will not have to act as a spokesman for the Cruscans, the "Infarinato" (whose identity was yet unknown to Pellegrino) will express views quite contrary to those he has voiced, for argument's sake, in the *Stacciata prima*: "E vedrallo Vostra Signoria in esso medesimo Infarinato, il quale in altre sue scritture, dove da senno favellerà di cose di poesia, sarà in molte cose contraria a quella che avrà detto per ragion di disputa sostenendo i detti

dell'Accademia [della Crusca]." For Salviati's entire letter, see Solerti, *Vita di Torquato Tasso* 2:263.

18. As his 1582 letter to Giovanni de' Bardi attests (see note 15), Salviati was championing the *Furioso* before the question of the merits of Tasso's rival epic entered the debate.

CHAPTER SEVEN

OTHER DEFENSES OF *ORLANDO FURIOSO* IN THE 1580s

1. *Difese dell'Orlando Furioso dell'Ariosto fatte dal Sig. Horatio Ariosto*, in *Apologia del S. Torquato Tasso in difesa della sua Gierusalemme liberata, a gli Accademici della Crusca, con le accuse, & difese dell'Orlando Furioso dell'Ariosto* . . . (Ferrara: G. Vasalini, 1586), p. 203. Henceforth, page references to this edition (the first edition appeared in 1585) will immediately follow the citations.

2. Tasso responded to Orazio's *Difese* in a short pamphlet entitled *Delle differenze poetiche* (1587), reprinted in *Le prose diverse di Torquato Tasso, nuovamente raccolte . . . da Cesare Guasti* (Florence: Le Monnier, 1875), pp. 431–41.

3. *Trattato di M. Francesco Caburacci da Immola. Dove si dimostra il vero, & novo modo di fare le imprese. Con un breve discorso in difesa dell'Orlando Furioso di M. Lodovico Ariosto* (Bologna: G. Rossi, 1580), pp. 75–77. Henceforth, page references to this edition will immediately follow the citations. For more on Caburacci's treatise see Klaus Hempfer, *Diskrepante Lektüren*, pp. 139–43.

4. See, for example, the more conventional list of the poem's defects cited in Malatesta's *Della nuova poesia* (1589), which I quote at the beginning of Chapter 5.

5. "L'intentione dell'Ariosto," as Caburacci puts it, "non fu mai di comporre una Epopeia; argomento ne sia, che non ha seguiti i precetti di quella; ma studiò bene di produrre una nuova poesia, sapendo quanto nella novità stia di forza poetica. Et vedendo le tre specie semplici, cioè la Tragedia, l'Epopeia, & la Comedia essere già note, & trattate da tutti, rivolse l'animo a mescolare tutte le materie loro insieme, regolandole però con il modo Epico [It was never Ariosto's intention to compose an epic poem, which is why he did not follow epic rules. But he worked hard at producing a new poetry, knowing how much poetic force comes from novelty. And seeing that the three simple genres, namely, tragedy, epic, and comedy, were already known and treated by all, he turned his mind to mixing all their subject matters together, regulating them, however, by writing in an epic manner]" (pp. 81–82).

6. Even though it was published in 1589, Malatesta's dialogue is set in 1581. It is possible that the author set it at this earlier date, the year in which Tasso's *Gerusalemme Liberata* first appeared, in order to avoid comparisons between Ariosto and Tasso, as well as to stay free of the quarrel that erupted between their respective supporters.

For Weinberg's comments on the dialogue see his *Literary Criticism*, pp. 662–66, 1043–45. But see also the more useful, albeit scattered, comments on Malatesta in Hempfer, *Diskrepante Lektüren*, pp. 86–89, 102–4, 109–11.

7. I cite the list of complaints at the opening of Chapter 5.

8. *Della nuova poesia o vero delle difese del Furioso, dialogo del Signor Gioseppe Malatesta* (Verona: S. delle Donne, 1589), p. 42. Hereafter page numbers to this edition will immediately follow the citations.

9. For Speroni's account of the genesis of the *Furioso* see ibid., pp. 55–59. Shortly after, Speroni qualifies the clear distinction he draws between the two genres by maintaining that the chivalric romance can possess epic attributes such as "gravità" and "adempie benissimo le parti dell'epica maestà" (p. 62).

10. Speroni maintains "che sia diversa la pluralità delle attioni di Statio, e degli altri da quella dell'Ariosto . . . , & concedero, che questo suo modo di poetare sia nuovo, & non più visto, nè sentito giamai. Ma soggiungero bene, che di questo nè il Signor Abbate, nè altri deve farsene punto maraviglia, però che l'Arte Poetica ha ritrovata in esso Ariosto, & negli altri romanzieri quella mutazione che, come Arte, era di necessità, che trovasse [that the multiplicity of actions in Statius and other ancient poets is different from that in Ariosto . . . , and I will admit that [Ariosto's] mode of writing is new and never previously seen or heard. But I will also add that neither Signor Abbate nor others should be at all surprised by this, since in Ariosto and other romance poets the art of poetry has undergone the change that, as an art, it necessarily has to undergo]" (pp. 105–6).

11. On the issue of *docere* and *delectare* as ends of poetry in sixteenth-century poetics, especially in interpretations of Horace's *Ars poetica*, see Garcia Berrio, *Teoría literaria moderna*, pp. 331–410. See also Bernard Weinberg's useful remarks concerning later sixteenth century views about the end of poetry in his "Nota critica generale," in *Trattati di poetica e retorica del Cinquecento*, vol. 1, esp. pp. 553–54. He points out that exponents of hedonistic theories were able to enlist Aristotle's authority in their arguments against traditionalist advocates of poetic didacticism given that in the *Poetics* Aristotle maintained that the effect of proper mimesis was pleasure. Nonetheless, the rhetorical orientation of the culture meant that poetry's ends continued to be conflated with those of oratory. "*Docere, movere, delectare*," Weinberg writes, "restavano i punti principali di riferimento quando si consideravano i fini della poesia. A questa tradizione si aggiunse (sopratutto coll'avvento della Controriforma) il potere delle autorità ecclesiastiche, che si opponevano all'estensione del principio del *delectare*, insistendo su quello del *docere*" (ibid., p. 554).

12. One can perceive how unacceptable Malatesta's hedonistic theory of poetry remained to more traditional theorists, outside his dialogue, by the vociferous rebuttal made against the specific claims advanced by his spokesman Speroni in the first of Faustino Summo's *Discorsi poetici . . . Ne quali si discorreno le piu principali questioni di poesia . . .* (Padua: F. Bolzetta, 1600). Summo's attempt to refute Malatesta's claims about the end of poetry, more than ten years after *Della nuova poesia* was published, further illustrates that the subject of debate between rival theorists was no longer Ariosto's poem but the new definitions of poetry the *Furioso* was shown to either exemplify or violate.

13. The same is true, incidentally, of Malatesta's *Della poesia romanzesca* (Rome: G. Faciotto, 1596), which was presented as the immediate continuation of the dialogue in *Della nuova poesia*, even though the second and third days of discussion that it records were published only seven years later. In this later sequel one finds, once again, that the *Furioso* is a "pre-text" used to confirm the basic argument of the treatise: the inadequacy of the epic in modern times in comparison to

the romanzo. The so-called second day of discussion devotes much more attention to Homer's and Virgil's epics (most of it criticism of their lack of *varietà*, and of their breaches of modern decorum in the representation of Achilles and Aeneas) than to the *Furioso*, which is brought up only to reassert the desirability of multiplicity of actions, and of adherence to current "usanza."

It should be said that in *Della nuova poesia* the speakers do bring up the issue of Ariosto's scabrousness at the end of the dialogue, but the ensuing defense of the so-called dirty episodes in the *Furioso* (see pp. 274–78) constitutes one of the very few occasions on which particular aspects of the poem are discussed in Malatesta's work.

14. Statements like the following assume that Ariosto was fully conscious of Aristotle's *Poetics* and its limitations: "Et havendo l'Ariosto con occhio molto ben sano vedute queste imperfettioni dell'Arte Aristotelica, volse fuggirle prudentissimamente [Having seen with a sure eye these defects in Aristotle's art of poetry, Ariosto most prudently sought to avoid them]" (p. 137). On more than one occasion Malatesta's speakers also presume that there already existed in Ariosto's time an awareness of generic categories and boundaries that were not, in fact, even defined or discussed until some time after Ariosto's death.

CHAPTER EIGHT
HARINGTON'S ENGLISH REFRACTIONS OF *ORLANDO FURIOSO*

1. For more information on the Spanish translations of the *Furioso* and on its reception in sixteenth-century Spain see Maxime Chevalier, *L'Arioste en Espagne (1530–1650): Recherches sur l'influence du "Roland Furieux"* (Bordeaux: Institut d'études iberiques, 1966). On the reception of the *Furioso* in sixteenth-century France see Enea Balmas, "Note sulla fortuna dell'Ariosto in Francia nel Cinquecento," in his *Saggi e studi sul Rinascimento francese* (Padua: Liviana, 1982), pp. 75–103. See also the relevant pages in Alexandre Cioranescu, *L'Arioste en France: Des origines à la fin du XVIIIe siècle* (Paris: Editions des Presses Modernes, 1939). Crude and erroneous though it was, the French prose translation of the *Furioso* was commercially successful: it enjoyed twelve reprintings between 1543 and 1571, and if one adds Chappuys's prose translation, which was largely a reworking of the earlier anonymous one, six more editions were published between 1576 and 1600. The affiliation between the *Furioso* in this prose translation and the Spanish *Amadís* was made explicit on the title page: "Si d'Amadis la tresplaisante histoire / Vers les Francoys a eu nouuellement / Tant de faueur, de credit, et de gloire. / Parce qu'elle est traduicte doctement. / Le Furieux, qui dit si proprement / D'Armes, d'Amours, et de ses passions / Surpassera, en ce totallement/ Auilissant toutes traductions."

Du Bellay urges his fellow poets to elevate the French language to the illustrious levels of Greek and Latin "comme a faict de nostre tens en son vulgaire un Arioste Italien, que j'oseroy (n'estoit la saincteté des vieulx poemes) comparer à un Homere & Virgile" (*La deffence et illustration de la langue francoyse*, ed. Henri Chamard [Paris: Didier, 1970], p. 128).

2. *Orlando Furioso, Translated into English heroical Verse by Sir John Harington (1591)*, ed. McNulty, p. 9. Hereafter page references to this edition will immediately follow the citations.

3. I cite more fully from Clemente Valvassori's preface in Chapter 2.

4. The first modern scholar to point out Harington's debt to Fornari was Susannah McMurphy, in *Spenser's Use of Ariosto for Allegory* (Seattle: University of Washington Press, 1924). Other studies that discuss Fornari's *Spositione* as a source of Harington's notes to every canto as well as of his prefatory defense are: Townsend Rich, *Harington and Ariosto: A Study in Elizabethan Verse Translation* (New Haven: Yale University Press, 1940); Robert McNulty, in the introduction to his edition cited above; and John Spevak, "Sir John Harington's Theoretical and Practical Criticism: The Sources and Originality of His Apparatus to the *Orlando Furioso*," Ph.D. diss. (University of Chicago, 1978). Spevak also demonstrates the importance of the commentaries in the Franceschi edition (Venice, 1584) as sources for Harington's apparatus, especially Lavezuola's "Osservationi" which I discussed in Chapter 3.

5. See Fornari, *Spositione*, pp. 40–43.

6. Ibid., p. 38.

7. Minturno particularly objected to the untimely interruptions that break up romance narrative, and if Harington had read the following passage, in which Minturno eventually denies that these abrupt suspensions can produce any pleasure, he could have deduced that the practice described was particularly common in the *Furioso*: "Ma non concede [il tempo] che impresa una battaglia, o cominciata una tempesta, o qualunque altra cosa, nel meglio s'interrompa, e quando più se n'attende il fine, si tralasci per trattar d'alcuna altra facenda, la quale ad altre persone, in altra parte, nel medesimo processo di tempo avvenuta sia; com'hanno propriamente in costume i romanzatori senza riguardo di ciò, che 'l tempo ricusa, e del desiderio, che lascian negli animi degli ascoltanti anzi molesto, che dilettevole. Percioché a niuno ragionevolmente dee piacere, che alcuna cosa interrota gli sia, quanto più gli diletta" (*L'arte poetica*, p. 35). I discussed this passage in Chapter 5. Gregory Smith proposed years ago (in his edition of *Elizabethan Critical Essays* [Oxford: Oxford University Press, 1904], 2:425) that Harington may have borrowed his definition of "peripetia" from Minturno's *De poeta* (1559), the Latin antecedent of the *Arte poetica*; and John Spevak ("Sir John Harington's Criticism," pp. 93ff.) presumes, as I do, that Harington knew the *Arte poetica* equally well.

8. Malatesta, *Della nuova poesia*, p. 17. As already noted in Chapter 5, the speaker, Scipione Gonzaga, describes the objectionable narrative shifts as "il segnar le materie, che narra intempestivamente, & quando il lettore aspetta ogn'altra cosa, che di vedersele toglier dinanti." Harington's knowledge of Malatesta's dialogue was first pointed out by Margaret Trotter in "Harington's Sources," *TLS* (30 December 1944), p. 631. She showed that Harington's defense of Ariosto's chasteness reiterated claims made in *Della nuova poesia* (pp. 240–41) and also resembled Scipione Gonzaga's defense of Ariosto's modesty (pp. 269–80).

9. Townsend Rich (*Harington and Ariosto*, pp. 50–69) showed that *Orlando Furioso* (Venice: F. de Franceschi, 1584) was the Italian edition most used by Harington. Aside from appropriating the Porro engravings in the Franceschi edition to illustrate his translation, Harington drew most of his concluding "Briefe and Summarie Allegorie" of the poem from the "Allegoria di Gioseffo Bononome sopra il Furioso" also included in the Franceschi edition.

10. As I have shown in Chapter 3, Lavezuola's "Osservationi" were devoted primarily to Ariosto's imitations, but in the course of his commentary he occasionally referred to critical opinions provoked by certain aspects of the poem. It was usually from Lavezuola that Harington learned about these opinions. For instance, in a marginal note to *OF* 25.51 (when Ricciardetto tells Fiordispina that he is really his twin sister Bradamante transformed into a male by a fairy) Harington writes: "This is a frivolous tale devised by him to blear her eys, and therfore it is not requisite it should be probable, though Castelvetro, an Italian wryter, found fault with this because, he sayth, it should have had more probabilitie." Harington learned about Castelvetro's reaction from Lavezuola's comment on canto 25: "È tassato in questa favola l'Ar.[iosto] nel Commentario della Poetica d'Arist. dicendo che non par verisimile."

11. John Spevak is one of the few scholars to have stressed the difference between the "moral" and "allegorical" interpretations Harington provides. See "Sir John Harington's Criticism," esp. pp. 162ff.

There has been a tendency in modern commentary on Harington's translation to doubt the good faith of Harington's allegorizations. A corollary view is that it was Harington's "mauvaise conscience" that prompted him to append tropological and allegorical readings to the poem as a way of appeasing censurers who might consider the poem "wanton" and frivolous without them. See, as a representative, albeit subtle, example of such a modern view, T. G. Nelson, "Sir John Harington and the Renaissance Debate over Allegory," *Studies in Philology* 82 (1985): 359–79. I do not share Nelson's view that Harington's moralizations betray doubts about *allegoresis* as a way of interpreting and justifying poetry. In my opinion, Harington took his interpretive project most seriously because he was convinced of the didactic value of the poem, and also because he realized that the value of his translation depended quite directly on the moral and educational benefits that the poem was shown to possess.

12. For example, Harington's "moral" to book 15 begins by commenting on Ariosto's own moral observations in the *proemio* to canto 15. See, for additional examples of Harington's tendency to elaborate on Ariosto's proemi, the morals to books 5, 11, 16, 21, 36, and 38, among others.

Starting with Dolce's, I discuss the *allegorie* prefacing each canto in Italian editions of the poem in Chapter 2. Aside from reiterating some of Fornari's moralizations (which, for some reason, only began in the *Spositione* at canto 12), Harington seems to have appropriated a number of Clemente Valvassori's *allegorie* which accompanied the poem in the several editions published by G. A. Valvassori in the 1550s.

13. See, for additional examples, *OF* 22.28 as compared to Harington 22.23, and *OF* 10.73, which Harington virtually omits.

14. An example of Ariosto's facetious effort to make his more fantastic creations seem part of the actual world can be found in the first description of the marvelous Hippogryph in canto 4:

> Non è finto il destrier, ma naturale,
> ch'una giumenta generò d'un grifo:
> simile al padre avea la piuma e l'ale,

li piedi anteriori, il capo e il grifo;
in tutte l'altre membra parea quale
era la madre, e chiamasi ipoogrifo;
che nei monti Rifei vengon, ma rari,
molto di là dagli aghiacciati mari.

(4.18)

Again, the amusing insistence about the real existence of this fabulous creature ("Non è finto il destrier, ma naturale . . . nei monti Rifei vengon, ma rari . . .) only serves to highlight its fantasticalness. Harington retained these truth claims in his translation. But his rendering suggests that he wanted such claims to be read quite literally:

But yet the beast he rode was not of art
But gotten of a Griffeth and a Mare
And like a Griffeth had the former part,
And wings and head and clawes that hideous are
And passing strength and force and ventrous hart,
But all the rest may with a horse compare.
Such beasts as these the hils of Ryfee yeeld
Though in these parts they have bene seene but seeld.

(4.13)

A notable instance of Harington's effort to make the marvelous events or characters that he does not interpret allegorically part of this world occurs in the notes to book 43, when he tries to authenticate the fairy Manto. First he cites historical records ("I finde written of her that when Thebs was razed by *Alexander*, this *Manto*, daughter of Tyresia, being learned in magick as well as her father, came unto that part of Italy where Mantua is now . . ."), and then he points out that strange tales about such creatures are told by "credible persons."

15. In his *Spositione* Fornari maintained from the start that the basis of Ariosto's poem was historical, since authoritative chronicles confirm the actual existence of Orlando, Rinaldo, and the other knights. Harington's serious treatment of Turpin's authority could only have been reinforced by Fornari's further claim that the historical veracity of Ariosto's Carolingian matter was attested by his frequent references to Turpin. Ariosto, writes Fornari, "così anchora in abbracciar materia che tenga del fondamento verace, non fu mica negligente. Et di qui viene, che tante volte cita Turpino Arcivescovo, il quale pienamente scrisse le chroniche delle cose di Francia [so also in appropriating matter with a truthful basis, was not at all negligent. And this is the reason that he cites so many times the Archbishop Turpin, who chronicled fully the matters of France]" (*Spositione*, p. 77).

For examples of Ariosto's facetious references to Turpin and Harington's earnest rendering of same, see *OF* 23.38 and Harington's translation at 23.28; or *OF* 26.22–23 versus Harington 26.9. Again, a representative example of Harington's unironic use of Turpin's authority occurs in canto 44, when Astolfo sends home the Nubian troops who helped the Christians conquer Biserta. The narrator reports that the horses of these warriors turned back into the stones they were before Astolfo miraculously transformed them into steeds. Here, as elsewhere in the poem (and as Boiardo already did before him), Ariosto facetiously cites Turpin's text to authenticate this incredible event:

> Scrive Turpino, come furo ai passi
> de l'alto Atlante, che i cavalli loro
> tutti in un tempo diventaron sassi;
> si che, come venir, se ne tornoro.

(*OF* 44.23)

Harington translates the passage quite faithfully:

> *Turpino* writes that they [the Nubians] no sooner came
> Unto the mountaine Atlas stonie roote
> But that their horses stones againe became,
> And so they all went home againe on foote.

(44.20)

One can infer from the context how seriously Harington takes Turpin's authority. When, two stanzas earlier, the narrator describes how the ships Astolfo had magically created out of branches also return to their leafy state, Harington, not having Turpin's authentication to rely on, adds as a marginal explanation, "Looke in the Allegorie of myracles," referring to his allegorization of Astolfo's miraculous metamorphoses in canto 38. Further proof that he believes, or at least assumes that his readers believe, Turpin's authentication is that he does not provide in his notes any allegorical interpretation of this extraordinary retransformation. Given the care with which he usually allegorizes all that is incredible (including Astolfo's prior transformation of these stones into horses), the absence of allegorization in this case indicates that Turpin's word suffices to give the event historical veracity.

16. On Harington's rationalization of Ariosto's fabulous episodes see Judith Lee's final pages in "The English Ariosto: The Elizabethan Poet and the Marvelous," *Studies in Philology* 77 (1980): 277–99. In this respect, as in so many others, it is likely that Harington was influenced by Fornari's earlier efforts to rationalize and authenticate some of Ariosto's overtly fabulous episodes. For example, in his commentary to canto 6 Fornari had taken pains to show that Alcina's island was probably somewhere near Japan, and later he tries to make geographically intelligible Astolfo's itinerary as he returns from Logistilla's realm.

17. Harington's assumption that readers will relate even the more fantastic of Ariosto's fictions to their lives is made explicit in the proem to canto 7, where he maintains that, strange as the ensuing events may be, discrete readers will see in them "as in a glasse their acts and haps." The "fond and simple common sort," as Harington translates the proem,

> Beleeve but what they feele or see with eyes;
> Therfore to them my tale may seeme a fable,
> Whose wits to understand it are not able,
>
> But carelesse what the simple sorts surmise,
> If they shalle deeme it a devise or deede,
> Yet sure to those that are discreete and wise
> It wil no wonder nor no passion breed.

> Wherefore my tale to such I do devise
> And wish them to the same to take good heed,
> For some there are may fortune in this booke
> As in a glasse their acts and haps to looke,
>
> For many men with hope and show of pleasure
> Are carrid far in foolish fond conceit
> And wast their pretious time and spend their treasure
> Before they can discover this deceit.

(7.1–3)

His translation significantly alters the Italian text. In the original the narrator does suggest that his better readers, initiated in allegorical reading, will discern his deeper meaning, but he says nothing about the fiction's moral bearing on their lives:

> Poco o molta ch'io ci abbia, non bisogna
> ch'io ponga mente al vulgo sciocco e ignaro.
> A voi so ben che non parrà menzogna,
> ch 'l lume del discorso avete chiaro;
> et a voi soli ogni mio intento agogna
> che 'l frutto sia di mie fatiche caro.

(*OF* 7.2)

18. Sassetti, "Discorso contro l'Ariosto," pp. 498, 499. Some of the neo-Aristotelian critique of allegorization as justification for incredible fictions that Harington may have known is briefly discussed in Robert Montgomery, "Allegory and the Incredible Fable: The Italian View from Dante to Tasso," *PMLA* 81 (1966): 45–55.

19. In the proem to canto 11, for example, the narrator comments on Ruggiero's sudden urge to rape Angelica following his rescue of the damsel from the Orca at the end of the previous canto. Harington's translation reads as follows:

> The gallant courser in his full carrire
> Is made by man to stop with slender raigne,
> But man himselfe his lust and fond desire
> Is seldome drawn by reason to refraine.
> Tis hard to stop but harder to retire
> When youthfull course ensueth pleasure vaine,
> As Bears do breake the hives and weake defences
> When smell of honie commeth to their sences.

(11.1)

Characteristically, Harington begins his "moral" of canto 11 by elaborating on Ariosto's *proemio*: "In the beginning of this eleventh booke is a notable morall of temperance with two comparisons, one of the horse, another of the beare, which I judge fit for this place rather to be repeated then expounded. If (saith he) a horse with a little snaffle may be stopt in his full carire, what shame it is for a man not to bridle his discordant affections with reason but to be like a Beare so greedie of honie that he breakes down the hyves and devoureth the combes till his tongue, eyes, and jawes be stoung readie to make him runne madd: so do young men devoure with extreme greedinesse these sensuall pleaures of venerie, surfeiting, drinking, pride in apparell, and all intemperance till in the end they may be plagued with sicknesse, povertie, and many other inconveniences to their utter ruine and confusion" (p. 130). I refer to more examples in note 12.

20. Sir Philip Sidney, *An Apology for Poetry*, ed. Geoffrey Shepherd (London: Nelson, 1967), p. 101.

CONCLUSION

1. Lodovico Dolce, *Osservationi nella volgar lingua, divise in quattro libri* (Venice: G. Giolito, 1550), pp. 111r–111v.

2. *Bellezze del Furioso di M. Lodovico Ariosto scielte da Oratio Toscanella*, sig. *3v.

3. See my earlier comments on this section of Pigna's "Life" in Chapter 2.

4. Dolce's account appears in his "Discorso . . . sopra il Furioso" that prefaces the 1568 Venice edition of *Orlando Furioso* published by Giorgio Varisco. The year 1568 was also the year of Dolce's death.

5. I have not been able to consult this work, but Fatini (*Bibliografia della critica ariostea [1510–1956]*, no. 39) notes that Luna considers Ariosto's poem as the "Furiosa Eneide," which is why he includes Ariosto with the great Tuscan authors.

6. The work that Ruscelli refers to in the prefatory letter of the Valgrisi *Furioso* (1556) is his *Commentarii della lingua italiana*, published posthumously in 1581.

Vincenzio Borghini's attack against Ruscelli is to be found in a work unpublished until the end of the nineteenth century, his *Ruscelleide ovvero Dante difeso dalle accuse di G. Ruscelli*, ed. C. Arlia (Città di Castello: Lapi, 1898), p. 23. Borghini recognizes that Ariosto "in vero è tale per ingegno, per arte, per un certo spirito alto e gentile accorto e giudizio che ha pochi pari," and that Ruscelli banked on this reputation "a chiudere la bocca ad ognuno" who might challenge Ruscelli's promotion of Ariosto as the arbiter of the Italian language. However, according to Borghini, Ariosto himself would refute Ruscelli's claims. "Io son certissimo, che se io dicessi all'Ariosto stesso, che e' non è buon maestro, né sicuro di lingua toscana, ch'e' me lo concederebbe" (p. 24).

7. Camillo Pellegrino, *Il Carrafa*, in *Trattati di poetica e retorica del Cinquecento*, ed. Weinberg, 3:343.

PRIMARY WORKS CONSULTED

Alunno, Francesco. *La fabrica del mondo di M. Francesco Alunno da Ferrara.* . . . Venice, 1548.

———. *Della fabrica del mondo di M. Francesco Alunno da Ferrara.* . . . Venice: F. Rampazetto, 1562.

Ariosto, Ludovico. *Orlando Furioso di Messer Ludovico Ariosto con la giunta, novissimamente stampato e corretto. Con una Apologia di M. Lodouico Dolcio contro ai detrattori dell'Autore.* . . . Venice: M. Pasini et F. Bindoni, 1535.

———. *Orlando Furioso di Messer Ludovico Ariosto, con la giunta, . . . con la citatione de la maggior parte de i luochi, d'onde il Conte Matteo Maria Boiardo, e Messer Ludovico Ariosto hanno tolto i soggetti.* . . . Venice: F. Bindoni et M. Pasini, 1542.

———. *Orlando Furioso di M. Ludovico Ariosto novissimamente alla sua integrità ridotto & ornato di varie figure.* . . . Venice: G. Giolito, 1542.

———. *Orlando Furioso di M. Lodovico Ariosto con molte espositioni illustrato.* . . . Florence: B. Giunta, 1544.

———. *Orlando Furioso di M. Lodovico Ariosto ornato di varie figure.* . . . Venice: G. Giolito, 1551.

———. *Orlando Furioso di M. Lodovico Ariosto. ornato di nuove figure, & allegorie in ciascun canto.* . . . Venice: G. A. Valvassori, 1553.

———. *Orlando Furioso de M. Ludovico Ariosto, dirigido al principe Don Philippo N. S. Traduzido en romance castellano por el S. Don Hieronimo de Urrea.* . . . Venice: G. Giolito, 1553.

———. *Orlando Furioso. Di M. Lodovico Ariosto, tutto ricorretto, e di nuove figure adornato.* . . . Venice: V. Valgrisi, 1556.

———. *Orlando Furioso di M. Ludovico Ariosto, diviso in due parti.* . . . Lyon: G. Rouillio, 1556.

———. *Orlando Furioso di M. Lodovico Ariosto. . . . annotationi, imitationi & avertimenti sopra i luoghi difficili di M. Lodovico Dolce, & d'altri.* Venice: G. A. Valvassori, 1566.

———. *Orlando Furioso ornato di varie figure, con alcune stanze.* . . . Venice: C. da Trino di Monferrato, 1567.

———. *Orlando Furioso di M. Lodovico Ariosto, corretto e dichiarato da M. Lodovico Dolce.* . . . Venice: G. Varisco, 1568.

———. *Orlando Furioso . . . nuovamente ricorretto; con nuovi argomenti di M. Lodovico Dolce.* Venice: D. & G. B. Guerra, 1568.

———. *Orlando Furioso, con gli argomenti in ottava rima di M. Lodovico Dolce.* . . . Venice: Horatio de' Gobbi, 1580.

———. *Orlando Furioso di M. Lodovico Ariosto, nuovamente adornato di figure di rame da Girolamo Porro.* . . . Venice: F. de Franceschi, 1584.

———. *Orlando Furioso di M. Lodovico Ariosto; delle annotazioni de' più celebri autori che sopra esso hanno scritto.* . . . Venice: S. Orlandini, 1730.

————. *Orlando Furioso, Translated into English Heroical Verse by Sir John Haring-ton (1591)*. Ed. Robert McNulty. Oxford: Clarendon, 1972.

————. *Orlando Furioso*. 2 vols. Ed. Emilio Bigi. Milan: Rusconi, 1982.

————. *Roland Furieux composé premierement en rhyme thuscane . . . et maintenant traduict en prose francoyse*. . . . Lyon: S. Sabon, 1543.

Ariosto, Orazio. *Difese dell'Orlando Furioso dell'Ariosto fatte dal Sig. Horatio Ariosto*. In *Apologia del S. Torquato Tasso in difesa della sua Gierusalemme liberata*. . . . Ferrara: G. Vasalini, 1586.

Aristotle. *La poétique*. Text, translation, and notes by Roselyne Dupont-Roc and Jean Lallot. Paris: Seuil, 1980.

Bardi, Giovanni de'. "In difesa dell'Ariosto." In *Della Imp. Villa Adriana e di altre sontuosissime già adiacenti alla città di Tivoli*. Florence: Magheri, 1825.

Bembo, Pietro. *Prose della volgar lingua (1525)*. In *Trattatisti del Cinquecento*, ed. Mario Pozzi. Milan and Naples: Ricciardi, 1978.

Borghini, Vincenzio. *Ruscelleide ovvero Dante difeso dalle accuse di G. Ruscelli*. Ed. C. Arlia. Città di Castello: Lapi, 1898.

Caburacci, Francesco. *Trattato di M. Francesco Caburacci da Immola. Dove si dimostra il vero, & novo modo di fare le imprese. Con un breve discorso in difesa dell'Orlando Furioso di M. Lodovico Ariosto*. Bologna: G. Rossi, 1580.

Castelvetro, Lodovico. *Poetica d'Aristotele vulgarizatta e sposta*. 2 vols. Ed. Werther Romani. Bari: Laterza, 1978–1979.

Dante Alighieri. *La divina comedia di Dante . . . con argomenti et allegorie per ciascun canto*. . . . Venice: G. Giolito, 1555.

Denores, Jason. *Poetica di Iason Denores*. . . . Padua: P. Meietto, 1588.

Dolce, Lodovico. *Osservationi nella volgar lingua, divise in quattro libri*. Venice: G. Giolito, 1550.

Fornari, Simone. *La spositione di M. Simon Fornari da Rheggio sopra l'Orlando Furioso di M. Lodovico Ariosto*. Florence: L. Torrentino, 1549.

————. *Della espositione sopra l'Orlando Furioso parte seconda*. Florence: L. Torrentino, 1550.

Giraldi Cintio, Giovambattista. *Discorsi . . . intorno al comporre dei romanzi, delle comedie, e delle tragedie*. . . . Venice: G. Giolito, 1554.

————. "Lettera a Bernardo Tasso sulla poesia epica." In *Trattati di poetica e retorica del Cinquecento*, ed. Bernard Weinberg, vol. 2. Bari: Laterza, 1970.

————. *Scritti critici*. Ed. Camillo Guerrieri Crocetti. Milan: Marzorati, 1973.

Guarini, Battista. *Delle opere del cavalier Battista Guarini*. 4 vols. Verona: G. A. Tumermani, 1737–1738.

Homer. *L'Ulisse di M. Lodovico Dolce da lui tratto dell'Odissea d'Homero et ridotto in ottava rima*. . . . Venice: G. Giolito, 1573.

Malatesta, Gioseppe. *Della nuova poesia o vero delle difese del Furioso, dialogo del Signor Gioseppe Malatesta*. Verona: S. delle Donne, 1589.

————. *Della poesia romanzesca, overo delle difese del Furioso, Ragionamento secondo*. Rome: G. Faciotto, 1596.

Minturno, Antonio. *L'arte poetica del Sig. Antonio Minturno*. Venice: G. A. Valvassori, 1564.

Ovidius Naso, Publius. *La Metamorfosi d'Ovidio . . . di G. A. dell'Anguillara*. Venice: G. Griffio, 1561.

————. *Le Metamorfosi d'Ovidio di G. A. dell'Anguillara . . . rivedute e corrette con le annotationi di G. Horologgi.* Venice: F. de Franceschi, 1563.

————. *Metamorphoses, cum commento Raphaelis Regii.* Venice: S. Bevilaqua, 1497.

————. *Metamorphoses.* Ed. W. S. Anderson. Leipzig: Teubner, 1977.

————. *Il primo libro delle Trasformationi d'Ovidio, da M. Lodovico Dolce in volgare tradotto.* Venice: F. Bindone et M. Pasini, 1539.

————. *Le Transformationi di M. Lodovico Dolce.* Venice: G. Giolito, 1555.

Pellegrino, Camillo. *Il Carrafa, o vero della epica poesia. . . .* In *Trattati di poetica e retorica del Cinquecento,* ed. Bernard Weinberg, vol. 3. Bari: Laterza, 1972.

Piccolomini, Alessandro. *Annotationi . . . nel libro della Poetica d'Aristotele.* Venice: G. Guarisco, 1575.

Pigna, Giovanni Battista. *I romanzi di M. Giovan Battista Pigna.* Venice: V. Valgrisi, 1554.

————. "Messer Giovambattista Pigna a Messer Giovambattista Giraldi." In G. B. Giraldi Cinzio, *Scritti critici,* ed. Camillo Guerrieri Crocetti. Milan: Marzorati, 1973.

Ricci, Bartolomeo. *Operum Bartholomaei Riccii Lugiensis. . . .* Batavia: J. Manfré, 1747–1748.

Ruscelli, Girolamo. *Tre discorsi di Gerolamo Ruscelli a M. Lodovico Dolce.* Venice: P. Pietrasanta, 1553.

————. *De' commentarii della lingua italiana.* Venice: D. Zenaro, 1581.

[Salviati, Lionardo.] *Lo 'nfarinato secondo ovvero dello 'nfarinato accademico della Crusca, risposta al libro intitolato Replica di Camillo Pellegrino ec. Nella qual risposta sono incorporate tutte le scritture, passate tra detto Pellegrino, e detti Accademici intorno all'Ariosto, e al Tasso. . . .* Florence: A. Padovani, 1588.

Sassetti, Filippo. "Il discorso contro l'Ariosto di Filippo Sassetti, edito per la prima volta di su l'originale magliabechiano. . . . Nota di Giuseppe Castaldi." *Rendiconti della R. Accademia dei Lincei,* Classe di scienze morali, storiche e filologiche, 22 (1913): 473–524.

Sidney, Sir Philip. *An Apology for Poetry.* Ed. Geoffrey Shepherd. London: Nelson, 1967.

Speroni, Sperone. *Opere di M. Sperone Speroni degli Alvarotti tratte da' Mss. originali.* 5 vols. Venice: D. Occhi, 1740.

Statius, P. Papinius. *La Thebaide di Statio Ridotta del Sig. Erasmo di Valvassone in ottava rima.* Venice: F. de Franceschi, 1570.

————. *P. Papini Stati Thebaidos libri XII.* Ed. D. E. Hill. Leiden: Brill, 1983.

Summo, Faustino. *Discorsi poetici dell'Eccell. Sig. Faustino Summo Padovano . . . Ne quali si discorreno le piu principali questioni di poesia. . . .* Padua: F. Bolzetta, 1600.

Tasso, Bernardo. *L'Amadigi di Gaula del S. Bernardo Tasso.* Venice: G. Giolito, 1560.

————. *Delle lettere di M. Bernardo Tasso.* 2 vols. Padua: Comino, 1733.

Tasso, Torquato. *Apologia del S. Torquato Tasso in difesa della sua Gierusalemme liberata, a gli Accademici della Crusca, con le accuse, & difese dell'Orlando Furioso dell'Ariosto. . . .* Ferrara: G. Vasalini, 1586.

————. *Delle differenze poetiche per risposta al Signor Orazio Ariosto.* In *Le prose diverse di Torquato Tasso, nuovamente raccolte . . . da Cesare Guasti.* Florence: Le Monnier, 1875.

———. *Discorsi dell'arte poetica.* In *Prose,* ed. Ettore Mazzali. Milan and Naples: Ricciardi, 1959.

———. *Rinaldo.* Ed. G. Bonfigli. Bari: Laterza, 1936.

Terracina, Laura. *Discorso sopra tutti i primi canti d'Orlando Furioso.* Venice: G. Giolito, 1549.

Toscanella, Oratio. *Bellezze del Furioso di M. Lodovico Ariosto. . . .* Venice: P. dei Franceschi, 1574.

Trissino, Giovanni Giorgio. *L'Italia liberata dai Gotthi.* Rome: V. e L. Dorici, 1547.

Varchi, Benedetto. *Lezzioni di M. Benedetto Varchi. . . .* Florence: F. Giunti, 1590.

Vergilius Maro, Publius. *The Aeneid of Virgil.* 2 vols. Ed. R. D. Williams. London: Macmillan, 1972.

———. *L'Enea di M. Lodovico Dolce tratto dall'Eneida di Virgilio.* Venice: G. Varisco, 1568.

———. *P. Virgilii Maronis . . . Opera accuratissime castigata et in pristinam formam restituta. . . .* Venice: L. A. Giunta, 1533.

INDEX